THE PROMISE OF PIETY

THE PROMISE OF PIETY

Islam and the Politics of Moral Order in Pakistan

Arsalan Khan

CORNELL UNIVERSITY PRESS   ITHACA AND LONDON

Copyright © 2024 by Cornell University

All rights reserved. Except for brief quotations in a review, this book, or parts thereof, must not be reproduced in any form without permission in writing from the publisher. For information, address Cornell University Press, Sage House, 512 East State Street, Ithaca, New York 14850. Visit our website at cornellpress.cornell.edu.

First published 2024 by Cornell University Press

Library of Congress Cataloging-in-Publication Data

Names: Khan, Arsalan, author.
Title: The promise of piety : Islam and the politics of moral order in Pakistan / Arsalan Khan.
Description: Ithaca [New York] : Cornell University Press, 2024. | Includes bibliographical references and index.
Identifiers: LCCN 2023013391 (print) | LCCN 2023013392 (ebook) | ISBN 9781501773525 (hardcover) | ISBN 9781501773570 (paperback) | ISBN 9781501773563 (epub) | ISBN 9781501773556 (pdf)
Subjects: LCSH: Islam and politics—Pakistan. | Islamic ethics—Pakistan. | Piety. | Muslim men—Pakistan—Conduct of life.
Classification: LCC BP173.7 .K4853 2024 (print) | LCC BP173.7 (ebook) | DDC 297.2/72095491—dc23/eng/20230509
LC record available at https://lccn.loc.gov/2023013391
LC ebook record available at https://lccn.loc.gov/2023013392

To my mother, Tanveer Anjum

Contents

	Acknowledgments	ix
	Introduction: Islam, Hierarchy, and Moral Order	1
Part 1	**THE MODERNITY OF PIETY**	
	1. Colonial Secularism and the Making of Scriptural Traditionalism in British India	27
	2. Dawat as a Ritual of Transcendence in an Islamic Nation	48
Part 2	**THE SEMIOTICS OF PIETY**	
	3. Islamic Iconicity, Moral Responsibility, and the Creation of a Sacred Hierarchy	75
	4. The Ethics of Hierarchy and the Moral Reproduction of Congregational Life	101
Part 3	**THE PROMISE OF PIETY**	
	5. Certain Faith, the Pious Home, and the Path to an Islamic Future	129
	6. Pious Sovereignty in Times of Moral Chaos	153
	7. The Ethical Affordances of Piety and the Specter of Religious Violence	172
	Conclusion: The Politics of Sovereign Transcendence in Modernity	189
	Notes	201
	References	205
	Index	217

Acknowledgments

The contours of this book were developed when I was in the Department of Anthropology at the University of Virginia. The research for this book was funded by the Wenner-Gren Foundation, The Graduate School of Arts and Sciences at the University of Virginia, the Department of Anthropology at the University of Virginia, and Union College. Parts of this book were previously published as "Pious Masculinity, Ethical Reflexivity and Moral Order in an Islamic Piety Movement in Pakistan," *Anthropological Quarterly* 91, no. 1: 53–78.

I am deeply indebted to my colleagues at the University of Virginia, who provided me with a nurturing and intellectually rigorous space to develop as a scholar. My deepest debt is to my mentor, Richard Handler, for his unwavering support and encouragement throughout my career and for reading many iterations of this manuscript over the years. This book is a dialogue with key ideas that I learned from Richard about modernity. I am also grateful to Dan Lefkowitz, from whom I learned a great deal about language and performance, and Peter Metcalf, who helped me ground my theoretical arguments in ethnography. I would also like to thank Eve Danziger for helping me navigate the literature in linguistic anthropology that has been critical for the framing of this book. The pages of this book are filled with lessons about anthropology that I learned from Ira Bashkow, Ellen Contini-Morava, Fred Damon, Ravindra Khare, Susan McKinnon, Wende Elizabeth Marshall, George Mentore, John Shepherd, and Kath Weston. I thank them for their support and encouragement.

I was fortunate to find an intellectually vibrant network of scholars at the University of Virginia. Jason Hickel and I spent many years discussing the theoretical significance of hierarchy in modernity, a central theme in this book. Discussions with Anna Eisenstein on language and semiotics proved particularly fruitful. Members of my writing group Roberto Armengol, David Flood, Julie Starr, Jack Stoetzel, and Rose Wellman deserve special mention for their thoughtful engagement with my work. My thinking has been enriched by conversations with Feyza Burak-Adli, Sena Aydin, Erika Brant, Mrinalini Chakrovarty, Jacqui Cieslak, Richard Cohen, Allison Christin, Dannah Dennis, Stephanie de Wolfe, Jennie Doberne, Nauman Faizi, Mehr Farooqi, Emily Filler, Andy Graan, Adam Harr, Elina Hartikainen, Nathan Hedges, Chris Hewlett, Jim Hoesterey, Carolyn Howarter, Yu-chien Huang, Peter Kang, Nadim Khoury, Sue Ann McCarty, Betsy Mesard, Nathalie Nahas, Neeti Nair, Amy

Nichols-Belo, Geeta Patel, Kristin Phillips, Alessandro Questa, Grace Reynolds, Giancarlo Rolando, Liza Sapir, Omar Shaukat, Justin Shaffner, Deepak Singh, Holly Singh, Sheena Singh, Lydia Rodriquez, Claire Snell-Rood, Erik Stanley, David Strohl, Todne Thomas, Clare Terni, Michael Wairungu, Lue Ann Williams, and Rizwan Zamir.

Over the years, I have benefited greatly from commentary and feedback on my work in many forums. I am deeply grateful to David Gilmartin and Jim Hoesterey for carefully reading the final manuscript and providing thorough feedback and suggestions for improvement. The manuscript is considerably richer and more coherent as a result. I would also like to thank Radhika Govindrajan and Jon Bialecki for their helpful suggestions on the introduction. Parts of the manuscript have been published in article form and benefited from suggestions by Will Dawley, Matthew Engelke, Naomi Haynes, Jason Hickel, Saba Mahmood, Neeti Nair, and Brendan Thornton. Many sections of the manuscript were presented as papers at conferences, and I received helpful feedback from Josepeh Alter, Christopher Ball, John Bowen, Ayala Fader, Ashley Lebner, William Mazzarella, and Andrew Shryock.

I could not have asked for a more supportive academic community than the one I have found at Union College. I am grateful to my colleagues in the anthropology department Karen Brison, George Gmelch, Sharon Gmelch, Aaron Kappeler, Steve Leavitt, Robert Samet, Jeff Witsoe, Michelle Osborn, and Gregory Deacon for their consistent support. I have learned a great deal from each of them about both anthropology and the art of teaching. I would also like to thank Peter Bedford, Lewis Davis, Joyce Madancy, Jen Mitchell, and Eshi Motahar for providing a supportive community at Union College. Teaching undergraduate students has given me a deeper understanding of the value of framing arguments in a simple and intelligible manner and has improved the clarity of my thinking and writing. I would like to thank my undergraduate students at Union College for their engagement in my classes.

My work has been enriched by conversations with academics from a variety of disciplinary perspectives working on religion, Islam, South Asia, and Pakistan. I want to thank Kamran Asdar Ali for his comments on my work and for his mentorship over the years. I have benefited greatly from the intellectual camaraderie of Noman Baig, Waqas Butt, Mariam Durrani, Ghazal Asif Farrukhi, Aisha Ghani, Erum Haider, Khurram Husain, Sohaib Ibrahim Khan, Nida Kirmani, Ping-hsiu Alice Lin, Ameem Lutfi, Sana Malik, Faiza Mushtaq, Taimoor Shahid, Omer Shaukat, and Sarah Waheed. I would also like to thank Majed Akhtar, Maira Hayat, Danish Khan, Tahir Naqvi, Natasha Raheja, Mubbashir Rizvi, and Adeem Suhail for their engagement with my work and for the productive dialogue on Pakistan in our Pakistan studies workshop. I have also benefited from conversations with Nosheen Ali, Sher Ali, Nausheen Anwar, Girish Daswani, Sarah Eleazar, Laurent Gayer, Becky Goetz, Natalie Gummer, Geoffrey Hughes, Rajbir Singh Judge, Hikmet Kocamaner, Salman Hussain, Hafeez Jamali, Umair Javed, Ajmal Kamal, Omar Kasmani, Ward Keeler, Saad Lakhani, Darryl Li, Candice Lucasik, Diego Malara, Nicholas Martin, Ali Altaf Mian, Katherine Miller, Naheed Mustafa, Nauman Naqvi, Anastasia Piliavsky, Sonia Qadir, Ali Usman Qasmi, Tariq Rahman, Ali Raza, Zahra Sabri, Sam Shuman, Niloufer Siddiqui, and Anand Taneja.

My intellectual engagement with journalists, lawyers, development professionals, artists, and activists in Karachi has been immensely productive and enriched my thinking. I am especially grateful to Moneeza Ahmed, Zebunissa Burki, Alia Chughtai, Fahad Desmukh, Nadir Hassan, Nadia Hussain, Zahra Malkani, Rabayl Mirza, and Shaheryar Mirza for enriching discussions on Pakistan and for their friendship. I also thank Awais Dhakkan, Osman Farid, Faraz Hussain, Muzaffar Manghi, Ramish Noorani, Fawad Parvez, Manoj Sawlani, and Tasmiah Sheikh for always making Karachi feel like home.

My friend Talha Zahid brought me into the world of the Tablighi Jamaat, taught me the purpose of *dawat*, and connected me to many of the Tablighis who appear in the pages of this book. I am immensely grateful for his faith in me, and I hope he will see in this work an effort to create understanding across differences. The Tablighis who engaged with me did so with the characteristic humility and patience that I describe in this book as central to ethical life in the Tablighi Jamaat. Tablighis may not agree with all the arguments in the pages that follow, but I hope they see that I have tried to write this book with the same spirit of generosity with which I was received in the Tablighi congregation.

My deepest gratitude is reserved for my family, who provided me with the emotional and intellectual support to see this long project to fruition. My Khalas, Mamu, and cousins all make returning to Karachi a joyful experience. My Khala Tazeen Erum and I regularly engaged in spirited discussions about my research that helped me hone my ideas. My brother Mansoor Khan has always served as an inspiration for my intellectual pursuits, and my trips to Brooklyn were both intellectually and emotionally invigorating. My stepfather Afzal Ahmed Syed has been a patient supporter and interlocutor and a model for careful study and scholarly commitment. All my academic pursuits have been shaped by my mother Tanveer Anjum who taught me to recognize the value of scholarship and encouraged me to pursue my passions and interests. This book would never have been possible without the immense sacrifices that she has made for our family.

My late Nani always pressed on me the importance of giving back to the communities that have nourished us. This book is my modest contribution to the fraught debates about Islam in public life in Pakistan. I can only hope that those invested in creating a more just and equitable world in Pakistan and beyond will find some value in it.

THE PROMISE OF PIETY

Introduction

ISLAM, HIERARCHY, AND MORAL ORDER

The car stopped on the side of the main road on our way to the grand mosque complex (*markaz*) of the Tablighi Jamaat. We were heading to the Thursday night (*shab-e-jumma*) congregation where practitioners of the movement, or *Tablighis*, spend the night praying, giving sermons and listening to sermons (*bayan*), and creating connection (*jor*) with other members of the congregation. In the car was my high school friend Talha, now an active and staunch Tablighi, and three Tablighis from his area mosque whom I knew only superficially. We waited on a fourth to arrive from his house in the adjacent street when suddenly Talha began to move the car forward as he looked intently in his rearview mirror. In Karachi, phone and car snatching are regular occurrences, and we knew something was amiss. A motorcycle with two riders had stopped a car not far behind us, a white Toyota Corolla with black tinted windows. The robbers on the motorcycle had picked the wrong car. The motorcycle suddenly zipped past our car, and a few gunshots were fired. We all took cover. The car zipped past us in chase behind the motorcycle. The robbers lost control of the motorcycle, hurling the riders onto the street. One robber took off on foot into the adjacent neighborhood, while the other, seemingly injured from the fall, tried to pick himself up. The white Corolla pulled up next to him. Three armed men exited the car, grabbed the injured robber, and hurled him into the backseat of the car. They then sped away, leaving the motorcycle in the middle of the street.

While this was certainly no ordinary event, seeing armed gunmen in cars with tinted windows is also not exceptionally uncommon in a highly volatile and militarized city like Karachi where, on top of criminal organizations, wealthy and powerful people often roam with armed guards and political parties have militant wings and a history of armed conflict. "Alhamdulillah," we all repeated, as we calmed our nerves. "May Allah have mercy," one compatriot said. We all heaved a sigh of relief. The ride to the Tablighi markaz was quiet, each of us in the car left with our own thoughts, our companions in silent recitation of the Quran. We arrived in time for the *maghrib* prayers. Then we sat down to listen to sermons given by the pious Elders (*buzurg*) of the congregation. After the sermons, Mohsin, one of the Tablighis who was in the car with us, came and sat next to me. "Arsalan," he said, "look at how calm and peaceful it is in this mosque. Everyone is at ease." I nodded in agreement. "You know why? Because this is Allah's house (*Allah ka ghar*) and all the people sitting here know that nothing happens without Allah's will. Not even a twig can be moved from one place to another without Allah's will. Today someone is around, tomorrow they are gone because that is what Allah has written for us." Again, I nodded in affirmation. "What happened today," Mohsin continued, "shows that Allah is not happy with us. Do you know why Allah is not happy with us?" No, I said. "Because we have abandoned our religion (*din*) and we are chasing after 'the world' (*dunya*). We have given up the Prophet's way (*rasool ka tariqa*) and we have adopted the ways of others (*doosron ke tariqe*). If we want to free ourselves from these troubles, we must return to religion, the one bestowed to our Prophet by Allah. We must cultivate our faith (*iman*). You must join us on this path and you, too, will see what benefits it brings to your life."

What Mohsin was engaging in was not a dialogue about what happened on our drive to the markaz. Instead, he was using the event as an occasion to frame the problems of crime and violence as a product of Muslims straying from the path of God. Mohsin was doing *dawat*, a distinct form of face-to-face preaching that is the hallmark of the Tablighi Jamaat. Tablighis can be seen walking through Pakistan's villages, towns, and cities in groups of ten or twelve dressed in the traditional *shalwar-kameez*, pant-legs raised above their ankles, with long flowing beards and a white Muslim cap, an image that is immediately discernable to Sunni Muslims as being in the Prophet's example (*sunnat*). Dawat literally means "calling" or "inviting," and it is used interchangeably with the term *tabligh*, which means to "convey." The Tablighi invites Muslim addressees to come to the mosque to pray and listen to sermons with the aim of incorporating them into the movement and turning them into Tablighis. Tablighis insist that Muslims have abandoned religion for the world and that this has thrust the world into a state of moral chaos (*fitna*), a condition in which moral relationships among Muslims have entirely broken down. All the problems that Muslims face in the world can be traced back to this foundational problem. Ultimately, it is only by drawing fellow Muslims back to Islamic practice and specifically encouraging them to take up the calling of dawat that moral relationships can be regenerated in Islamic life and moral order restored.

The Tablighi Jamaat emerged in the 1920s in North India and is now one of the largest Islamic movements in the world (Sikand 2002). It has a major presence in many parts of the world, but especially in South Asia and where there are large South Asian populations. Pakistan is one of the four major centers of Tablighi Jamaat activities, with millions of people from Pakistan and around the world attending the annual congregation (*ijtima*) at Raiwind and hundreds of thousands attending the other annual congregations in various cities across the country. Since the 1980s, the Tablighi Jamaat has grown dramatically in Pakistan. The large mosque complexes (markaz) that have sprung up in all the major cities are a testament to this, the largest of which can host up to fifty thousand worshippers. These complexes serve as key institutional nodes in a network of mosques that, either formally or informally, are affiliated with the movement.

The concept of dawat has deep roots in Islamic theology and can be found in the Quran. The Quran states: "Who could be a better person than the one who 'called' (*da'a*) toward God and acted righteously" (41:33), and "There should be a group of people among you who 'call' (*yad'una*) to [do] good, enjoining good and forbidding evil" (3:104). Tablighis interpret these Quranic injunctions to mean that it is the duty of every individual Muslim to preach the virtues of Islam to their fellow Muslims, just as the Prophet did, to keep Muslims focused on God and "religion" (din) and protect them from the ploys of the Devil and "the world" (dunya).

Tablighi conceptions of dawat, however, are not simply about the spreading of Islamic content. Rather, Tablighis insist that it is the very form or "method of preaching" (*tariqa-e-tabligh*) that is Islamic because it follows the Prophet's example (sunnat). The Prophet is an exemplary being (*insan al-kamil*) whose every deed and action was divinely inspired and carries in it great benefits; thus, these deeds must be meticulously replicated in the lives of Muslims. Because dawat as a method of preaching is inspired by the Prophet's example, it is uniquely capable of soliciting God's mercy (rehm) and grace (barkat) and thus affording one "success in both this world and the next" (*donon jahan mein kamiyabi*). It is only through dawat, they insist, that Islamic virtue can be spread and God's will communicated. Early Tablighi accounts suggested that the "method" came to the founder of the movement, Muhammad Ilyas, in a dream, implying that it was a direct gift from God, but Ilyas himself never said this. He did note, however, that it was a blessing from God and that "the closeness and the help and blessings [of God] is not to be found in the case of other methods" (cited in Sikand 2002, 131). The efficacy of dawat in soliciting divine intervention is thus seen to depend on it being conducted in precisely the form that it was prescribed and fulfilled by the Prophet and his Companions. It is by following this precise method of the Prophet that dawat becomes a religious deed or practice (*dini amal*) that is exclusively efficacious in spreading Islamic virtues, regenerating moral relationships, and creating an Islamic community.

The Tablighis' commitment to their own form of preaching stands out in a country like Pakistan where state sovereignty is directly linked to Islam, where the state sees its role as one of promoting Islamic values, and where Islamic revivalist activism flourishes in public life. The Objectives Resolution of the Constitution of the Islamic Republic of Pakistan passed in 1949, only two years after the founding of the nation-state, states: "Whereas sovereignty over the entire universe belongs to Allah Almighty alone and the authority which He has delegated to the State of Pakistan, through its people for being exercised within the limits prescribed by Him is a sacred trust." Islamist political parties have drawn on this constitutional commitment to move Pakistan in the direction of an Islamic state (*Islami riyasat*). Islamists have historically claimed that Islam is a total system for life and that this necessitates creating an Islamic state governed by Islamic law (*shariat*), one that enforces Islamic codes and injunctions and actively creates the space for Muslims to live according to Islamic precepts. In recent years, Islamists have increasingly turned toward creating institutions of "market Islam" (Rudnyckyj 2009) like corporations, welfare trusts, new educational institutions, and NGOs, and have become an active presence in mass media such as radio, television, newspapers, and the internet.

The Tablighis' insistence that only dawat performed and taught in their own congregation can spread Islamic virtue and is the basis for creating a genuine Islamic community challenges the many forces of the Islamic revival that compete for Islamic authority in Pakistan. Tablighis reject the Islamist claim that they are spreading Islamic virtue through participation in the state or in democratic politics. This came up early in my fieldwork. When I first arrived in the field, I had decided that I would try to build in a strong comparative dimension to my research examining both Tablighi piety as well as a range of Islamist political parties, particularly the Jamaat-e-Islami with which I had some prior connections. As I pursued this comparative dimension, I was told repeatedly by Tablighis that I would not come to any understanding of Islam through involvement with Jamaat-e-Islami as they were not "doing religion" but were instead involved in "politics" (*siyasat*). Islamists, Tablighis insist, conflate "worldly activities" (*dunyavi kam*) with "religious practice" (dini amal) and thus are incapable of spreading Islamic virtue, as it can only be spread through practices that are themselves religious. Tablighis argue that confusing religion for politics has undermined the spread of Islamic virtue and created fissures and fragmentation of the Islamic community.

The historian Barbara Metcalf (2004), a foremost scholar of the Tablighi Jamaat, has described this position as "quietist," but the boundaries that Tablighis draw between religion and the world underpin an ethical response to the crises that afflict life in postcolonial Pakistan. *The Promise of Piety* leverages this tension within the Islamic revival in Pakistan to explore how Tablighis constitute the domain of religion (din) and the distinct form of moral order that they imagine against what they construe as the "moral chaos" of life in Pakistan. Drawing on the Deobandi tradition of Islamic thought, Tablighis understand religion to be a set of practices authorized by the sacred sources, the Quran, Prophetic tradition (sunnat), Islamic jurisprudence (*fiqh*) and Islamic law (shariat) as it has been developed by Islamic scholars (*ulama*). They advocate for a return to the pure and original Islam of the Prophet, which they say has been corrupted by innovations (*biddat*), a position that places them within the broad currents of Islamic reform in South Asia. However, the Tablighis' insistence that their own form of dawat is modeled on Prophetic example gives a distinct institutional form to their congregation. Tablighis note that the entanglement of Islam with modern institutions of the state and market has failed to produce pious subjects and regenerate moral relationships. This Tablighi stance takes us beyond religion as a matter of doctrinal content to the mediational means for constituting pious subjects and pious relationality and the institutional structure of the domain of religion.

Some questions arise: What is at stake ethically, morally, and politically in the way that Tablighis draw the boundary between religion and the world, and how does this construction of religion shape their moral intervention in the world and their vision of moral order? These questions take us into an examination of how dawat as a set of mediational practices through which distinct pious subjects, pious relationality, and ultimately pious authority and sovereignty come to shape Pakistan's social and political landscape. Dawat is what Birgit Meyer (2011) has called a "sensational form," a set of organized practices, techniques, and tools for mediating a relationship to transcendental power and therefore creating the conditions for divine presence in the world. This book argues that the ritual forms of dawat constitute a distinct form pious relationality organized around what I call the "ethics of hierarchy," a hierarchical vision of moral relatedness in which the Tablighi learns to enact Prophetic example by submitting to the authority of pious others. The ritual ideology that frames dawat creates a hierarchical organization of the movement that must be inhabited and embodied in submission to pious authority. This submission is enacted in both ritualized forms of listening to sermons and everyday acts of citationality that situate pious authorities as a model of life to be emulated in the realization of proximity to God (see Robbins 2001). The ethics of hierarchy, I argue, then becomes the basis for an ethical engagement with the problems of kinship conflicts and political fragmentation that Tablighis see as emblematic of the state of moral chaos. The sacred hierarchy constructed in the Tablighi Jamaat and the effort at ethical engagement with the world then come to be seen as an alternative form of sovereign power to the powers of the Islamic state and the corporate institutions of the market. I show how the ethics of hierarchy is a mode of ethical reflexivity that aims to domesticate the powers of modern life and, thus, is understood by Tablighis as the basis for transcending the political fragmentation and violence that shapes life in postcolonial Pakistan.

The question of hierarchy is of course an old one in anthropology and one that can trace back to Louis Dumont's (1980) theorization of the Hindu caste system in his classic *Homo Hierarchicus*. Dumont famously argued that the "paramount value," or the primary normative principle of Indian society is purity, and this sets the terms for the ranking of people and things. Dumont shows that the Hindu caste system organizes castes in terms of their relative purity and that this can be contrasted with the egalitarianism and individualism of the West (Dumont 1986). Critics of Dumont have long noted that Dumont creates an ahistorical image of Indian society locked in tradition as opposed to a historically changing and dynamic West and that, far from reflecting Indian realities, his portrayal of India replicates a distinct Brahmanical worldview (see Das 1997). However, Dumont's argument that hierarchy cannot be understood purely as a top-down exercise of power but instead must be thought of as a shared value to which people are, relatively speaking, committed as a moral principle remains important. Saba Mahmood's (2005) argument that feminism's prescriptive project of liberating women from relations of subordination has hampered the analytic project of understanding forms of agency like that of Islamic pietist women who see pious submission as a form of pious agency rather than simply a capitulation to power and a form of domination (see also Strathern 1988). The normative egalitarianism of our dominant approaches to social and political life has in other words prevented analysts from understanding how hierarchy can be a value in social life (see, however, Ansell 2014; Ferguson 2015; Hickel 2015; Haynes and Hickel 2016; Keeler 2017; Khan 2016, 2018; Piliavsky 2020).

The Promise of Piety takes up the question of the moral value placed on hierarchy and the ethical reflexivity this engenders among Pakistani Tablighis. Tablighis see hierarchy as a basis for responsibility and care, not domination and exploitation, and indeed they see their movement in converting a world of domination and exploitation into one based on the responsibility and care that they understand to be intrinsic to Islam and generated in dawat. The book examines how Islamic piety as a form of hierarchical relationality is constituted, legitimated, and naturalized in the practices of dawat and how hierarchy becomes a basis for the ethical reflexivity that structures Tablighi approaches to social and political life. It shows how the ethics of hierarchy builds on a distinct ritual and semiotic ideology and becomes an ethical resource that Tablighis see as a basis for addressing the crisis of political fragmentation and violence in Pakistan. The book then opens the question to how people throughout the world constitute hierarchies, how this serves as a basis for ethical action in the world, and how this shapes different conceptions of moral order in modernity.[1]

Anthropology in the Space of Cultural Intimacy

He wore a starched and crisply ironed white *kurta* and sported a long flowing beard with his mustache shaved, a style that was immediately discernable to anyone in Pakistan as being in the example of the Prophet (sunnat). For years, my friends—our mutual friends—had been telling me that Talha had become a *maulvi*, a term that means a religious scholar but is also sometimes used derisively by more liberal and secular-oriented people as someone who is excessively religious, closed-minded, and even fanatical. Some said this sympathetically, some with mild amusement, and some with a measure of disappointment. Talha and I had met in high school, and we became very close friends over the next few years. He was quiet and contemplative and generally thoughtful about the world. We shared an interest in politics, something that I shared with him more than I did with our other mutual friends. Like the rest of us, Talha indulged in activities that this person standing in front of me who was crafting himself in the image of the Prophet would later describe to me as "way outside the bounds of Islam." Now, we stood in front of each other on what is sometimes construed as opposite ends of an incommensurable divide between Islam and secularism. But, as we embraced each other in the courtyard of the Makki Masjid, the grand mosque complex in Karachi of the Tablighi Jamaat, the discomfort dissipated, and a sense of intimacy and familiarity resurfaced. "Come, let's pray, Arsalan, and then we will catch up."

When I returned to Pakistan for fieldwork, my goal was to seek out a Tablighi mosque to which I had absolutely no attachment, preferably in a working-class area. This somehow fit with my idea of what it meant to be in "the field." From my pre-field experience, I had come to realize that doing research among Tablighi was going to be difficult because they actively opposed being the objects of research and rarely engaged intimately with scholars or journalists. They saw my research as an obstacle to dawat as an Islamic practice. It was clear to me that more than simply being uninterested, my questions to them posed a peculiar kind of threat to their faith. During my preliminary fieldwork, I met several Tablighis at the two grand mosque complexes in Karachi, Makki Masjid and Madni Masjid. Of the many Tablighis that I tried to build relationships with, only two agreed to meet with me beyond the mosque. All the others told me I should seek out Tablighis in my own neighborhood and that understanding dawat required "coming to Islam properly." In meetings that happened in and around the market where they worked, we exchanged pleasantries, and after I explained to them the aims of my research, they would tell me that dawat is not something to be grasped through the mind (*zehn*) but only something that one can understand through "doing," and it is only through participation that I would gain the understanding I was seeking. Then they would narrate the virtues of dawat as they did to anyone seeking guidance about how to live an Islamic life. These encounters would end with them insisting that I create "connection" (jor) with the congregation in my own neighborhood mosque and begin to participate in mosque activities.

I will have much more to say about these features of Tablighi ritual ideology and process in the chapters to come. Here I simply want to point to not only how this shaped my ethnographic approach but also what it can help us think about in terms of cultural intimacy between different positions in Islamic or Muslim life in Pakistan. The mosque in my own neighborhood, an upper-middle- to upper-class area, had very few Tablighis, and the area itself does not have the kind of neighborly intimacy that one finds in older parts of the city. I considered moving to an area with a more vibrant Tablighi congregation, but I also knew that moving to an area simply to conduct research would be viewed with suspicion. In the age of the Global War on Terror, a young man with no kinship ties to a neighborhood suddenly arriving to conduct research would surely have aroused suspicion. At the time that I was struggling to find Tablighis who were willing to engage with my research, Talha and I had reconnected, and he expressed an interest in meeting. He came to my apartment on a few occasions, usually close to dusk prayer times (maghrib), and we would go to the mosque and then venture out for juice or tea, and sit in the car and talk, sometimes about dawat and sometimes about our own friends and families. It was obvious that Talha was invested in drawing me to dawat, but he also wanted to rekindle an old friendship. I suspect that he thought my research would ultimately serve to bring me to Islamic practice and that I would find myself less interested in my research and more interested in moving on the path of piety. This created a space between us that allowed me to both ask him substantial questions about the Tablighi congregation and for him to give me dawat in a manner that was in keeping with his ideas about Islam.

Talha was a close confidant, caregiver, and "son" to a prominent Tablighi Elder (buzurg) who sat on both the city and national councils (*shura*) and was highly revered and extremely influential throughout the congregation. He went by the title Hazrat, a term of respect that Pakistani Muslims use as an honorific before the names of Prophets, including the Prophet Muhammad. Hazrat was an authorized Sufi sheikh of the Chisti order. He could trace his unbroken spiritual lineage back to the Prophet Muhammad through the founder of the Chisti order. As an authorized sheikh, Hazrat had "followers" (*murids*) in the thousands who devoted themselves to him through an initiation called *bayt*, which entails a formalized commitment to follow the sheikh's every instruction. Hazrat maintained a spiritual house (*khanqa*) where he received people who needed his guidance. The spiritual house was also a space of special Sufi practices, including various forms of remembrance (*zikr*) that are not trained in the broader Tablighi Jamaat. Hazrat's followers were not all Tablighis, but he encouraged them all to be and believed, as other Tablighis do, that dawat was a foundational practice based on which all other practices were built and thus was a necessary condition for all spiritual reform and realization (*islah*). He insisted that esoteric knowledge (*ilm*) was no substitute for dawat, and he regularly went on dawat tours to stay on the right path. In this way, Hazrat insisted that dawat superseded all other Islamic activities.

Hazrat took a liking to me and told Talha to bring me with him to the khanqa. From then onwards, I was treated as Hazrat's "guest," and this is an identity I carried with me into many Tablighi spaces. I will venture to say that Hazrat saw some potential in me as a Tablighi, but he also recognized that Talha wanted me to be part of his world, and this led him to extend an extra level of generosity and kindness toward me. This did not go unnoticed by others in Hazrat's network. Several Tablighis told me that they did not fully understand why Hazrat had taken such a liking to me, and I could tell that this inspired a level of jealousy in them. In any case, Hazrat's endorsement of me became pivotal for my research, as people who knew of my relationship with him simply accepted or had to accept my presence. They could not go against Hazrat's wishes, and many of them assumed that he had a purpose that they could not fully understand. Through Hazrat's khanqa, I made my way to the Al-Aqsa Mosque, which was close by, and each week Hazrat delivered a sermon there that was attended by hundreds of people. The Al-Aqsa Mosque has one of the largest congregations of Tablighis that I have found anywhere in Karachi, and they all attributed this first to Allah's grace and then to being under Hazrat's "shadow." Hazrat, they said, had singlehandedly created the passion for dawat in this area starting some three decades ago. They frequently recalled how in decades past, Hazrat would wander alone from house to house in the scorching sun inviting people to mosque when nobody knew anything about dawat, and the fruits of this labor could now be seen in the fact that the Al-Aqsa neighborhood was a model for other neighborhoods throughout the city and country.

I begin on this note of personal intimacy because it speaks directly to the aim of this book to understand how Islamic piety in the Tablighi Jamaat exists in relation to other moral possibilities of being Muslim in Pakistan. Tablighis assumed that we belonged to the shared tradition of Islam and that the differences between us did not pose some incommensurable divide. We had simply been led down distinct paths and distinct ways of understanding the world. For Tablighis, their path was God's path (*Allah ka raasta*), while mine was a fallen path that one took when one had become seduced by "the world." But, it was our shared position as Muslims with divergent historical experiences that created the threshold of similarity and difference that both united and divided us. We were, ultimately, not incommensurable people but rather interchangeable, and it was our interchangeability that could make me an object of the moral transformation of dawat.

My interlocutors were not wrong that our lives were, relatively speaking, interchangeable. I spent a good part of my life living in an old middle to upper-middle class neighborhood in Karachi that was relatively conservative called Nazimabad. Various forms of Islamic piety, including commitment to the Tablighi Jamaat, were ubiquitous and going to the mosque was a daily part of neighborhood life. When I moved to the relatively more affluent part of the city in my teenage years, I found that the daily strictures of Islamic piety were significantly less stringent. But, the pursuit of piety was not absent here either. Over the years, I witnessed countless friends become more and more explicitly pious, increasingly committed to religious practice and indeed to encouraging others to fulfill their religious duties. Many of them ventured, at least for some time, to the Tablighi Jamaat. Some of them ultimately concluded that this pursuit of piety was "too much" and that one should learn to balance religion (din) and the world (dunya). Some became deeply disenchanted and left with significantly less commitment to religious practice than when they arrived. The possibilities of these moral and ethical shifts are a constant feature of life in Pakistan.

The fact that I was participating in dawat was a significant source of consternation and fear for many of the closest people in my life, especially my mother, who was deeply worried that I would internalize the normative commitment to piety, particularly its gender norms, and that this could create strains in our relationship. Some friends teased me for growing a beard and joked about how any day now I would be preaching to them. Such fears are built on the recognition that Islamic preaching is a powerful force of transformation in people's lives and that many people just like me could easily be pulled into the orbit of Islamic piety. On the other hand, Tablighis felt that engagement with impious people could easily undermine their faith and pull them into untoward activities. Indeed, this was why when Talha first began to commit to the Tablighi Jamaat, he distanced himself from many of his old friends, including me. Tablighis avoid excess contact with people who they believe are involved in un-Islamic activities, and indeed this was one of the principal dangers of my research as it could lead to questioning their own commitments and could therefore undermine their faith. It is, after all, reason that the devil uses to lure people away from commitment to religion.

My research depended on this presupposition of shared religious tradition as well as cultural sensibilities. As one Tablighi explained to me, Hazrat has only accepted my research despite its potentially deleterious effects because he thinks I have "good attributes" (*achei sifaat*) and could do good things for Islam if only I would commit myself to dawat. Indeed, almost everyone accepted that eventually I would be transformed by dawat and would either give up my research or be so thoroughly transformed that I would use my own position as a professor as the basis for drawing others to Islam. The encounter between us, they hoped, was one in which the differences between us created by my investment in "research" (*tahqiqat*) rather than dawat, would eventually be erased. In other words, it was built on the presumption of cultural intimacy. What I mean by cultural intimacy here is not the actuality of sameness but the possibility of a common future created through the subjunctive encounter of dawat.

This provides a theoretical entry point into the debates about modernity that are central to Pakistani social and political life. I point to this cultural, and indeed personal, intimacy to lay out the context for an argument about how Islamic piety as it is manifest in the Tablighi congregation is a moral stance within the shared but contested field of modernity. Despite the now well-known critique of the culture concept and radical alterity, my anthropological training coincided with the immense and sudden popularity of what came to be known as the "ontological turn" in anthropology. Those advocating for the need for a turn to ontology argued that cultural relativism and the concept of culture itself was an inadequate analytic tool for understanding how people inhabited and experienced radically different realities. Culture, it was argued, treats distinct "ontologies" as simply different understandings of the same underlying reality, which grants "our" modern Western scientific rationality a privileged place in accessing this reality, while the West's "Others" are assumed to remain under the veil of false consciousness. The task set forth by the ontological turn was to recognize that people inhabit different realities rather than just different epistemologies or understandings of reality (Holbraad and Pederson 2017). Ontologies were reality, and the theoretical task was ultimately to invent an analytic language that could bring such ontologies into a comparison without reducing the one reality to the other (de Castro 2004).

I knew from my own experience growing up in Pakistan that indeed the Tablighi Jamaat was sufficiently different from what we in anthropology too often gloss as "Western" ontology with its association with an autonomous, bounded, and authentic individual and therefore a good candidate for thinking about cultural alterity. I was particularly attracted to the more ritualized nature of Tablighi practice and to understanding the role of ritual as a form of agency in social life, one that was different from modern scientific rationality. Yet, having seen many people, including members of my own family, venture into Islamic piety movements, I always understood that the differences that are often characterized as "ontological" were not incommensurable differences but of a more subtle variety, and shifts between moral commitments are a common feature of life for most people in Pakistan and occur at various points in their life and in response to a range of complex circumstances. Moreover, I knew that such shifts are also reversible, fraught with difficulties and anxieties, and thus never quite settled. Indeed, many Muslims take up the moral project of Islamic piety with great alacrity, while others can dabble in it, and still others can become radically opposed to such a stance, and all these people can exist within the bounds of the same families, classes, and communities. Islamic piety is, therefore, not an ontological shift but a shift in ethical stance in a shared world of moral possibilities (Graeber 2015).

The Promise of Piety explores how piety is mediated and created through a distinct ritual and semiotic ideology in the context of Pakistan, the ethical sensibilities and stances engendered in the pious practices of dawat, and how they compete with other ethical stances and moral possibilities that animate social and political life in Pakistan. The Pakistani Tablighis whom I describe in this book are not radically Other, certainly not for someone raised in the same Islamic tradition and in the same country as them. Islamic pietists are "the repugnant cultural Other" (Harding 1991) of the modern liberal and secular subject not because they represent a radically different ontology but rather because they posit recognizable and familiar truths and these truths lay claim to the same reality as liberal and secular traditions lay claim. They, too, claim that their worldview has universal significance for humanity, and they offer solutions that are appealing to many of the same people who might otherwise be liberal and secular, or for that matter of different denominations, sects, and religions. It is the familiarity with and possibility of an interchangeability of our moral perspectives that makes the Islamic pietists (or Christian or Jewish ones) repugnant to liberal and secular sensibilities, not their radical otherness. The repugnant cultural Other is always an intimate Other.

The Promise of Piety focuses on the question of hierarchy and hierarchical relatedness, a question that has unfortunately been too closely attached to the notion of radical cultural alterity, most notably in Dumont's contrast between hierarchy and holism and egalitarianism and individualism (see Piliavsky 2020). Rather than focus on how Islamic piety in the Tablighi Jamaat represents a radically distinct ontology, the book focuses on how Islamic piety competes for space in a diverse field of Muslim and Islamic possibilities and is embedded in the shared architecture of modernity. The focus on "vernacular" or "alternative" modernities is a well-developed theme in anthropology (Gaonkar 2001; Knauft 2002), but as Joel Robbins (2001) notes, when anthropologists speak vernacular modernity, they often fail to state explicitly what makes a particular vernacular form "modern." Drawing on Björn Wittrock's (2000) definition of modernity as a set of "promissory notes," Robbins notes that modernity "points to the possibility of creating new 'assumptions about human beings, their rights and agency'" (Robbins 2001, 903). In his work on Christianity among the Urapmin of Papua New Guinea, Robbins (2001, 2004) shows how Christianity becomes a vehicle for the transformation of the self and for creating a rupture between the present and the past, thus opening the possibility for imagining an alternative future. Robbins argues that it is this aspiration for self-transformation and the moral transformation of social and political life that is characteristic of modernity.

In Pakistan, as Naveeda Khan (2012) has noted, one of the key sites for this aspiration is Islam. As I will show in the next section, Islam affords the possibility for aspiration because it enables people to imagine a "direct" relationship to transcendental power and thus creates the possibility for moral transformation. The question that arises then is how the relationship with transcendental power is mediated and thus gives a distinct form to aspiration. This book explores how dawat in the Tablighi Jamaat becomes the means for mediating a direct relationship to God and thus transcending the world. It is this promise of piety that draws Muslims in Pakistan from across caste, class, and ethnicity to the Tablighi Jamaat to realize their aspirations to become the pious agents of an Islamic moral order.

The Semiotics of Piety and the Making of an Islamic Moral Order

The Promise of Piety examines the aspiration for Islamic piety among Pakistani Tablighis who regard dawat as the basis for transcending the problems that afflict Muslims in Pakistan and throughout the world. The problems that Tablighis identify in Pakistan are immediately recognizable and often lamented by many non-Tablighis, such as the breakdown of moral relations in and between families, ethnic communities, and Muslim nations. The Tablighi Jamaat provides a framework for understanding these problems as a consequence of a deficit of faith and provides the means, dawat, for their remedy. Indeed, the moral force of Islamic piety and the fears that it sparks among Pakistani liberals and secularists and the challenge perceived in it by Islamists is precisely because it provides a potent and compelling answer to millions of Pakistani Muslims about how to address the many problems that afflict life in postcolonial Pakistan. What does everyday life look like from the vantage point of the practices of Islamic piety and the forms of relationality that are materialized in dawat? What does the vision of Islamic piety do for its adherents against other normative possibilities for Muslim and Islamic life? What is the form of moral order that the practices of piety engender? These are the questions that animate this book. Answering them requires understanding how Tablighis constitute the domain of "religion" (din) in the ritual and performative space of dawat, how they separate it from "the world" (dunya), and how the ethical sensibilities crafted in this space come to be the basis for the moral transformation of the pious subject and the creation of moral order.

To understand how the religion/world distinction is constituted and, thus, how this moral intervention into the problems of the world takes shape requires recognizing religion as a distinctly modern domain but not one exclusively tied to secularism. Understanding the Tablighi vision of moral order requires moving beyond the focus on secularism that has become so central to the anthropology of Islam. As is well known, Talal Asad (1993, 2003) challenged Clifford Geertz's conceptualization of religion as a system of symbols in which religious symbols serves as vehicles for "moods and motivations," arguing that this erases the authorizing discourses and disciplines through which the boundaries of religion are constituted. The category "religion," Asad argues, is constructed as a universal and transhistorical category even though it presupposes a distinctly Protestant model of religion as an inward and immaterial set of beliefs to which an individual gives assent. In his later work (2003), Asad argues that the religion/secular binary is itself integral to the disciplinary power of secularism insofar as secularism aims not only to separate religion and state and limit religion to the private sphere but crucially also to transform nonliberal and nonsecular traditions into "proper" religions organized around Protestant conceptions of privatized, interior belief. Secularism strips religions of their embodied and material dimensions, subordinating these other forms of life to the secular sensibilities of modern life.

Building on these insights, Saba Mahmood (2005) and Charles Hirschkind (2006) show how the Islamic revival in Egypt has stridently resisted this liberal-secular project of transforming Islam into a matter of private belief. Drawing on Foucault's (1994) conception of ethics as "technologies of the self" by which he means those practices through which an individual constitutes oneself as an ethical subject, Saba Mahmood shows that women in an Islamic piety movement in Egypt understand religious practices to be the disciplinary means for molding subjectivity, cultivating a habitus that directs a person toward ethical action in the world. These practices of ethical self-cultivation, Mahmood shows, defy liberal-secular conceptions of agency and freedom in which agency is about realizing autonomy against rules imposed by society (see Strathern 1988). The women in Mahmood's piety movement aim to replicate in their lives the ideals that they derive from the Islamic tradition. Similarly, Charles Hirschkind (2006) shows that sermon-listening in the Islamic Revival in Egypt creates a "counterpublic" to that of the secular public enforced by the secular state. Hirschkind shows that sermon listening is not merely about acquiring the content of Islamic knowledge but rather an embodied practice that hones the senses and orients a person to God's command, thus making him or her capable of living an Islamic life.

My argument draws on these critical insights about the relationship between the Islamic tradition organized around embodied practices that aim to cultivate pious sensibilities that enable a Muslim to live an Islamic life. Indeed, Tablighis are deeply committed to creating an Islamic habitus through the meticulous and careful modeling of oneself on the norms embodied in the textual sources of Islam and the example of the Prophet. As Mahmood and Hirschkind rightly note, Islamic pietists believe and say that their practices cultivate Islamic virtues like sincerity, humility, and pious fear. Yet, the Foucauldian concept of ethical self-cultivation comes perilously close to replicating the ideological claims of Islamic pietists like Tablighis and erases the problems, tensions, and indeterminacies within this process. Tablighis, for instance, insist that God puts faith in the heart in exchange for the sacrifices made in dawat, and this faith is the fount for virtuous dispositions that cannot be created by any other means. But, as we learn quickly in the Tablighi Jamaat and other movements of Islamic piety, this faith does not always materialize and is cut through with what Mathijs Pelkmans (2017) calls "fragile conviction." Moreover, Tablighis recognize that practice is not conducted solely by an individual on him or herself but is also about creating a connection (jor) between Muslims that allows Muslims to come to "stand together on the good." In other words, Islamic piety in the Tablighi Jamaat is also about creating an Islamic community and specific types of pious relationships between Muslims, or what I will call pious relationality. Pious relationality is not always materialized, and even when it is, it requires constant effort and upkeep without which it can unravel.

Much of the criticism of the anthropological literature on the "piety turn" and pious self-cultivation has centered on how this literature erases the plurality of moral lives that Muslims live and the ambiguity, ambivalence, and tensions that animate "everyday" Muslim life. Samuli Schielke (2015) argues that the work of scholars on Islamic piety fails to examine the multiple "moral registers" available to Muslims because it assumes a singular, underlying moral imperative and ignores how morality "is not only situational, unsystematic, and ambiguous" but "also does not have clear boundaries" (56). Schielke argues that morality follows "situational logics" and is not reducible to a single imperative (59). By contrast, he argues that what is needed is to attend to how Muslims wrestle with these multiple moral registers and thus attend to the complex, ambivalent, and conflictual ethical decision-making that characterizes "everyday" Muslim life. Sadia Abbas argues that the literature on Islamic piety essentializes the Islamic tradition, reducing it to a monolithic whole, ignoring the fault lines, tensions, and conflicts that characterize Muslim societies. In these accounts, Muslim selves should be thought of as "unstable" (Marsden and Restikas 2013) and "multidimensional" (Simon 2014) rather than defined by the imperatives of Islamic piety (see Kloos and Bleekers 2018 for an overview). Such critiques dovetail with broader calls within the anthropology of ethics to focus on ethical reflexivity, or the ability of people to step away from social norms to reflect on them, and to locate individuals within a field of diverse moral possibilities (Laidlaw 2014).

The critique of the piety literature raises some important concerns about how the project of Islamic piety must be situated in relation to other forms of Muslim life and to other ways of constructing Muslim identity (Silverstein 2003; Bangstad 2009). However, as David Kloos (2018) has aptly argued, Muslims are not "locked in or struck by a condition of insoluble moral tensions and unattainable futures (12)." Kloos shows that the failure to achieve pious ideals does not in itself negate the quest for piety; rather, moral failure itself becomes a focus of reflexive attention and efforts to resolve the tensions that exist between the pursuit of piety and other "everyday" concerns. Following Kloos (2018), *The Promise of Piety* focuses on how ambivalence, tension, and ambiguity arise in the aspiration for Islamic piety among Pakistani Tablighis. The argument I develop here is that the tensions that arise are not simply features of living in a plural moral space. Rather they are products of a structural tension within the ritual ideology of dawat that must be managed through specific techniques (cf. Schielke 2015). These tensions arise from the effort to model life around the Prophetic ideal and the potential for change in every iteration of that model in dawat, change that departs from the model and thus threatens to undermine its efficacy. This basic internal problem, I show, is managed through pious companionship (*sohbat*) structured around what I call the "ethics of hierarchy." The Tablighi, recognizing his own limitations, submits to the authority of pious others in ritualized acts of pious listening as well as in "everyday" forms of citationality that constitute and reproduce a hierarchical form of pious relationality that is at the center of Tablighi congregational life. What we see is not just the constitution of pious selves but also the creation of an institutional structure that gives a distinct shape to domain of religion (din). *The Promise of Piety* then turns to how the pious relationality structured by the ethics of hierarchy serves as the basis for transforming both domestic and public life to create what Tablighis understand to be an Islamic moral order.

Addressing the issues raised here requires a theoretical shift away from self-cultivation to one that emphasizes piety as a relational form and an intersubjective achievement realized in practices of semiotic mediation. The literature on semiotic mediation in anthropology can be traced back to an effort to overcome the limits of a Sassurian grammar and to create a dynamic, pragmatic, and socially grounded theory of language. This approach informs a broad literature in linguistic and semiotic anthropology on reflexive sign use (Jakobson 1971; Silverstein 1976; Mertz 1985; see Agha 2007). Our focus here is on "religion as mediation" or as a set of reflexive practices, sensorial forms, and material objects that stand between in order to create a relationship between people as well as between people and nonhuman or spiritual beings (Engelke 2010; see Meyer and Moors 2006 and Meyer 2009). I argue that dawat is what Birgit Meyer (2011) has called a "sensational form" or "relatively fixed modes of invoking and organizing access to the transcendental" (29). Sensational forms are structured by distinct semiotic ideologies, or cultural understandings of what signs are and how they work, and this defines how they conceptualize and value various semiotic media as vehicles for divine presence (Keane 2003).

Anthropologists working across the Abrahamic traditions have focused on linguistic and semiotic mediation (Engelke 2007; Eisenlohr 2018; Fader 2009; see Stasch 2011). Niloofar Haeri's (2003) careful examination of Arabic as simultaneously a sacred and ordinary language provides a model for this in the anthropology of Islam. As a sacred language, it is seen as a nonarbitrary means for the creation of a relationship with God, and therefore as a means for divine presence. Brinkley Messick (1992) shows that Islam is structured around what he calls "recitational logocentrism," the idea that the human voice is the unmediated means for the creation of divine presence. Scholars working across Abrahamic traditions have stressed how a "direct" relationship to transcendental power is one of the hallmarks of modernity (see also Mazzarella 2006). In his work among the Masowe Apostolics in Zimbabwe, Matthew Engelke (2007) shows how the sharp distinction between spirit and matter creates a perennial and almost obsessive concern with the "thingification" of religiosity, the turning of an inner and immaterial expression of spirit into an "object" that becomes an obstacle to a "live and direct" relationship and experience with God. In the study of mediation among Mauritian Muslims of the Barelwi denomination, Patrick Eisenlohr (2006, 2018) shows how they use *naat* or devotional songs in praise of the Prophet as a means for a relationship of immediacy or directness with God. Building on these arguments, this book examines how dawat serves as a basis for mediating a direct relationship to God as well as a means for the creation of a distinct form of pious relationality between Muslims that Tablighis say allows Muslims to "stand together on the good."[2]

The concept of self-cultivation has had the unfortunate effect of reproducing the notion of an individuated and bounded subject who acts on him or herself (see Mittermaier 2011). It, therefore, has backgrounded the relational dynamics of subject formation, the indeterminacy in the creation of piety, and the wider political implications of creating an Islamic moral order in a plural social and political context like Pakistan. The approach of semiotic mediation is able to address all of these issues. We have long known from Goffman (1959) that a person is always performing for others and that a person's sense of themselves is shaped by how they are perceived by others. *The Promise of Piety* examines Islamic piety as an intersubjective achievement by focusing on how piety is realized in recognition from others, and not just any others but very definite types of pious others, those who have pious authority within the Tablighi congregation (chapters 3 and 4). The book shows how a distinct form of pious relationality is constituted in the ritual practices of dawat and in the congregational life of the Tablighi Jamaat. This pious relationality must be created and sustained against both internal tensions and the threats posed by other possibilities of configuring Islam and Muslimness, and we focus on the reflexive techniques through which these problems are addressed (chapters 4 and 5). Crucially, Islamic piety is not only a self-making project but also a world-making one in which transformations of the self are intimately bound up with the transformation of others. This means that Islamic piety is a hegemonic project of transforming and subordinating other forms of relationality and remaking the world. We will examine how the ethics of hierarchy structures dawat as a moral intervention in domestic and public life. This book shows how the distinct constitution of religion around pious relationality in dawat becomes the ground on which Tablighis erect an Islamic moral order that they believe can transcend the political fragmentation and violence of life in postcolonial Pakistan (chapters 5, 6, and 7).

Chapter Overview

The Promise of Piety shows how the broad features of the Islamic tradition reconfigured by the historical particularities of modernity are materialized in specific practices of dawat. It further explores the political implications of the Tablighi project of creating an Islamic moral order in the diverse and contested political landscape of Islam in postcolonial Pakistan. Toward this end, this book is broken into three sections. Section 1 entitled "The Modernity of Piety" focuses on how religion (din) comes to be defined under British colonialism and in postcolonial Pakistan. In chapter 1, I outline how British colonialism created the conditions for the rise of the scriptural traditionalism of the Deobandi ulama out of which Tablighi Jamaat emerges. Specifically, I show how the British efforts to codify Islamic law in the nineteenth century sharpened the distinction between "religious" (dini) and "worldly" (dunyavi) domains and reconfigured the domain of religion around scriptural authority, displacing the emphasis on sacred genealogy that had been central to religious authority in South Asian Islam. The distinction between religious and customary law created the conditions for the rise of a broad project of Islamic reform that aims to purify Islam of customary practices, particularly those associated with the Sufi emphasis on the intercessory powers of saints. Moreover, colonial modernity and specifically the wide availability of print created new possibilities for the creation of Islamic authority and thus opened a field of possibilities for mediating a relationship to God and creating Islamic authority. In this contested Islamic public sphere, the Tablighi Jamaat takes up this project of Islamic reform by emphasizing dawat as an embodied means for the realization of a direct relationship to God.

Chapter 2 explores the political relevance of directness in contemporary Pakistan against the backdrop of Pakistani nationalism. Pakistani nationalism has been structured around a genealogical imaginary that assumed that high-caste (*ashraf*) Muslims were purer Muslims and that it was their task to uplift low-caste (*ajlaf*) Muslims as well as reform their religious practices. This logic frames caste, class, and ethnic hierarchies that exclude a range of people from occupying positions as proper Islamic subjects of the Islamic nation. By reenacting the Prophet's example, dawat returns the Tablighi to the time of the Prophet, the original generative movement of Islam, thereby creating a direct relationship to God. In doing so, dawat obviates and even reverses the hierarchies that structure Pakistani political life. Dawat extends Islamic authority to those who were previously denied it by the terms of Pakistani nationalism, allowing them to become the bearers of a pure, authentic Islam. I argue that dawat is a ritual of transcendence that allows people defined as "low" in the caste, class, and ethnic hierarchies of the nation to transcend their "worldly" origins and become agents of Islamic moral order. This promise of piety explains the millions of Pakistani Muslims that flock through the gates of the Tablighi Jamaat.

Section 2 entitled "The Semiotics of Piety" turns to how this direct relationship is materialized in semiotic and performative practice and how it structures pious relationality within the congregation. Dawat is a "sensational form" or a set of organized practices, techniques, and tools for mediating a relationship to transcendental power and therefore creating the conditions for divine presence in the world (Meyer 2011). Chapter 3 outlines the relationship between the ritual ideology of dawat and the hierarchical structure of the congregation. Built on a creed paradigm (Keane 2007), dawat functions as a mode of ethical self-cultivation precisely because it is a performance of Prophetic example that draws the gaze of others. I show that dawat mobilizes iconic signs associated with Prophetic example and creates a sense of moral responsibility in the Tablighi for living up to the ethical entailments of Islamic iconicity. Performance transforms Islamic iconicity, a relationship of similarity with the Prophetic model, into an indexical relationship or a relationship of contiguity with that model. Through the repeated performance of dawat, one creates proximity to God, which is manifest in one's words becoming "heavy" with divine agency, allowing one to affect others and draw them to the congregation. As one's words become heavy with divine agency, one ascends the sacred hierarchy of the Tablighi Jamaat. Ascending the sacred hierarchy transforms one from being primarily a pious listener of the words of others to a pious speaker. Piety, then, can be thought of not only as a means of ethical self-cultivation but also as a sacred hierarchy that structures the Tablighi congregation and movement.

Chapter 4 examines the role of pious companionship (sohbat), which manages and mediates the tensions that arise in the performance of dawat. At the heart of the ritual ideology of dawat is a tension between, on the one hand, the idea that Islamic tradition is complete and perfect, and, on the other, the possibility that every iteration can create new meanings that depart from the original, a problem captured in the dangers of "innovation" (biddat). This tension threatens to produce fragmentation in the movement that must be managed through participation in congregational life and specifically in acts of pious companionship. Piety requires adopting a stance of submission to pious authority and being "acted upon" by pious others. This involves not only ritualized acts of listening to sermons but learning more everyday forms of citationality of pious others who serve as exemplars of pious becoming. The humility and patience manifest in pious listening and citationality is what I call the ethics of hierarchy, and it is central to pious relationality in the Tablighi Jamaat. Pious relationality I show regulates the creation of pious authority and slows the temporality of pious becoming, and thus manages the fissures and dispersal of the Tablighi congregation. The ethics of hierarchy is therefore the basis for the moral reproduction of the Tablighi congregation.

The third and final section titled "The Promise of Piety" shows how this pious relationality that is created in dawat and defines the domain of religion for Tablighis becomes the basis for the moral transformation of the world. Chapter 5 focuses on how "certain faith," the ideal to which Tablighis strive, depends on creating an Islamic home organized around pious male authority. An Islamic home subsumes patriarchal authority in the family within the authoritative voice of the congregation's pious Elders, creating a single line of authority from God to Elders to father to son. This creation of a pious home is understood by Tablighis as the basis for sustaining piety. While some Tablighis can create a pious home, for many this is unrealizable, and this creates in them religious doubt. I show that the value of piety is unevenly distributed between familial and non-familial Tablighis, and this is experienced as a difference in the capacity to embody certain faith. However, the ethics of hierarchy stresses the limits of pious agency to transform others and reframes and valorizes the struggle against doubt as a sacrifice for God. This secures commitment even from those who are not able to establish model families and thus certain faith. I argue that the recognition of the limits of pious agency and the emphasis on individual striving help to manage the problem of doubt and accept living in spaces of cultural and religious plurality. The ethics of hierarchy, therefore, enables the Tablighi Jamaat to incorporate people from diverse backgrounds and thrive in diverse social and political contexts and is thus a condition for the growth of the movement.

Chapter 6 outlines how Tablighis understand the ethics of hierarchy as a basis for remedying the communal discord and violent ethnic and sectarian fragmentation that characterizes political life in Pakistan. Tablighis understand this political context through the idiom of moral chaos (fitna) and see dawat as the exclusive basis for the moral regeneration of the Islamic community. Tablighis mobilize this logic against the *politiks* of modernist Islamist groups, who they insist conflate religion and the world and therefore fail to spread Islamic virtue and undermine the creation of an Islamic community. The Tablighi rejection of politiks is based on the idea that it represents a worship of the self and thus a source of unruly and surplus agency. I argue that the sharp contrast that Tablighis draw between dawat and politiks must be understood as a reflexive response to the constitutive role of Islamic governmentality in deepening ethnic and sectarian divisions and the intense competition over Islamic authority in a bourgeoning Islamic public sphere. While scholars have defined the Tablighi Jamaat as an "apolitical, quietist movement" (Metcalf 2004, 266), I show that Tablighis engage in a form of pious mediation that aims to remedy conflicts and regenerate moral relationships among Muslims and thus recreate the conditions for an Islamic life. In contrast to the hierarchies and forms of authority that define political life in Pakistan, dawat is understood as a freely made sacrifice for God that comes with no material gain. Pious authority is, therefore, understood by Tablighis to escape the twin ills of political life: self-interest and domination. In dawat, religion comes to be anchored in pious authority, and this becomes the basis for domesticating the powers of modern life. By offering an alternative conception of sovereignty to the Islamic state, dawat carries the promise of transcending the violence and fragmentation that afflicts life in postcolonial Pakistan.

The final chapter takes up the relationship between religious violence and popular politics by focusing on the rising incidence of blasphemy accusations in the past few decades. Vigilante and mob violence against blasphemy accused has become a perennial feature of political life in Pakistan. This violence is framed in liberal-secular discourse as "religious violence," a concept that presumes that the problem of violence arises from excess passions and the absence of reason in religion. I argue that understanding the relationship between religion and violence in contemporary Pakistani life requires attending to how religious practices generate their own ethical affordances, the potential for distinct ethical responses to social and political situations. I show that while blasphemy politics depends on the sacralization of the state and law, and collapsing the distinction between the Pakistani state and the sacred law of the shariat, dawat depends on expanding the gap between the current Pakistani state and the moral state of Islam, pushing the latter to the future. For Tablighis, the violence of blasphemy politics only hardens the boundaries among Muslims and between Muslims and non-Muslims and thus undermines *dawat* as a means for the circulation of sacred bodies and words. Although Tablighis recognize blasphemy as a form of moral injury, they redirect efforts toward reproducing the conditions for dawat. While the Tablighi response does not transcend the structural conditions for "religious violence" toward sectarian and religious minorities, it does mitigate the violence of blasphemy politics. To understand "religious violence," we must locate it at the intersection of state sovereignty and popular politics.

The Promise of Piety shows how religion is constituted in Tablighi Jamaat and how this becomes the basis for a moral intervention into social and political life in Pakistan, but this also raises a broader question about the relationship between religion and modernity. I argue that it is the capacity for transcending one's social origins and reimagining oneself as a different subject than what one was in the past that makes Islamic piety in the Tablighi Jamaat decidedly modern. In liberalism, the hegemonic and canonical form of modernity, it is the sovereign individual who is "set apart" and, through the exercise of autonomous reason, becomes an agent for moral order. This, however, is only one possible conception of modernity, and there is a range of other ways to configure transcendence. Dawat enables the Tablighi to stand apart from and above the world to then act on it to create moral order, and it is, therefore, best understood as an alternative form of sovereign transcendence. An examination of Islamic piety in the Tablighi Jamaat points to how religious and hierarchical forms of sovereign transcendence compete for the mantle of moral order in modernity.

Part 1
THE MODERNITY OF PIETY

1
COLONIAL SECULARISM AND THE MAKING OF SCRIPTURAL TRADITIONALISM IN BRITISH INDIA

The Tabighi Jamaat was founded in the 1920s by Muhammad Ilyas, an Islamic scholar (*alim*) trained in the Dar-ul-Uloom madrassa in the town of Deoband in North India. The ulama at Dar-ul-Uloom, also known as the Deobandi ulama, were key forces in the colonial era in pursuing the purification of Islamic practices from what were deemed "innovations" (biddat) on the original Islam of the Quran and Prophetic tradition (sunnat). Historians of South Asia describe this effort to purify Islamic life and return to the "original" Islam of the Quran and Prophetic tradition as the project of Islamic reform. This project took on great urgency in the minds of Muslim elites and Islamic authorities in the period after the Rebellion of 1857 and the transference of sovereign power from the East India Company to the British Crown after the passing of the Government of India Act of 1858. The loss of Muslim sovereignty under British rule created a new urgency for Islamic reform and vitalized a diverse array of traditionalist and modernist Islamic movements (Zaman 2018). The term reform or *islah* means "correct" and is often invoked by Deobandi ulama to mean the inculcation of Islamic values and virtues rooted in Islam as it is embodied in the scriptural sources, the Quran, understood as the word of God and the Prophetic tradition (sunnat). This Islam of the Prophet, they believed, has been corrupted through association with local traditions and customs and especially through interactions with Hinduism. The term for reform is often used alongside the term "renewal" (*tajdid*), understood as a process of reviving the past and making the present conform to the exemplary past.

Drawing on the teaching of the Deobandi ulama, Muhammad Ilyas aimed to purify Islam and return Muslims to the original Islam as it was embodied in the Quran and Prophetic tradition and teach them to live according to the broad normative framework of the shariat as it had been articulated by the ulama. For Ilyas, the purpose of dawat was not primarily to convert non-Muslims but to strengthen the faith (iman) of Muslims themselves, which had become weak from living among non-Muslims. For Ilyas and for early recruits to the Tablighi Jamaat, many Muslims remained only nominally Muslim and unaware of even the most basic tenets of Islam, and this was especially true for "new Muslims" (ajlaf) or those who had more recently converted to Islam and had roots in local practices and Hinduism. The new Muslims were especially in danger of drifting away from Islam as they had never really been weaned off their customs. The Tablighi Jamaat was founded on the premise that it was the responsibility of "old Muslims" (ashraf), or those whose families had been Muslims for long periods of time and could trace their roots to the Middle East and Central Asia, to deliver to them the basics of Islamic knowledge and practice. For Ilyas, dawat would be the means through which the ashraf or high-caste Muslims with greater knowledge and purer Islamic practices would draw the ajlaf or low-caste Muslims with less knowledge and "impure" forms of Islamic practices to the Islam of the Quran and Prophetic tradition.

The central aim of the Islamic reform movements today is to purify Islam of corruptions or innovations (biddat) that have seeped into the lives of Muslims, corruptions or accretions that many Muslims in Pakistan associate with Hinduism. Even today, the boundary between pure, upper-caste Muslims and impure customary practices of lower-caste Muslims shapes many currents of Islamic thought and is central to the purification project of the Tablighi Jamaat. In this chapter, I argue that while this scriptural traditionalism can be traced back to the precolonial period, the drive for purification was less central to Islamic practice in South Asian Islam prior to colonialism and flourished into a defining feature of Muslim politics under British colonialism. Our purpose here is not to provide a comprehensive history of Islamic forces under colonialism but to chart out the broad parameters of scriptural traditionalism in the Deobandi tradition from which the Tablighi Jamaat emerges and to situate this in the political contestation over Islam in postcolonial Pakistan.

The project of Islamic reform that has been zealously pursued by a range of Islamic movements in Pakistan depends crucially on the construction of religion as a distinct domain of knowledge and practice defined primarily in relation to the Islamic textual sources: the Quran, Prophetic tradition (sunnat), and Islamic jurisprudence (fiqh) are understood as the authoritative sources for the true and authentic Islam. This creation of the domain of religion cannot be understood without understanding the role of British colonial governance that produced the shift in value toward a scripturalist conception of Islam. The colonial effort to create a unified and standardized Islamic law helped convert scriptural knowledge into an autonomous and primary source of Islamic authority, severing the ties between scriptural and genealogical forms of authority. This shift in focus to the autonomy and authority of scriptural sources created new possibilities for Muslims to acquire Islamic knowledge and authority regardless of caste and class origins. This conception of Islam furnished the grounds for the development of the modern madrassa and created a flurry of diverse and competing efforts to define and objectify Islamic knowledge, efforts that became themselves entangled in a broadening Islamic public sphere made possible by the wide availability of new print technologies.

Within this broad transformation, the Deobandi ulama retained and elaborated a key aspect of the Islamic tradition; they insisted that the truth of scriptural knowledge could only be realized by creating an embodied relationship to the sacred past, and they argued that it could only be understood by a moral person as only those who fulfill their ritual duties were capable of understanding and interpreting the sacred textual sources. In emphasizing the ritualized and embodied nature of Islamic knowledge, the Deobandi ulama set themselves against not only custom but against modernist Islamic alternatives that emphasized the primacy of reason and rationality (Ingram 2018; Stephens 2018). The Tablighi Jamaat conceptualization of dawat as deed or practice (amal) aims to purify Islam of what it sees as the corruptions of Sufism and Sufi-adjacent forms of Islam, but it emphasizes embodied practice against what it sees as the excess value placed on reason (*aql*) in the modernist conceptions of Islam that are central to the Islamic revival in Pakistan.

The Tablighi Jamaat

The early twentieth century witnessed an explosion of religious revivalist and proselytizing activity among Muslims, Hindus, Sikhs, and Christians in the Indian subcontinent. The period was marked by intense competition between Hindu, Muslim, Sikh, and Christian groups for conversion. Scholars trace revivalist and proselytizing activity to the competition over bodies that resulted from the classification and enumeration of religious communities under British colonial rule (Pandey 1990; Appadurai 1996). The British imagined India to be made of up of "religious" communities with distinct traditions and philosophies, an assumption and approach that organized British census categories (Cohn 1996) and language policy (Lelyveld 1993) and ultimately served as the basis for Indian electorates (Jalal 1995). The drawing of these boundaries by colonial governments created, rather than just reflected, Indian realities in that it pushed

Hindus and Muslims to imagine themselves as essentially distinct, mutually exclusive communities, a fact that we know historically led to the rise of divergent nationalist movements. Colonial governmentality spurred an intense competition for delineating the proper boundaries of the religious community and created the grounds for competition over membership of these respective religious communities. In other words, it helped spur a broad politics of authenticity that aimed to define what constitutes the appropriate form and content of religion and thus define the boundaries of the religious community. The competition that erupted during the late nineteenth and early twentieth centuries spurred elite efforts to reform religious practices and bring them into the proper boundaries of religion, and these efforts focused on drawing in members of low-caste groups who were perceived to be ambiguous and ambivalent in their religiosity, neither properly Muslim nor Hindu, into the fold of communal boundaries.

In the British colonial imaginary, Indian civilization was essentially Hindu and could be traced back to the Vedic period. Islamic civilization, by contrast, had its roots in the Middle East and Central Asia and arrived in India through a series of raids and conquests (see Eaton 2003). Muslims were thus outsiders to India. For the British, Islamic rule over "native" Hindu civilization was despotic and had driven a spiritually rich and flourishing civilization into moral decay and dissolution (Breckenridge and Van der Veer 1993; Van der Veer 1994). When the British established direct rule over India after the Rebellion of 1857, known in British historiography as the Mutiny, Mughal rule understood as "Muslim" was made the explicit point of contrast to British rule. The British construed themselves as liberating Indians from the yoke of Muslim rule and reestablishing the grounds under which Indian civilization could be restored to its past glory. The British promised to uplift Hindus from their deplorable state of servitude to Muslims, but they also said that this required the elimination of backward customs like child marriage and bride immolation. The British narrative of civilizational decline articulated with Brahmanical ideas about cosmological decline, situated Brahmans as natural leaders, and placed Muslims at the center of Brahmanical anxieties about moral decay and destruction. As Peter Van der Veer (1994) has shown, this resulted in a call for Hindu revival and reform and an effort to recuperate India's lost glory of Vedic times. From the middle of the nineteenth century onwards, India witnessed what M. N. Srinavas (1956) called "Sanskritization" of social life or the "gradual reshaping of local beliefs and practices in the direction of Brahmanical ideals" (Van der Veer 1994, 166). Hindu reformers, for instance, those associated with the Arya Samaj (Noble Society) that launched the *shuddhi* or purification movement, called for the elimination of the corrupting influences of Islamic rule from Hinduism.

A comparable sensibility took hold among Indian Muslim elites. Muslims developed a sense that they were indeed a diasporic people whose true origins were in the Middle East and Central Asia and whose religion had fallen into a state of disarray as a result of the corrupting influences of Hinduism.[1] Fears of both Hindu revivalism and Christian missionary work, which Muslims and Hindus both imagined to be directly tied to the colonial state, spawned several forms of preaching efforts, one of which was the Tablighi Jamaat in North India (for a detailed account, see Reetz 2006, 151–60). The Dar-ul-Uloom madrassa of Deoband launched a Department of Preaching around the same time as the Arya Samaj launched its purification movement and began propagating their ideas through journals like the *al-Qasim* and *al-Rishad* as well as through the establishment of Quranic schools and field offices. The prominent Deobandi alim Ashraf Ali Thanwi established an organization called The Association for the Protection of Muslims (Majlis Siyanatul Muslimin) in Saharanpur, the task of which was to help "reform" Muslim practice by bringing it in line with Islamic textual sources, which they saw as a way to protect against the efforts of the Arya Samaj to lure Muslims away from Islam. Similarly, the Barelwi sect established a Society Pleasing to the Prophet Muhammad, and the ulama of Firangi Mahal, a Sufi-oriented Islamic madrassa, also established its own preaching organization. The Ahmadiyya community, who were condemned by the other Sunni groups for being heretics, began as a missionary movement, and they quickly turned their attention to defending the Rajput Muslims from the efforts of the shuddhi movement.

In keeping with the teachings of the Deobandi ulama, Muhammad Ilyas believed that "old" or high-caste Muslims (ashraf), those who had deep Islamic genealogies, have a fundamental duty to teach "new" or low-caste Muslims (ajlaf) who had converted more recently to the fundamentals of Islam. The true Islam, for Ilyas, could be located exclusively in three sources: the Quran, the hadith literature (documented sayings and acts of the Prophet), and Hanafi jurisprudence (fiqh) as articulated by the ulama. Ilyas recognized that low-caste Muslims could not learn the basics of Islamic knowledge and practice in the madrassa, so it was the duty of those with access to Islamic sources to deliver the message directly to them. The Tablighi Jamaat's first project was the Meos, a population who lived in the region of Mewat, sixty-five kilometers southwest of Delhi. Like the Rajput Muslims targeted by the Arya Samaj's shuddhi movement, the Meos identified as Muslims and most were from low-caste backgrounds and maintained many practices that Islamic reformers understood as Hindu corruptions, except they did maintain Islamic circumcision as well as Islamic forms of burial. The Meos' history was also cut through by recurring conflict with the Muslim rulers of Delhi (Sikand 2002). This shaped Muhammad Ilyas's perspective on the Meos as only nominally Muslim and therefore particularly open to Hindu efforts at conversion. As one Tablighi ideologue would later write, "The Meos were even unaware of the appearance of namaz (mandatory prayer) itself. If perchance, a Muslim entered their territory, they would all gather together in amazement and wonder what he was up to, thinking that he might have a pain in the stomach or that he had lost complete control over his senses, because of which he was repeatedly standing up and sitting down" (cited in Sikand 2002, 110). The Meos clearly fit the model of a community that was seen as having never adopted the correct Islam. Even today, the Meos occupy a central place in Tablighi narratives as a community that transformed itself from being nominally Muslim to becoming a model of Islamic piety for all other Muslims.

For Ilyas, creating Muslims who had a proper relationship to the sacred past was the basis for restoring the power of Muslims. Ilyas believed that Muslims had fallen into a state of internal division and disarray because of the accretion of corruptions in the Islamic tradition that had developed from interactions with Hinduism. This was a position that Ilyas took from the Deobandi ulama who drew a line connecting themselves to the eighteenth-century Islamic reformer Shah Waliullah (d. 1762) (see Metcalf 1982). Muhammad Ilyas's conception of dawat was not just instrumental in terms of delivering a message alone. Ilyas's writings state that dawat was a fundamental duty for every individual Muslim (*farz-i-ayn*), and his goal was not only to give dawat to the Meos but also to train them to give dawat to each other, which he insisted was how they would be able to sustain their faith and remain Muslim. Ilyas insisted that the efficacy of dawat came from the fact that it was grounded in the Prophet's example (sunnat) and was, therefore, a practice (amal) in its own right. As an Islamic practice, it had to be conducted in the manner (tariqa) that the Prophet himself conducted it. I will have much more to say about this method in chapters 3 and 4, but for now, it is worth noting that the Prophet was the exemplary human being (*insan al-kamil*) and the perfect embodiment of God's command. This meant that his actions were divinely inspired, and it is the duty of all Muslims to replicate them as closely as possible in daily life. According to at least one account by an early Tablighi, the "method of preaching" (tariqa-e-tabligh) was also divinely inspired and came to Ilyas in a dream. Although Ilyas did not himself say this, he insisted that dawat was a blessing from God and that "the closeness and the help and blessings [of Allah] is not to be found in the case of other methods" (cited in Sikand 2002, 131).

Central to Ilyas's movement was the idea that dawat had to be conducted in a face-to-face manner, just as the Prophet had done. Ilyas believed the Prophet gave dawat even before the revelation of the form and method of five daily prayers and even before the entirety of the Quran was revealed to the Prophet. This made dawat a foundational practice in Islam. For Ilyas, giving dawat was not only to spread Islam to others, though it was surely for this as well, but also for the "correction" (islah) of the person giving the dawat. In the process of giving dawat, a Tablighi was strengthening his own "faith" (iman). Ilyas conceived of dawat as a disciplinary practice; it disciplines the "lower self" (*nafs*) and orients a person toward his "spirit" (*ruh*), transforming the Tablighi in the very act of attempting to transform others. This commitment to a distinct, fact-to-face embodied and ritualized form of dawat positioned Ilyas, as it does the Tablighis who would follow, against Islamic actors who would use print as their primary means of dissemination, which Ilyas believed was creating factionalism and divisiveness. By contrast, he believed that dawat conducted in the way of the Prophet drew people together and unified the Islamic community. This form of dawat would restore the strength of the Islamic community and lead to the triumph over Hindu and Western powers.

The emphasis on embodied practice for Ilyas built on the Deobandi ulama's critique of print technology. As Brannon Ingram (2014) argues, the Deobandi ulama utilized printed pamphlets to circulate their message, but they nevertheless were deeply concerned about the possibilities latent in print to create centrifugal forces and were fearful that print materials would spur challenges to their authority. Ingram (2014) notes that these pamphlets continued to emphasize the importance of orality and positioned themselves as devices to facilitate an oral tradition (856). Ilyas's approach, then, drew directly on these concerns and represented a self-conscious effort to transcend the ideological discord within Muslim communities, discord that resulted from the availability of print technology and a growing circulation of texts. The association Ilyas drew between ideological discord and the negative impact of texts as a medium fundamentally shaped his commitment to dawat as a face-to-face and embodied practice. We will take up the issue of the ritual ideology that shapes Tablighi praxis in chapter 3, but first, it is necessary to look at the conditions that created the broader impetus to purify Islam that grounds not only the Tablighi Jamaat but also an array of other Islamic reform movements that have emerged in South Asia. This desire for a pure or authentic Islam depended crucially on the assumption of religion as a distinct, bounded sphere of activity. Far from being an inevitable part of the Islamic tradition, this conception of religion was constructed in relation to the colonial state, and specifically as an effect of the colonial state's project of governing Muslims through Islamic law.

Colonial Secularism and the Making of Scriptural Traditionalism

The notion that Islam is a "religion of the Book" is a widely accepted truism among Muslims and non-Muslims alike. It therefore seems obvious that command over textual knowledge should constitute the primary source of authority in Islam. A closer look at the history of Islam in South Asia, however, shows a more complex relationship between textual and genealogical forms of authority. Textual knowledge, while an integral part of Muslim life in South Asia, remained largely subsumed within and subordinate to genealogical forms of authority. In other words, command over textual knowledge itself was closely tied to the authority of influential elite families. Textual knowledge was tied to the morality of the persons interpreting them, and the morality of said persons was itself tied to their kinship and genealogical origins. It was the colonial transformation of the domain of religion that lent autonomy and vitality to textual authority and created the conditions for the rise of the ulama as a class of "religious experts" overseeing a distinct sphere of religion (see Zaman 2002). A key dimension of this transformation was the British effort to codify "religious law." The codification of Islamic law was part of a broad policy of what Julia Stephens (2018) calls "colonial secularism," an explicit effort to separate the religious and political spheres and subordinate the former, limiting the scope of religious law to the regulation of kinship. Religious law was codified against "customary law," which shifted the emphasis from a conception of moral personhood rooted primarily in kinship and genealogy (*nasb*) to one in which pious deeds (*hasb*) and pious consciousness (*taqwa*) could be separated from kinship and genealogical origins. In this section, I outline how this shift enabled the rise of the project of Islamic reform from which emerged the Tablighi Jamaat.

Understanding this shift requires a brief examination of the history of Islam in South Asia and the codification of Islamic law that happened under British colonialism. Sufi Islam had dominated the religious landscape of South Asia throughout much of the precolonial era and was central to the organization of the power of the Mughal empire. Sufi orders proliferated across the Muslim world during the twelfth and thirteenth centuries. The spread of Sufism to India was largely a result of the Mongol invasions, which drove influential Sufi spiritual leaders (*shaikhs*) out of Arab lands and into the Islamic sultanates of India. In India, Sufi leaders or *pirs* managed to establish their own domains of spiritual authority (*wilayat*) and came to wield tremendous power. The powers of Sufi pirs grew to such an extent that local rulers were compelled to recognize their authority and would even negotiate with them about jurisdiction over territory (Eaton 2002). Under the Mughal empire, the shrines of Sufi pirs became key sites of sovereign authority, and Mughal emperors and local rulers patronized these shrines to shore up their own authority. Azfar Moin (2012) argues that notions of sacred kinship that merged kinship and sainthood were central to the organization of Mughal rule, as it was for the Safavid dynasty in Iran. This link was clearly articulated in the reign of the Mughal emperor Akbar (1556–1605) who established himself as a spiritual guide to all within his realm and established a system of imperial discipleship that came to be known as the Divine Religion (*Din-i-Ilahi*) (Moin 2012, 17). Contrary to scholarly accounts that limit this dispensation to the rule of Akbar, Moin argues that this was a theme that ran throughout the Mughal empire. Mughal rule, he shows, drew its power not through its emphasis on scriptural authority but through patronage of a network of shrine complexes across the South Asian landscape and by mobilizing the symbols of sacred kinship.

Sufism in South Asia had long been organized around spiritual genealogy, which anchored a hierarchical cosmology that placed overarching value on descendants of the Prophet (*syeds*), followed by descendants of the Companions of the Prophet (*sahaba*), descendants of early converts (shaikhs) of Arab descent, followed by those who could trace their roots to Central Asia (Mughals and Pathans), and, finally, those that were seen as local converts from Hinduism, regarded as workers (*kammi*), and sometimes even referred to as "small Muslims" (*mussalli*) (see Eglar 2010). A broad distinction could be drawn between the nobility (ashraf) with "foreign" origins and commoners (ajlaf) of native (i.e., Indian) origins. This division was simultaneously marked by a distinction between landowners (zamindars) and those who worked the land or handled the plow (Eglar 2010 [1960]; Eaton 2002; Ho 2006). Hierarchical distinctions were maintained through asymmetrical marriage exchange in which wife-takers were superior to wife-givers and a theory of procreation in which essence and identity passed through patrilineal descent (Alavi 1972; Eglar 1960; Lefebvre 2014). Among this nobility were hereditary Sufi pirs known as *sajjada nishin* (literally, keepers of the prayer rugs) and their descendants who maintained the shrines devoted to their ancestors. These shrines were and remain crucial sites of worship for much of the population, including Hindus and Sikhs. Not only were these shrines sites for intercession with God but descendants of the Prophet were seen as capable of fairly adjudicating conflicts within clans, often between brothers and/or cousins over patrimony, and between competing clans over land and patronage. In this sense, sacred genealogy was integral to the functioning of precolonial and colonial South Asia (see Eglar 1960).

At the apex of this cosmological hierarchy were descendants of the Prophet (syeds). Although not all Sufi pirs are descendants of the Prophet, the most powerful are, and their power to intercede on behalf of supplicants was and continues to be predicated not only on the quality of their character or even their mastery of mysticism, but crucially on relations of descent to the Prophet. As Engseng Ho (2006) shows, the Prophet's descendants are said to have blood that carries divine light (*nur*) that grants them miraculous powers, both in the world and beyond. Most fully elaborated in the writings of Ibn-al-Arabi, the theory argues that Muhammad, the last of the Prophets, was the first being to be created from divine light, the primeval creation, which is the source of all subsequent beings. Divine light is the vital essence that animates the world and its creatures. In South Asia, the transmission of Prophetic descent conceived in terms of light, essence, and substance followed customary patrilineal channels and was upheld by Islamic law. Saintly light is transmitted through agnatic blood from the line of the Prophet to his descendants, and the patriline is conceived as the fount of divine vitality (Ho 2006).[2]

Devotional practices aimed at soliciting the intercession of Islamic saints have been integral to organizing social life for Muslims, Hindus, and Sikhs in South Asia. These practices entail giving alms or making supplications to living and dead saints who would then intercede (*tawassul*) on behalf of the practitioners to grant boons in the form of wealth, fertility, and healing. Sufi saints are regarded as channels of divine grace (*barakat*) due to their proximity to God (*qurbat*). They have the power to command spiritual agents such as *muwakkil* and *jinn* who possess people, especially women, and lead them down the path of madness and impropriety. For this reason, the saint is understood to be a protector of the honor (*izzat*) of families. Especially powerful saints can perform miraculous feats like providing fertility to infertile women, bringing rain in times of drought, and facilitating growth and protection of crops. Throughout the year, saint shrines (*mazaar/durgahs*) draw pilgrims from distant corners of South Asia who consult the saint on crucial matters of life and death. Saints are consulted or invoked during major life cycle rituals such as birth, marriage, and death. The powers of saints are greatly augmented after their death when they return to God, which is itself construed symbolically in terms of the marriage (*'urs*) of the saint to God. The death anniversaries of saints are celebratory events, and they are seen as occasions for earning religious merit and grace through sacrifice and giving (Werbner 2005; Werbner and Basu 1998; Lindholm 1998). Living saints are generally less powerful than dead ones, but they too perform everyday miracles, issue protective amulets (tawiz), and have the unique power to see into the hearts of people (Gilsenan 1982).

The decline of the Mughal empire in the late eighteenth and early nineteenth centuries and the growth of British power created a flurry of Islamic revivalist activity. On the one hand, the period witnessed the enhancement of the powers of Sufi pirs, especially away from the former imperial center of Dehli, for instance in Sindh and the Punjab. As the Mughal Empire unraveled and power was decentralized in the hands of local rulers, these rulers became increasingly dependent on influential pirs for their legitimacy. On the other hand, the period witnessed the rise and strengthening of a reformist ulama who called for purifying Islam of corruptions and innovations (biddat), which they regarded as having developed through close contact with Hinduism. While no sharp dichotomy can be drawn between Sufism and the practices of the ulama, the cult of saints was regarded by eighteenth-century reformers like Shah Waliullah (1703–1762) to be the product of Hindu influence and thus a target for reform (van der Veer 1992). Barbara Metcalf (1982) argues that the decline of Mughal rule created the deep anxieties of a loss of cultural standing among ulama who had once enjoyed patronage from the imperial center. These ulama articulated the notion that Islam was in decline because it had been corrupted by local customs and that only a return to the true Islam of the time of the Prophet could restore Muslim power. The growing availability of print technology enabled the reformist ulama to begin outreach efforts mobilizing instructional literature under the belief that ordinary Muslims could come to better understand the tenets of Islam. However, unlike the pirs and the landed aristocracy, their influence remained limited until the British crown took direct control of India in 1858.

It would of course be too simplistic to suggest that textual authority had no role in the precolonial period or that Sufism has no basis in the scriptural tradition. Islamic scholars had of course long debated the proper parameters of the religious tradition based on textual exegesis of the scriptural sources, but, as Muzaffar Alam (2004) notes, "jurists and theologians rarely had supreme legal authority" (14). The Mughal empire was not organized around a single authoritative Islamic law, and shariah was variable and attuned to local context and power structures. When the British took formal control of India, they hoped to maintain order by relying on and incorporating "traditional" authorities and began the project of codifying Islamic law. As Julia Stephens (2018) notes, the period after the Rebellion of 1857 established in the minds of the British that the best way to preserve order was to protect the "religious" sentiments of the native population by separating secular and religious affairs and granting autonomy to the religious sphere, which would become a central feature of secular governmentality under British colonialism (52).

In urban areas, the British sought to rule through the institutionalization of religious law and later through modes of democratic self-representation based on religious identities. This project assumed an encompassing distinction between Muslims and Hindus as bounded, mutually exclusive religious communities each with their own respective religious traditions. By contrast, British administrators assumed that rural areas were governed less by religion than by custom. This distinction between religion and custom was articulated in the socio-evolutionary paradigm developed by the Legalist Henry Maine (1861) and elaborated by the American ethnologist Lewis Henry Morgan (1877). In this socio-evolutionary paradigm, societies evolve from a primitive state in which social norms and solidarities are structured by kinship understood in terms of "blood" relations to ones in which people maintain primary allegiance as individuals through contractual relations, or, in the words of Maine, from status (*societas*) to contract (*civitas*), a movement that entails the separation of kinship from legal-jural domains. In the moral geography of British colonialism, this also mapped onto rural and urban space and became the basis for the tripartite distinction between customary, religious, and civil law that structured the colonial legal order.

British colonial policy varied significantly across colonial India, making it difficult to generalize, but it is clear that in regions with large rural Muslim populations like the Punjab and the Uttar Pradesh, Bengal, and Sindh, the British depended on the Muslim landed nobility and influential pir families to connect them to the mass of rural peasants (Gilmartin 1988). While the British maintained an overarching vision of British India as divided between "religious communities," British administrators were skeptical that "religion" captured the ethnographic reality of rural life. Shaped by a socio-evolutionary paradigm that viewed rural areas as locked in an earlier stage of development, colonial authorities understood rural social organization and life to be structured around "race" and "tribe." In 1872, the British passed the Punjab Laws Act, which established that rural order was governed not by "religion" but by "custom" and that this should be the basis for laws of personal status, which would regulate familial affiliation, marriage, and inheritance. After passing this law, revenue collectors were instructed to conduct surveys to empirically verify customary practices so the laws could be codified (Anderson 1993). The lieutenant-governor of the Punjab, Sir Robert Egerton, exclaimed in 1878 that "the most fundamental basis for the division of the population in this part of India is tribal rather than religious, and should rest, not upon community of belief or ceremonial practice, but upon ancestral community of race, in which, whether it be genuine or only suppositious the claimants of a common origin equally believe" (cited in Gilmartin 1981, 152). British administrators acted as de facto ethnographers, claiming to have understood the underlying principles that structured Muslim social life in rural areas. One prominent British official in the Punjab, C. L. Tupper, argued that "Native society . . . will be happier as long as it can be held together by the bonds of consanguinity" (cited in Gilmartin 1981, 153). Tupper claimed that Punjab had a "tribal" system in which "kinship and the land combine to determine and regulate the form and practice of our communities" (Gilmartin 1981, 154).

British administrators' understanding of kinship drew on Henry Maine's formulation of "patriarchal theory" from his work *Ancient Law* (1861), which he defined as "the theory of the origin of society in separate families, held together by the authority and protection of the eldest valid male ascendant" (192–93). For British administrators in the Punjab, rural Muslim social life was organized around kin-based loyalties of "tribes" and "clans," which they sometimes spoke of also in terms of "races," held together by bonds of agnatic blood and theories of common origin. C. L. Tupper argues that the kinship system was predicated on clan exogamy in which daughters were married "outside the closely drawn limits of the clan, but within the looser, but still remembered, circle of the tribe or race of origin" (Gilmartin 1981, 154). Tupper imagined a scenario in which giving daughters in marriage functioned to connect various "clans" to maintain "the sense that the clan had expanded from the family of a common ancestor" (Gilmartin 1981, 155). This system of alliances between clans, according to Tupper, is what undergirded the entire Punjabi rural social system. According to Tupper, rural social order depended on this system of alliances, but this system necessitated that inheritance pass exclusively through the male lines and that daughters be barred from inheritance. As Gilmartin (1981, 1988) shows, customary laws depended on excluding a great deal about local understandings of kinship, a fact that British administrators themselves occasionally noted. Nevertheless, in the interest of maintaining a stable set of traditional political brokers and a steady stream of land revenue, the "agnatic theory" was defended, becoming the foundation for the development of case law in the Punjab (Gilmartin 1988).

This agnatic theory of kinship was designed explicitly to facilitate the maintenance and consolidation of land to secure a stable and steady flow of taxation, with minimum military involvement (Washbrook 1981). Customary law exempted agricultural classes from the obligations to give rights of inheritance to women, which ensured that marriage could be contracted without fear that it could lead to the breakup of landholdings, thereby ensuring that land be retained in the hands of fewer intermediaries. The Punjab Alienation of Land Act of 1901 made land belonging to "agricultural tribes" inalienable and barred nonagricultural classes from acquiring land (see Nelson 2011). This policy not only enabled an unprecedented consolidation of land but also produced the effect of singling out some of the nobility as "natural" leaders in rural areas, many of whom were themselves *sajjada nishin*. This relationship with "traditional" authority would structure the politics of rural Punjab throughout the colonial period and become an enduring feature of the politics in postcolonial Pakistan, where land remains highly concentrated in the hands of aristocratic families and where Sufism remains integral to the legitimacy of rural social order.

If the colonial state's efforts to govern and regulate social life in rural areas revolved around the concept of custom, in urban areas it was framed around the category of religion. Well before the British state had taken formal control of India, the East India Company began formulating religious laws to help with administration in territories under its control. The Hastings Plan of 1772 established the colonial law court to adjudicate matters that fell under the areas controlled by the East India Company, stating that "in all suits regarding inheritance, succession, marriage and caste and other usages or institutions, the law of the Koran with respect to Mahomedans, and those of the Shaster with respect to the Gentoos [Hindus] shall be invariably adhered to" (cited in Zaman 2002, 21). As Anderson (1993) argues, the presumption that a single set of legal rules could apply to all persons professing adherence to Islam was far removed from both Islamic theory and the practice of Islamic law in South Asia. Confronted by a dizzying array of diversity of legal forms and authorities and driven by the theory that native communities should be governed by their own indigenous laws, the British aimed to create a "unified" Islamic law based on what they considered to be the authoritative texts of Islam (Zaman 2002), just as they did for Hinduism (Mani 1998).

In a rich historical account of the development of Islamic law in South Asia, Muhammad Qasim Zaman (2002) shows how what came to be known as the "Anglo Muhammadan Law" was built on a narrow set of Islamic sources and premised on the notion that the courts could not go beyond these authoritative sources to earlier ones, thereby greatly limiting the range and flexibility of juridical practice that had characterized the practices of the ulama in the precolonial period (Zaman 2002). British judges were frustrated by what they perceived as a complete lack of consistency in judgment on the part of native scholars, leading them to assume that "pure integrity [was] hardly to be found" among the natives who made up the law according to their own whims (Zaman 2002, 44). Deep mistrust of native authorities and frustrations with what they understood as inconsistent interpretations of the law led the British to focus on translation and standardization of textual sources and an insistence on relying on a very narrow set of sources deemed authoritative. As a result, Zaman argues that Islamic law under colonialism assumed a highly rigid quality and came to strongly emphasize the principle of *taqlid*, the following of judgments of authoritative figures of the past. If the logic undergirding precolonial juridical practice was context-specific, sensitive to persons of different social standing, particularly as it related to genealogy, then "the law" as the British now conceived it was invariant, equally applicable to every member of the community, and could be located in authoritative rulings of the past.

This history of the colonial state is important for our account of the Tablighi Jamaat because of the profound impact it had on native conceptions of religion (din) as a distinct domain of activity associated with the textual sources and the need to follow authoritative rulings of the past (taqlid). The reformist ulama in the late eighteenth and early nineteenth centuries had already articulated a program for purifying Islam of what were seen as corruptions and accretions upon an original, authentic Islam. This anxiety about the nature of Islam was spawned by the decline of Mughal rule and the quest for a new basis for Islamic sovereignty and unity. Reformist ulama made the case that common people should come to understand the basic tenets of Islam in order to live pious lives, but they could not conceive of commoners becoming the primary keepers or agents of Islamic knowledge. Shah Waliullah, the scholar to whom much of Islamic reformist thought in South Asia is traced, insisted on caste discrimination in determining the appropriateness of marriage. Moreover, the influence of the reformist ulama was of limited scope, and, broadly speaking, the lines between Sufi emphasis on genealogy and scriptural forms of Islam remained blurry (Metcalf 1982). The dominant forms of scriptural Islam remain tied to genealogical authority and are located in key ulama families like those of Firangi Mahal (Robinson 2001). This shifts significantly after the Rebellion of 1857 with the British efforts to construct an Islamic law becoming a full project of codification.

Scriptural Traditionalism and the Problem of Objectification

The loss of Muslim sovereignty after the Rebellion of 1857 and the codification of Islamic law created a new demand for Islamic education. The establishment of the Dar-ul-Uloom madrassa in the North Indian town of Deoband in 1867 marks a decisive moment in the growing emphasis on scriptural authority in South Asian Islam. The Dar-ul-Uloom madrassa became a model for madrassas across South Asia, spawning what is now called the Deobandi tradition. Unlike traditional Islamic learning, in which a student would train under a prominent alim who would impart knowledge about specific texts, after which he would move on to another alim to acquire mastery of other texts, the Dar-ul-Ulum was organized by classes, offered a curriculum, was staffed by a paid faculty, and provided living arrangements and necessities for its students. In this sense, it was modeled on European educational institutions and provided a standardized education for all students (Metcalf 1978). The colonial state, then, helped create the ulama as a centralized class of experts to oversee an object called "religion" (din) (Metcalf 1978).

While the codification of Islamic law opened some avenues for the ulama for state employment, the notion of the law as a fixed code also meant that the law could be administered by Muslims who were trained in British common law as well as by British magistrates themselves. In other words, despite the formal recognition of Islam in the law, the ulama experienced a decline in state patronage. In a rich study of the rise and spread of the Deobandi tradition, Brannon Ingram (2018) argues that the loss of state patronage pushed the ulama to engage directly with an emerging Muslim public sphere, made possible by the availability of new print technology. The ulama thus shifted from being state functionaries to keepers of public morality, an orientation reflected in the issuing of *fatwas* or religious edicts directly to Muslims in print literature. The ulama also established the now-widespread system of funding by collecting alms in an effort to establish the madrassa's autonomy from aristocratic families (Metcalf 1978). Indeed, one can see the push for financial autonomy of the madrassa itself as part of the effort to create the autonomy of religion from the influence of community authority and the ulama's claim of being answerable only to God rather than to the influence of human beings. Given that religious knowledge was the exalted form of knowledge that stood above all worldly knowledge, the ulama saw themselves as the rightful guides of the Muslim community who stood above worldly authority associated with genealogy and economic power.

Dale Eickelman (1992) argues that mass literacy transformed Muslim understandings of Islam from one that focuses on practice to one that focuses on Islam as a self-contained system that can be explicated in terms of its propositional content, a process he calls objectification. Indeed, the rise of new print publics addressing Muslims directly meant that the Deobandi ulama were competing with a number of other Islamic and Muslim orientations. For the ulama, the new possibilities of objectification of Islam were a paradoxical experience. On the one hand, the ulama could greatly augment their power by situating themselves as the keepers of public morality, but, on the other hand, the objectification of Islamic knowledge meant that Islamic authority could easily slip out of their hands and into the hands of lay Muslims who had access to this knowledge and even into the hands of non-Muslims. As Muhammad Qasim Zaman (2002) shows, the ulama adjusted to the new circumstances but retained key aspects of the Islamic tradition and were therefore what he aptly calls "custodians of change." Most notably, the ulama rejected the notion that Islam is a code to be deciphered by anyone, insisting that only pious Muslims were capable of interpreting and implementing the scriptural sources, and pious Muslims were those who fulfilled their ritual duties and lived according to the Prophet's example (sunnat). Non-Muslims would inevitably be drawn to false exegesis as would nonobservant Muslims. Hence, the ulama linked Islamic authority to moral personhood, and moral personhood was predicated on the fulfillment of the ritual obligations of Islam. Orthopraxy, or the idea that correct understanding or belief had to be based in correct practice (amal), became central to the ulama's conception of Islamic knowledge (ilm), a framework that for purposes of simplicity we can call scriptural traditionalism.

The scriptural traditionalism of the Deobandi ulama draws on an older logic of the primacy of orality and the dangers associated with textual practice, as well as the notion that reason (aql) cannot be separated from and extracted from embodied practices. In his remarkable study of Islamic textual practice in Yemen, Brinkley Messick (1992) argues that texts have a dual character in the Islamic tradition. On the one hand, Messick argues, text serves as a necessary "safeguard" for Islamic knowledge because it "permits preservation of life, memory, speech, event," but, on the other hand, "it harbors within a separation and a threat of falsehood" (213). Messick shows that in Islamic history, writing was seen as a kind of "temptation" that leads men to invent new truths that depart from the original divine intent of the Quran. Messick shows that inscription of Islamic knowledge in texts is understood as second-order representation of a primary oral reality and that this second-order representation harbors the threat of a departure from the original voiced presence of God. This means that the text as a medium is dangerous because it can produce distortions that circulate widely across time and space and therefore create a gap between the present and the sacred past, pulling Muslims away from the original presence of God. Hence, Islamic texts must be handled only by specialists who are themselves moral persons capable of effective transmission of Islam and resisting the temptations of the pen.

The logic of what Messick has aptly called "recitational logocentrism" is most clearly evidenced by how Muslims relate to the Quran as a ritual or performative text. The Quran, Messick notes, is not simply a receptacle for propositional truth, that is, a book in the conventional sense of the term: "The textual character of the Quran is quite different from that of the Bible, or at least the Gospels, which are considered humanly authored and which constitute a 'book' in a sense closer to the contemporary Western meaning. The Quran, by contrast, is a recitation-text. The Prophet was instructed by the Archangel Gabriel to 'recite,' and the Quran, an extended 'recitation,' was received by him and then orally reconveyed in this way to his companions" (Messick 1992, 22). The Quran is understood here as the direct word of God that was perfectly transmitted to the Prophet and therefore the perfect embodiment of divine intent. The Quran was initially transmitted orally and only later transcribed in order to preserve it. It remains primarily an oral text that Muslims must read and recite because the language of the Quran is untranslatable. Recitation of the Quran in its original language is integral to the performance of the mandatory prayers (*namaz/salat*). Correct form or style of recitation (*qirat*) is a necessary condition for its efficacy. The memorization of the Quran is referred to as protecting (*hifz*) the Quran, and someone that has memorized the entirety of the text is called a "guardian" of the Quran (*hafiz-i-Quran*). From the perspective of the ulama, a moral person is one who fulfills his daily ritual obligations including the mandatory prayer as well as reading and recitation among other ritual acts (see Graham 1993).

Central to the Deobandi ulama's conception of moral personhood was living according to the tradition of the Prophet (sunnat). The primary source of knowledge about the ways of the Prophet is recorded in the *hadith* literature. Rahman (1979) defines a hadith as a "narrative, usually very short, purporting to give information about what the prophet said, did, or approved or disapproved of, or similar information about his Companions, especially the senior Companions" (cited in Woodward 1989, 61). The power of hadith to authorize or prohibit certain practices in the Islamic tradition cannot be overstated, but precisely because they are so powerful, there is the risk that they will be invented. In one widely accepted hadith, the Prophet warns of the invention of hadith: "After my death more and more sayings will be ascribed to me, just as many sayings have been ascribed to previous prophets (without their having really said them). When a saying is reported and attributed to me, compare it with God's book. Whatever is in accordance with that book is from me, whether I really said it or no" (Goldzhier 1981, 42–43, cited in Woodward 1989). The Quran is the foundational basis of all religious knowledge, the final source of truth, but the Quran does not provide prescriptions for everyday life in the same manner as the hadith literature. Hence, a critical task of the ulama was to verify the authenticity of hadith. This required authenticating a chain (*isnad*) that leads from the present to the Prophet's time. This "chain" entails a series of men who have orally transmitted these accounts over the generations. According to Messick, verifying a hadith requires "knowing the men" who transmitted them, ensuring that these men were morally righteous and not prone to falsification. In this sense, each hadith encapsulates a moral genealogy of persons.

Drawing on this framework of knowledge, the Deobandi ulama claimed that Islamic authority must be anchored in moral persons and that only they could verify such knowledge and transmit it without falsification. The ulama stressed the importance of the faithful replication of authoritative reason or taqlid and stressed that individual interpretive reasoning or *ijtihad* should be conducted only by those with the requisite knowledge and moral standing. As Ingram argues, British utilitarianism had construed religious knowledge as largely useless and thus subordinate to rational scientific thought, but the ulama reversed this calculation insisting that religious knowledge was the only true knowledge. This was reflected in the emphasis they placed on learning the hadith sciences against philosophy (Ingram 2018, 52). The Deobandi ulama framed religious knowledge as pure knowledge against worldly knowledge. Moreover, it is the context of the threat posed by the possibilities of objectification that encouraged them to stress the link between ritual and reason and the embodied nature of knowledge of Islamic texts against disembodied reason or rationality (Stephens 2018).

We will return in subsequent chapters to the importance of orthopraxy, embodiment, and other features that Tablighis draw from the scriptural traditionalism of the Deobandi ulama like the importance of pious companionship (sohbat). What we have seen here is that the emphasis on ritual as the means for crafting pious bodies that are capable of correct moral reasoning is a transformation of the Islamic tradition under the conditions of colonial modernity (see also Rock-Singer 2022). Scriptural traditionalism presupposes an understanding of religion (din) as an autonomous domain defined by scriptural authority and one that should be purified of corruptions and accretions. This emphasis on the purification of religion was structured by the heightened emphasis on boundary-making between religious communities, Hindu and Muslim, created by colonial policies like the census, the codification of Islamic law, the rise of new educational institutions like the madrassa, new possibilities for the objectification of Islam created by the availability of print technology, and the emergence of an array of claimants to the mantle of Islamic authority in a burgeoning Islamic public sphere.

An Islamic Public Sphere and the Politics of Mediation

The scriptural traditionalism of the Deobandi ulama that I have outlined here is necessary for understanding the Tablighi approach to dawat and its social and political significance in Pakistan. Before proceeding to the specifics of the Tablighi Jamaat in Pakistan, it is important to frame the broader field of Islamic contestation that was engendered by colonialism and that persists in postcolonial Pakistan. As Zaman (2018) notes, what was unique about colonialism was not so much the demand for reform of Islam, which had existed before and elsewhere, "but the underlying view that a reinvigorated Islamic identity offered the most effective means of coping with the radically changed world in which the Muslims of India had come to find themselves" (15). The loss of sovereign power spawned an intense search for the ground of Islamic identity among Indian Muslims. This quest for Islamic identity created a renewed vitality in traditionalist understandings of Islam but also fostered deep debates and divisions about the form and nature of religion and religious authority that continue to shape contemporary Muslim life across South Asia. The British efforts to codify customary and religious law engendered a break between genealogical and scriptural authority, intensified tensions over the proper boundaries of religion, and created a new impetus for the objectification of Islam. The wide availability of print technology created a bourgeoning public sphere in which such differing interpretations of Islam were fiercely contested.

The period witnessed intense conflicts between Shia and Sunni movements as well as the formalization of divisions within Sunni Islam that crystallized around distinct ways or paths (*maslak*) (Ingram 2018). The Ahl-e-Sunnat-wa-Jamaat founded by Riza Ahmed Khan, also referred to as Barelwis, argued that the Prophet was "present and observant" (*hazir-o-nazir*) and argued for a scriptural basis for the veneration of saints (Sanyal 1996; Tareen 2020). This was against the Deobandi claim that the veneration of saints was a form of idolatry (*shirk*) adopted through contact with Hinduism. The Ahl-e-Hadith rejected the tradition of jurisprudence of the ulama, the four schools (*madhab*) of Islam, and the principle of taqlid on which it was based and accepted only the authority of Quran and the hadith, thus challenging the authority of both Deobandi and Barelwi ulama. The Ahmadiyya believed in the Prophethood of Mirza Ghulam Ahmad and were declared heretical by both Sunni and Shia ulama. Ahmad interpreted the notion of the finality of Prophethood (*khatmun nabbiyyin*) attributed to Muhammad as the "seal of the Prophets," arguing that Muhammad was the final law or book bearing Prophet, but there were nevertheless Prophets after Muhammad who carried forward the Prophetic mission set forth by Muhammad (Qasmi 2014). The Muslim modernists advocated for combining Islamic and Western scientific knowledge under the influence of Sir Syed Ahmad Khan (1817–1898). Muslim modernism flourished in the Muhammadan Anglo Oriental College in Aligarh founded in 1875. Islamism emerged from the thought of the journalist Abu Ala Maududi (1903–1979), founder of the Jamaat-e-Islami party, who argued that an Islamic society required the establishment of an Islamic state. Both Muslim modernists and Islamists stressed the ability of individuals to directly access the Quran, which was plain for any and all Muslims and thus challenged the authority of the traditionalist ulama.

These diverse Muslim and Islamic forces competing for the mantle of Islamic authority and representatives of the Muslim and Islamic community constitute an Islamic "public" as defined by Michael Warner (2002), a shared sense of belonging created by reflexive modes of address, meditational tools, and the circulation of discourse. The addressivity of the Islamic public, the "we" invoked in discourse, was the Muslim subject, and the struggle to define this Muslim subject drew not only on diverse doctrinal commitments but also modes of address and forms of mediation that aimed to simultaneously create a relationship to God as well as forge connections and bonds between Muslims. In other words, the contestation unleashed under colonial modernity was about correct doctrine, mediational techniques, and the form of the Muslim and Islamic community. This book takes up the place of the Tablighi Jamaat in this diverse and deeply contested religio-political landscape in Pakistan. The Tablighi Jamaat represents an effort to spread the scriptural traditionalism of the Deobandi ulama by, on the one hand, reforming Sufi practices of saint veneration and, on the other, challenging the objectification of Islam by Muslim modernists and Islamists whom they see as having undermined the tradition through an overriding emphasis on abstracted reason rather than embodied practices of the Prophetic tradition. The truth of Islam, Tablighis insist, must be realized in deeds or practice (amal) modeled on Prophetic example. Tablighis frame dawat through a ritual ideology that stresses that Islamic practices hone and cultivate the virtues and create the Islamic habitus that is needed to live an Islamic life (Mahmood 2005; Hirschkind 2006). The performance and replication of the Prophetic model in dawat, as we will see in later chapters, is seen as a basis for transcending the fragmentation that characterizes Muslim life in Pakistan and beyond, and the practices of dawat give a distinct institutional form to the domain of religion (din).

Before we turn to the specific structure and ethical entailments of dawat, we must frame the importance of the Tablighi Jamaat in the religio-political landscape of postcolonial Pakistan. The debates over the proper content and form of religion take on even greater intensity in the postcolonial Pakistani context where Islam has been integral to the definition of the nation-state and where the state has taken up the project of defining the proper boundaries of Islam. As we will see, Pakistani nationalism has been dominated by Muslim modernism that has excluded and subordinated people based on caste, ethnicity, and class against a normative upper-caste and class subject. Pakistani nationalism has denied lower-caste and lower-class Muslims and even those associated with specific ethnic communities the status of being proper subjects of the Pakistani nation and turned them into objects of reform. I show that dawat as a means to create a direct relationship with God allows the Tablighi to cultivate an Islamic habitus, obviating and even reversing the terms of a national hierarchy of religious virtue. This, I argue, attracts people from all walks of life to the Tablighi congregation as they pursue the promise of becoming authentic Islamic subjects.

2
DAWAT AS A RITUAL OF TRANSCENDENCE IN AN ISLAMIC NATION

This chapter examines the political significance of dawat in the context of the Pakistani nation-state and specifically in relation to its forms of hierarchy and exclusion. While Tablighis claim that dawat has nothing to do with politics, a theme we will thoroughly explore in subsequent chapters, I show here that dawat creates the possibility of transcendence of worldly status and thus allows people from all walks of life to realize the value of Islamic piety. In this chapter, I argue that dawat creates a direct relationship to God, allowing one to reshape one's lower self and cultivate faith, therefore creating a closeness to God. The political significance of this closeness must be understood against the cultural backdrop of Pakistani nationalism, which has been shaped by modernist Islamic sensibilities that deny the status of proper Islamic subject to people of low caste, class, and ethnic backgrounds. Dawat creates a temporal link between a Tablighi and the original generative moment of Islam, allowing the Tablighi to transform himself in the direction of Islamic ideals. Dawat obviates one's social origins and creates the conditions for transcending the hierarchies of caste, class, and ethnicity that structure Pakistani nationalism. It is this promise of transcendence, I argue, that has made the Tablighi Jamaat one of the most popular Islamic movements in urban Pakistan, drawing Muslims from all walks of life.

Postcolonial scholars of nationalism in South Asia have stressed the importance of attending to the colonial transformation of religion and the creation of anticolonialism nationalism organized around religious identity. Responding to Benedict Anderson's influential claim that nationalism displaces the religious community that precedes it, Partha Chatterjee (1993) shows how anticolonial nationalism in India developed by placing religion at the center of the national imaginary. Colonialism, Chatterjee argues, was predicated on the modernizing assumption that India was a "spiritual" land and that this was the source of its arrested development. This allowed the British to frame colonialism as a project to bring India into the modern age through the reform of Indian religious traditions. These reforms were centered around transforming what were deemed barbaric religious traditions, particularly those toward women such as *sati* (see Mani 1998). Chatterjee argues that anticolonial nationalism in India inverted this logic. If colonialism assumed that India was too "spiritual" and thus backward, anticolonial nationalism construed India's spirituality as the core of its moral superiority and the West's materialism as the source of its moral degeneracy. Anticolonial nationalism, Chatterjee shows, drew a distinction between the inner spiritual sanctum from which India drew its moral superiority over the West and a material sphere of science and technology in which the West had gained ascendancy and from which Indians had to learn. The tension, then, for Indians, was how to preserve the authentic inner core of Indian religious traditions while simultaneously acquiring the material trappings of the West.

We saw in the previous chapter that while colonialism designated religion as the central feature of communal identity, what constitutes religion among South Asian Muslims was never a settled matter and instead became the site of intense competition between various understandings of Islam. What we need to examine is how this inner spiritual sanctum is constituted and how a certain hegemonic view of religion arose. As Peter van der Veer (1994) argues, "religious nationalism" is structured by distinct religious traditions organized around different conceptions of personhood, ritual, and time. Muslim nationalism, I argue in the following sections, drew on Islamic concepts of personhood that divide the person between the spirit and the lower self, which map onto distinctions of inner/outer, pure/impure, and high/low, creating the basis for a hierarchically structured nation in which some are regarded as more or less proximate to pure Islam and thus to God. I show a genealogical model of religion in which Muslims with deeper Islamic pasts (ashraf) are seen as the proper keepers of Islam and are meant to rule over and guide lower-caste people (ajlaf). Even as the explicit importance of genealogy has diminished, ashraf values have come to frame ideologies of caste, class, and ethnicity in Pakistan, turning entire groups of people into objects of moral reform. It is by recognizing the hierarchical structure of Muslim nationalism that one can see why embodied practices of dawat have gained wide popularity across caste, class, and ethnic communities. By granting people direct access to transcendental power, dawat enables the Tablighi to become the universal subject of the Islamic community.

From Muslim Nationalism to Islamic Statehood

Historians of South Asia generally agree that Muslim anxieties about living in a Hindu-majority India grew deeper in the decades leading up to Indian independence. As Francis Robinson writes, "the Muslims feared that the Hindu majority would not only interfere with their religious practices such as cow-sacrifice, but also, out of religious hatred, would discriminate against them in a wider range of secular fields upon which their progress depended such as education and employment" (Robinson 1974, 13). In 1906, the All-India Muslim League was founded for the purpose of "safeguarding" Muslim interests. In 1909, the British established separate electorates for Hindus and Muslims, creating a quota system for electoral representation and issuing identity cards to uphold the distinction. This had the effect of greatly enhancing the power and prestige of the Muslim League. As Ayesha Jalal (1995) notes, this created the "political space without which invoking the nation from the podium of the All-India Muslim League would have been an exercise in futility" (75). By the 1930s, the Muslim League had emerged as the main political organ of Muslim representation in British India, and in that same decade began to advocate for the creation of Pakistan, a separate homeland for India's Muslims.

The rationale for a separate homeland for India's Muslims was provided by the "two-nation theory" that posited that Hindus and Muslims were distinct communities and that the Muslims could not live freely as a "minority" in a Hindu-dominated India. In his famous address to the All-India Muslim League Conference in 1940, Mohammed Ali Jinnah, the chairman of the League and subsequently the "father" of the Pakistani nation, stated "The Hindus and Muslims belong to two different religious philosophies, social customs, literatures. They neither intermarry, nor dine together, and they belong to two different civilizations which are based mainly on conflicting ideas and conceptions." Such essentialist divisions positing Muslims and Hindus as mutually exclusive communities with distinct religious, cultural, and linguistic heritage became the basis for the demand for Pakistan.

A key symbol of the Muslim nation articulated by the Muslim League was the Urdu language, which came to be associated directly with Islam, but this must also be understood in relationship to colonial language policies (Ayres 2009). David Lelyveld (1993) directs attention to the early role of British philologists and lexicographers who sought to create a stable orthography, grammatical structure, and unified lexicon for a national language that "extended over the whole of India" (195–96). The goal of these "language experts" was to identify a language that reflected popular language usage and would orient Indians away from the "elite" and "religious" languages of Arabic/Persian (Muslim) and Sanskrit (Hindu), which they considered to be instruments of traditional domination. These early language experts transformed language into an object of study, creating dictionaries, grammars, and scripts that began to circulate among British civil servants and native elites studying in British-run schools. When the British took direct control over administration, they began relying heavily on "native" administrators for the functioning of a growing colonial bureaucracy. By the late nineteenth century, the British colonial administration had largely abandoned the notion of a unified national language. They established English as the language of official communication and committed instead to developing distinct vernacular languages that represented the major "communities" of India. They settled on a distinction between the language of Muslims (Urdu) and the language of Hindus (Hindi), the former being marked by the greater use of Persian and Arabic, and the latter being associated with Sanskrit. This distinction was utilized in a widening circuit of print media. It became among the major points of conflict between Hindus and Muslims in the late nineteenth and early twentieth century as language comes to be the basis for employment in the colonial bureaucracy.

Muslim nationalism emerged as a cultural and intellectual movement in the last four decades of colonial rule, and the calls for a separate homeland for India's Muslims were made with greater frequency after the establishment of the All-India Muslim League in 1906. But the controversy over the establishment of Hindi as a "majority" language and the relegation of Urdu to "minority" status began much earlier. The gradual displacement of Urdu in print, that is, the removal of Persian/Arabic terms and the shift away from the Persian script in the second half of the nineteenth century, generated much anxiety among literate, middle-class Muslims. In 1870, the Muslim modernist Syed Ahmad Khan, to whom the idea of Muslim nationalism is often traced, wrote a letter to a friend that evidences the growing anxieties over Hindu domination:

> I understand ... Hindus are roused to destroy the Muslims' [cultural] symbol Musalmanun Key nishani embodied in the Urdu language and the Persian script. I have heard that they have made representation through the Hindu members of the Scientific Society that the Society's Akhbar (Journal) should be published in the Devanagari rather than in the Persian script, and that all translations of [foreign language] books should likewise be in Hindi. This proposal would destroy cooperation between the Hindus and the Muslims. Muslims would never accept Hindi and if Hindus persistently demanded the adoption of Hindi in preference to Urdu it would result in the total separation of the Muslims from the Hindus (cited in Malik 1970, 189).

Prominent Muslim thinkers had begun to understand language in terms normally associated with modern nationalism, as a representative cultural symbol and an essential feature of identity (see Ayres 2009).

Syed Ahmad Khan was instrumental in spreading these ideas through the establishment of the Muhammadan Anglo-Oriental College in 1875. Renamed the Aligarh Muslim University in 1920, the university educated a class of Muslim administrators and intellectuals who would later form the core of the Muslim nationalist movement. The purpose of the Aligarh Muslim University was to couple modern Western science with Islam and transform the latter into something that could lead to the economic and political life of Muslims (Lelyveld 1978). He developed a robust critique of the ulama's commitment to taqlid and argued that such an orientation to the past would keep Muslims from making progress (Zaman 2018, 27). Syed Ahmad Khan believed that Muslims' social and cultural life had degenerated because Muslims refused to adapt to the realities of the modern world and specifically because they failed to acquire education in modern science and had thus fallen behind their Hindu counterparts. Modern scientific education would not only strengthen the power of Muslims relative to Hindus, but it would also make Muslims attentive to the demands of the modern world and thus lead to a revival of Islam. Subsequent Muslim scholars like the poet-philosopher Muhammad Iqbal also coupled Islam and science, arguing that the creation of Pakistan would usher in a long process of modernization. Iqbal regarded Western scientific education as a prerequisite for the three principles of faith (iman), unity (*ittehad*), and discipline (*nazm*) with which the ideal of Pakistan was to be achieved (Verkaaik 2004). Muslim modernists understood formal and scientific education to be the basis for a modern Islam that would move Muslims beyond traditional forms of Islamic practices that they regarded as "backward" and "superstitious," linking scientific knowledge and education to the practice of proper Islam. Creating a modern Muslim nation, then, required the purification of popular religious practices and the acquisition of modern, scientific, and Western education (Verkaaik 2004).

While the formal demand for Pakistan was predicated on Muslim identity, the leadership of the All-India Muslim League, the main organ of the Muslim nationalist movement, did not envision a state governed on the basis of Islamic law (shariat) or imagine much of a role for ulama in the functioning of the state. Mohammad Ali Jinnah, the "father" of Pakistan, made his famous address to the Pakistan Constituent Assembly on August 11, 1947, in which he advocated for equal citizenship for all inhabitants of the territory of Pakistan regardless of caste, creed, or religion attests to the secular sensibilities of this leadership: "You are free; you are free to go to your temples, you are free to go to your mosques or to any other place of worship in this State of Pakistan. You may belong to any religion or caste or creed—that has nothing to do with the business of the State." Moreover, the fact that the majority of ulama considered the leadership of the Muslim League to be heretical and largely opposed the formation of Pakistan because it would leave India's Muslims divided has supported the case that the leadership's outlook was fundamentally secular. Today more than ever, Pakistani secularists invoke Jinnah's legacy to make the case that the Pakistani nation-state was built on "secular" and not Islamic foundations. Historians of Pakistan have also generally agreed that the movement for a Muslim nation was a "secular" rather than a substantively "Islamic" project (Jalal 1985; Jaffrelot 2002; Shaikh 2009; see, however, Dhulipala 2015).

Despite these secular sensibilities of the Muslim League leadership, David Gilmartin's (1988, 1998) work shows that Islam was also central to the campaign for Pakistan and shaped how the nation was imagined. Gilmartin's examination of the 1946 elections in rural Punjab in which the Muslim League defeated the anti-Pakistan Unionist Party, demonstrates that for rural voters in the Punjab, Islam was the ground for their support for the Muslim League's demand for Pakistan. Gilmartin (1998) argues that it was not just the fear of Hindu domination that created support for the Muslim League, but rather, "The moral necessity of Pakistan was rooted rhetorically in opposition to a very different Other—the specter of internal dissension and disorder among Muslims themselves" (422). While internal unity and integrity are arguably always a concern for nationalists, here the threat felt by those who supported the Muslim League and were committed to Islamic unity was much more specific. One flyer, for example, shows Jinnah imploring fellow Muslims to support Pakistan: "For the sake of Islamic *akhlaq* (morality), Islamic ittehad (unity), and Islamic *ta'limat* (teachings) . . . We can bear difference of opinions, but we cannot bear disturbance, riot, curses and lies" (Gilmartin 1998, 423). The fiercest attacks were made on the Unionist party, which the League insisted was playing on "tribal feeling" (*qabaili asabiyat*) and encouraging "moral disorder of the age of ignorance" (*fitna-i-jahiliyat*), which is the disorder that reigned over the Arabs before the advent of Islam.

The Muslim League constructed Pakistan as an "independent Islamic state" (*azaad Islami-riyasat*) that would defend Muslims against the threat not only from Hindu domination but also from the moral chaos and divisiveness that would surface when the British left India. "The enemies of the Muslims are two," proclaimed one flyer, "Color and genealogy (*rang o nasab*), that is, the fitna of tribes and biraderis," and "country and homeland (*mulk o watan*) that is the idol (but) of quamiyat and wataniat" (Gilmartin 1998, 425). This statement summarizes the opposition between Islam and Pakistan, on the one hand, and the more parochial loyalties of clan and ethnic identity on the other. It construes the nation in terms of the transcendence of these parochial loyalties deemed "worldly." As Gilmartin's sensitive reading of the historical record shows, even as the Muslim League leadership made secularist arguments, the capacity of Islam to unite Muslims by transcending worldly attachments and interests was routinely invoked. The Muslim League represented itself as the embodiment of the transcendental principles of Islam that stood above and beyond worldly attachments and interests that threatened to tear apart the Islamic community.

The construction of the nation as a transcendent unity that stands above and encompasses worldly attachments of kinship, caste, and ethnicity raises an important question about the proper or normative subject of the Islamic nation. In other words, who precisely embodies this transcendental Islamic unity and can thus serve as the vehicle for the nation's progress and realization? The answer that Muslim modernism provided is best embodied by Syed Ahmad Khan who argued that it was Muslims of noble or high origins (ashraf) who were the rightful keepers of the Muslim nation because of their greater cultural and moral standing. Syed Ahmad Khan had drafted a bill for the Viceroy's Legislative Council to make the estates of Muslim aristocrats inalienable, which he argued was necessary to uplift the Muslim community. "In India people with exalted status set examples of good conduct, because the common man looks up to them," he wrote (cited in Malik 1970, 134). Moreover, he believed that commoners should get limited education only appropriate to their vocations and that higher levels of education should be reserved for those from aristocratic backgrounds. As Faisal Devji (2013) notes, Syed Ahmad Khan's investment in social rank took primacy over his focus on the unity of Muslims as a religious community and, despite concerns over Hindu domination, he opposed nation-wide politics around Muslim identity, which would only be taken up after his death in 1898. Subsequent Muslim nationalists would incorporate the commitment to social rank into the very conception of the national community.

David Lelyveld argues that Mughal conceptions of respectability, or *sharafat*, took account of genealogy and lineage but were not defined by it. He writes, "it was better to be the progenitor of a great lineage than an unworthy descendent," and yet he finds that when one acquires respectability one is "quickly redefined in the vocabulary of honorable descent" (Lelyveld 1978, 30). In other words, genealogical descent remained a primary way to define social respectability even if the latter could be acquired in other ways. Lelyveld (1978) provides an apt description of the culture of sharafat:

> One usually defines Sharafat in terms of honorable descent. Sharafat also defined character, a sharif man was one who had honorable de-

scent, dignified temperament, self-confident but not overly aggressive, appreciative of good literature, music, and art but not flamboyant, familiar with mystical experience. Sharif social relations involved a pose of deference, but were above all a matter of virtuosity within the highly restricted bounds of etiquette (30).

Margrit Pernau (2013) argues, similarly, that genealogies were important in the precolonial period, but social status exceeded genealogies and genealogies could always be invented to fit newly acquired status. Colonialism opened new avenues for the acquisition of sharif status, particularly through the acquisition of education. The Aligarh Muslim University became a hub for the creation of a larger class of ashraf who were educated in the British tradition. This class with its rationalist sensibilities about Islam and its commitment to scientific education became central to the Muslim nationalist movement and would go on to profoundly shape the developmentalist politics of postcolonial Pakistan (Verkaaik 2004).

The twin principles of genealogy and education that were the mark of the ashraf shaped the Pakistani state's project of authoritarian modernization. This project linked the nation's progress to the elimination of so-called backward customs, particularly popular practices associated with Sufism, through a project of top-down reform. This worldview also became the basis for the racially charged approach adopted by the West Pakistani establishment toward Bengalis in East Pakistan. In 1954, the West Pakistani establishment amalgamated the provinces of the west wing of the country to form one administrative unit. The rationale for the One Unit policy was to counterbalance the size differential of East Pakistan. In 1958, General Mohammad Ayub Khan (1958–1969) dismissed President Iskander Mirza and imposed martial law under the doctrine of necessity out of fear of turning over control of the government to Pakistan to the majority in East Pakistan. In his autobiography, General Ayub Khan justifies this move by stating that the Bengalis "belong to the very original Indian races," "have been and still are under considerable Hindu cultural and linguistic influence," and "have not yet found it possible to adjust psychologically to the requirements of the newborn freedom" (cited in Verkaaik 2004, 29).

The West Pakistani elite, especially Punjabis and Urdu-speaking Muhajirs who dominated the military and civil bureaucracy, were hostile toward Bengalis and treated them contemptuously as un-Islamic or Hinduized. General Ayub Khan here draws on a long history of racialized colonial stereotypes about "effete" Hindu Bengalis who are incapable of asserting masculine control and domination in contrast to the "martial races" like Muslims, Sikhs, Rajputs, and Marathas, a division that shaped British colonial understandings of Hindus and Muslims more broadly (Sinha 1995; Streets 2004). The idea that Bengalis were of the "original Indian races" evokes the broad distinction between locally and more recently converted populations of Hindu origins, seen as new and impure, and Muslims with deeper genealogical ties to the Middle East and Central Asia, who are seen as old and pure Muslims. Since the early 1950s, the Bengali language movement had been demanding equal recognition for Bangla as a national language at par with Urdu, but West Pakistani elites regarded it as too "Hinduized" to be given the status of a national language, unlike Urdu which was coded as an Islamic language (Toor 2011; see also Ayres 2009). The inferior status of Bangla was confirmed in the minds of West Pakistanis because of its use of a Sanskrit-based script rather than the Arabo-Persian script of Urdu. The subjugation of Bengalis by the West Pakistani establishment drew on what Kurin (1988) calls a "culture of ethnicity" that imagined "high" language and culture to be linked to the purity of the "spirit" (ruh) while low origins are linked to the lower self (nafs). This culture of ethnicity also drew on racialized stereotypes developed under British colonialism to create a hierarchy of national purity.

The period following Pakistan's civil war witnessed a resurgence of ethnic nationalist forces in Balochistan, Sindh, and NWFP (now Khyber Pakhtunkhwa) demanding ethnic autonomy from the federal center. As Oskar Verkaaik argues, the dominant theory of nationalism that emerged after the civil war posited the nation as a conglomerate of different "ethnicities" (*quam*), each with its own cultural and linguistic identity rooted in territorial history (Verkaaik 2004). The newly elected Pakistan People's Party led by the charismatic Zulfiqar Ali Bhutto instantiated this shift away from Muslim nationalism organized around Islamic unity to ethnic nationalism conceived as a federation of ethnic communities. Bhutto stressed his own identity as a Sindhi and tied this identity to Sufi imagery and themes that he drew from Sindhi nationalists and placed a new emphasis on the shrines of saints as sites of cultural heritage. Democratization, then, placed an emphasis on precisely those aspects of life that Muslim modernist reformers had construed as problems associated with custom: the emphasis on identities shaped by blood such as kinship, caste, and ethnicity as well as on the intercessionary powers of saints. The resurgence of ethnic nationalism and the new emphasis placed on ethnolinguistic identity and Sufism by Bhutto's government generated a moral panic that the nation and Islam were being dismembered by the centrifugal forces of ethnic nationalism.

The opposition to Bhutto's Pakistan People's Party that emerged was led by Islamist political parties like the Jamaat-e-Islami. When General Zia-ul-Haq (1977–1988) overthrew the democratic government of Zulfiqar Ali Bhutto in a military coup, he adopted the Order of the Prophet (*Nizam-e-Mustafa*) platform of the Islamist-led Pakistan National Alliance, an alliance of opposition parties to the Bhutto government. While Islam had been acknowledged as the state religion since the Constitution of 1956, Islamization under Zia formalized the link between Islam and state sovereignty by establishing the Federal Shariat Court and elaborating the central place of Islamic law in the state. We will take up this theme of state-driven Islamization and its political implications thoroughly in chapters 6 and 7. For now, what is important to note is that the shift from the authoritarian modernization program of Muslim nationalism to one in which Islam was central to the definition of the state remained united by a shared commitment to creating the transcendental unity of Islam above and beyond what were seen as parochial loyalties of kinship, clan, and ethnicity. Both Muslim modernism and Islamism aim to transform society through the arms of a top-down, centralized state, and both represent efforts at eliminating what they see as the backward customs associated with Hinduism; this frames their understanding of poor, uneducated, and rural populations as well as the ritual practices of saint intercession and worship associated with Sufism.

By deepening the ties of state sovereignty to Islam, Islamization had the effect of drawing ulama into the project of building the Islamic nation-state and the *statist* project of Islamic reform. This has meant that the very contestation of Islamic public life outlined in the previous chapter is now clearly directed at the control and transformation of the state by different Islamic revivalist forces: modernist, Islamist, and traditionalist, each trying to define the form and content of Islam in their own ways. Moreover, state-driven Islamization has created the conditions for a proliferation of a wide range of Islamic revivalist forces, including Islamic militants, and institutions like Islamic corporations, banks, televangelists, educational institutions, and NGOs, creating a vitality to the Islamic public sphere that is much more intense than anything under British colonialism.

The Islamic revival is one of the central features of life in postcolonial Pakistan, and the Tablighi Jamaat is only one of the Islamic forces that attempt to define the content and form of Islam in public life. Like Muslim modernists, Islamists, and traditionalist ulama, Tablighis aim to purify religion of custom, but they have stayed clear of the top-down state project and other modern institutions like corporations and instead remain committed to what Ingram calls a "revival from below" through dawat (Ingram 2018). I argue that dawat provides the ritual means for self-reform (islah) and self-transformation and thus makes available ashraf values to people who are otherwise defined as low by virtue of caste and class and thus objects of reform in the national hierarchy. By connecting the Tablighi back to the original generative movement of Islam, dawat obviates and even inverts the hierarchical structure of the Islamic nation of Pakistan.

Before turning to this power of dawat, however, it is helpful to situate the Tablighi Jamaat in Karachi's urban landscape where many of the violent conflicts and contradictions in Pakistani nationalism are most acutely manifest.

Islamic Piety in a Landscape of Urban Crisis

With an official population of over 16 million inhabitants, Karachi is Pakistan's largest and fastest-growing city. A trading port on the Arabian Sea, Karachi is in Pakistan's province of Sindh. Prior to Partition and Pakistani independence in 1947, Sindh was split communally between an urban Hindu minority and a largely rural Muslim peasantry (Wright 1991). During Partition, the vast majority of Hindu Sindhis emigrated to India, while millions of Urdu-speaking Muhajirs, Muslim migrants from northern India, as well as Gujarati-speaking businessmen from Bombay and the west coast of India, migrated to urban centers in Sindh, primarily Karachi and Hyderabad. In the 1960s and 1970s, the number of Punjabi and Pashtun migrants from the northwest had been steadily increasing, and, during the 1980s, Karachi experienced a great upsurge in population and growing demand for housing, transportation, electricity, water, education, and employment. The arrival of Afghan refugees in the 1980s and increasing traffic of arms from Karachi to the Afghan Jihad added to the city's volatility, as communities jockeyed for decreasing urban space and a stake in a deteriorating urban infrastructure. The rise of massive poor settlements (*katchi abadis*) and the expansion of the informal economy are hallmarks of this period. In the last census in 2017, approximately 48.52 percent of Karachi's population identified itself as Urdu speaking, 10.73 percent as Punjabi speaking, 15 percent as Pashto speaking, 10.67 percent as Sindhi speaking, and 4.04 percent as Baloch speaking (Pakistan Bureau of Statistics 2017).

Population growth through migration in the 1970s and 1980s created intense competition for space and resources, and conflict manifested itself along ethnolinguistic lines. Until this point, the Muhajir population had been largely averse to politics along ethnolinguistic lines. They supported Islamist political parties like the Jamaat-e-Islami which as a result dominated the politics of Karachi. In 1984, a mass ethno-nationalist movement and later political party called the Muhajir Quami Movement (MQM) emerged to represent Urdu-speaking Muhajirs who feared they were being squeezed out of Karachi by new migrants. In 1985, mass riots broke out between Pashtuns and the majority Urdu speaking Muhajirs. The rioting and communal violence was sparked by the death of an Urdu speaking student of Bihari origins, Bushra Zaidi, when she was struck by a bus. Newly arrived Pashtun migrants had become central to the transport industry in the city. They were considered by many Muhajirs to be unruly and dangerous drivers and were blamed for the accident. The MQM party stoked Muhajir fears and anxieties about losing control of the city and framed the accident as an attack on the Muhajir community (Verkaaik 2016). The ethno-nationalist assertions of the MQM resonated with Muhajirs and led to the party sweeping the 1988 elections, handily defeating the Jamaat-e-Islami the Islamist party that Muhajirs had supported in previous eras. The MQM immediately assumed a militant cast and began to assert its control over the city through violence. In June 1992, citing the need to restore "law and order," the Army launched Operation Clean-up, in which thousands of MQM activists were extrajudicially killed. From 1992 to 1996, Karachi became the site of bloody street battles between the MQM, the MQM-Haqiqi, a breakaway faction of the MQM, and the Sindhi-dominated ruling Pakistan People's Party (PPP).

This history of violent ethnolinguistic conflict has left an indelible mark on Karachi's culture and politics with major political parties being associated with ethnic groups. At the time of the core of my research from 2010 to 2012, MQM was the most powerful political force in the city, representing the majority Muhajir population; the PPP was and remains the most powerful party at the provincial level, representing Sindhis, who are a majority in the province; the Awami National Party (ANP) represented the Pashtun population. These major political parties maintained their own militant arms, were linked to crime mafias, and routinely came into violent conflict with one another over land and resources, frequently attacking each other's workers in what have come to be known in Karachi as "target killings." The second year of my fieldwork, 2011, is considered one of the bloodiest in recent memory. The Human Rights Commission of Pakistan reports that at least 1,715 people were killed in politically motivated murders alone that year (HRCP Report 2011). Such killings almost always result in reprisals, and, at one time when the MQM was the dominant force in the city, they led to "strikes" in which the entire city was forcefully shut down. In recent decades, violent crime, including kidnappings and car- and phone-snatching, has reached unprecedented heights, related of course to rising inflation and levels of unemployment as more and more people migrate to the city. Moreover, sectarianism, which has been growing since the 1970s, has come to the forefront with the increased incidence of radical Sunni militants murdering Shias, especially educated Shias like doctors who are seen as community leaders. The threat of terrorism by several militant outfits, especially the Tehreek-e-Taliban Pakistan (TTP) and the more recent rise of the Barelwi militancy, particularly around issues of blasphemy, represented by the Tehreek-e-Labbaik Party (TLP), has added another dimension to the deep and pervasive sense of crisis in Karachi.

One might complain that framing the narrative of a city in terms of urban violence reinforces stereotypes of Karachi in the Western media as "the world's most dangerous megacity" (Khan 2013). Such depictions can erase other, equally salient, aspects of urban life and also flatten the nature of urban violence. However, Karachi's violence is indeed a significant aspect of life in this tumultuous city that informed my own fieldwork. It is no wonder that anthropologists and sociologists working in Karachi often center the questions of urban violence, insecurity, and ethnolinguistic conflict (Khan 2010; Kirmani 2015; Gayer 2014; Ring 2006; Verkaaik 2004). In an edited volume titled *Beyond Crisis: Reevaluating Pakistan*, Naveeda Khan (2010) argues that we need to move beyond reductive explanations for Pakistan's political predicament. In the afterword, Katherine Ewing astutely observes that there are cultural rather than just socioeconomic roots to the sense of crisis that people in Pakistan experience. As Ewing (2010) writes, "the image of crisis is thus itself an aspect of national imaginary" created by a "sense of failure associated with the pervasive sense of continuously being on the periphery" (539). In Karachi, the sense of crisis is exacerbated by the deep mistrust between ethnic and sectarian communities that derives from this history of violence. The insecurities of life create a fear that political life can degenerate into mass violence, and this is partly why many, especially in the middle and upper classes, accept and sometimes even advocate for the militarization of their respective ethnic parties and demand for police and military presence.

This book is not an ethnography of violence, but I draw attention to these aspects of life in Karachi because they were never far from conversations I had with people during my time in the field, and they informed the Tablighi conceptions of moral chaos (fitna). For Tablighis, Karachi's crisis—evidenced both by quotidian and dramatic forms of violence and by deep ethnolinguistic and sectarian divisions—was among the clearest signs that Muslims had abandoned Islam and had fallen into a state of moral chaos. It is against this background of Karachi's political crisis that the Tablighi Jamaat experienced such dramatic growth from the 1990s onward. While the sense of crisis does not necessarily lead Pakistanis toward desires for a transcendental Islamic community, the notion that a deeper commitment to Islam is a means for restoring Muslim unity extends well beyond the Tablighi Jamaat. Indeed, if Pakistani nationalism itself is conceived as a transcendental unity that stands above "worldly" attachments of blood, language, and territory, Karachi's urban conflict and crisis lays bare the limits of such nationalist imaginings. The appeal to Islamic piety is that it can create a transcendental unity above and beyond the parochial loyalties of language and ethnicity, and, as we will see, it is this desire to create a transcendental Islamic community that animates the Tablighi Jamaat.

Genealogy as the Moral Anchor of Islamic Habitus

Raheem and I traveled together to the national congregation or ijtima of the Tablighi Jamaat in Raiwind in 2010. A stocky Pathan,[1] who was raised in Karachi, Raheem was markedly humble. He spoke in a soft and comforting voice and had a very gentle demeanor, though he also often spoke proudly about the honorable virtues of being Pathan, such as manliness, pious fear, and hospitality. Raheem owned a real estate agency on the main road near the Al-Aqsa Mosque. His shop was adjacent to Shakil and Sultan's shop, who were both regulars in the Al-Aqsa congregation. They were all good friends, and, along with other business owners on the main road, they frequently ate and prayed together. Sultan had convinced Raheem to come on the forty-day tour (*chilla*) and Raheem had agreed, and over time Raheem became a regular presence in the Al-Aqsa congregation. Raheem did not, however, participate in congregational life daily and was thus not perceived by everyone else to be a particularly committed Tablighi. Raheem had a short beard when I met him, but he had accepted from his Tablighi friends the claim that if one keeps a beard it should meet the requirements of the Prophet's example (sunnat), and so he allowed his beard to grow and did not, to my knowledge, ever trim it down again. Despite his seeming commitment, Raheem did not identify as a Tablighi. He even cautioned that too much participation in tabligh made one disconnect from the world, and this was not good as people would lose sight of their responsibilities to their family and to other dimensions of their lives.

After months of cajoling, Raheem finally agreed to do an interview. As we sat down, Raheem's friend Mahmood entered the store. Mahmood was a thin man of approximately thirty-five years of age with dark skin, a small face, and sharp angular features and without a beard. Like Raheem, Mahmood was also a real estate agent and had an office a few shops down. "What is going on here?" Mahmood asked with a grin across his face. "An interview," I said. Raheem was visibly embarrassed and sheepishly introduced us. "Why would you interview him? This Pathan doesn't know what he is talking about!" Raheem laughed and replied, "Arsalan, do not listen to this Memon. Memon are always doing 'ethnicity worship' (*quam parasti*). A Memon will always stick to his own kind, no matter what happens. This is bad. They are selfish (*khudgarz*) people." Mahmood laughed. Raheem continued, "These people don't even have a country. Tell me, Arsalan, when you think of Pathan, do you think of a place, a country where they are from? Yes, you think of Afghanistan! We Pathan were royals, related to the highest emperors!" Mahmood retorted, "Ask him if he even knows who the Mughals were. These Pathan are always fighting among themselves. And they have sold off their own country to the Americans! They are all for sale. Would a Memon ever do such a thing? Never!" "Arsalan," Raheem protested, "These Memon were Hindus till one or two hundred years ago. They are *baniya*! Their faith is not strong like us Pathan." "So what if we were Hindus? What does that matter? *MashAllah*, we accepted Islam and read the *kalima*. You Pathan are always talking about what your grandfathers and great-grandfathers did. What have you done? You don't do anything but fight among yourselves and you have sold off your country!" Raheem laughed and batted his hand at Mahmood as if to dismiss the conversation. A grinning Mahmood, convinced that he had won the battle, said he would be back to discuss some important matter later and took his leave.

This jocular exchange between two friends highlights the significance of ethnic joking as a means of creating social harmony across ethnic and linguistic lines in a city as diverse as Karachi that has been and remains a hub of explosive ethnic tensions. In this context, ethnic joking plays on negative stereotypes, which are often the grounds for violent ethnic conflict, but transforms them into a source of friendship and camaraderie. When Mahmood left, I asked Raheem whether it was appropriate to differentiate Muslims on the basis of ethnicity given that we are all Muslims. Raheem insisted that it was not he who was differentiating based on ethnicity but actually Mahmood:

> These people are always differentiating themselves on the basis of their "ethnicity" and language. All Muslims that have read the kalima are brothers. There's a hadith that when the forces of the Prophet were fighting Abu Jahl, they had tied up all the prisoners. And one person said: "tie that one up tight. He is from a rich, powerful family." And the man protested: "but you are my brother!" It was his own blood brother who said it. He had converted to Islam. And the brother responded, "No! These are my brothers. The ones that fight with me for our Beloved Prophet!" So, you see, all Muslims are brothers, but these people don't understand this. It is because their faith is weak.

Mahmood is explaining here that it is not blood and kinship that define what it means to be Muslim but instead one's commitment to Islam and loyalty to the Prophet. Given that Mahmood had begun the teasing, Raheem seemed to have a point, but wasn't Mahmood the one saying there is actually no difference between Muslims as long as they have accepted Islam, that all Muslims are basically the same and differentiated only by their commitment to Islam? Raheem's response was that Memons have weak faith, so they are not able to recognize the importance of their relationships with other Muslims, and thus they fall prey to "ethnicity worship" (*quam parasti*). The term "worship" here is the same word that one uses for the worship of idols, and Raheem was saying that the failure to relate to other Muslims as brothers is itself a form of idol worship. In this sense, a failure to recognize one's relationship with other Muslims is tantamount to a failure to recognize one's relationship to God by confusing immanence for transcendence and worldly relations based on kinship or ethnicity for transcendent relationships defined by religion. I asked Raheem if his response was not also indicative of ethnicity worship, and he categorically denied it, saying that faith is the only basis for distinguishing Muslims, but their faith is weak, and this, Raheem believed, is a consequence of their more recent history of conversion. Raheem explained that Muslims with strong faith can see each other as true brothers in Islam beyond "worldly" criteria like "blood" (*khoon*) and "language" (*zabaan*). It was faith that allowed Muslims to transcend worldly ties and create religious ones. Faith is the grounds for the fashioning of genuinely Islamic relations and for constituting the transcendental Islamic community.

What appears at first like a contradiction in Raheem's thought, the accusation that Memons practice "ethnicity worship" but his own belief that Pathans have superior faith, is reconciled by a conception of faith (iman) linked to genealogical origins. Faith here is not a matter of belief but, As Talal Asad (1993) reminds us, a "constituting activity in the world" that is so central to the Islamic tradition (47). Faith in the Islamic tradition is a product of practice that grows through repetition, a material entailment sedimented into bodies over time through practice or an Islamic habitus. Drawing on Mauss, Asad (2003) argues that the human body is a "self-developable means by which the subject achieves a range of human objects—from styles of physical movement (for example, walking), through modes of emotional being (for example, composure), to kinds of spiritual experience (or example, mystical states)" (251–52). This is precisely the logic on which Raheem is drawing when he distinguishes Pathan from Memon according to how faith, as a material property, has accumulated and seeped into the bodies of people over time. But, for Rahim, this Islamic habitus is not an individual achievement but is seeped into the language, customs, and traditions associated with entire ethnolinguistic communities. In Raheem's quotation, faith derives from the longevity of one's Islamic past, which creates the ethical sensibilities to transcend parochial and worldly attachments, which in turn allows one to devote oneself to a transcendental cause. Included in these ethical sensibilities is the recognition that worldly ties of kinship and language are ultimately transient and that what counts is the relationship to each other as brothers in Islam. Those without a deep Islamic past, Raheem argues, lack the requisite faith to see beyond kinship and ethnicity and recognize themselves as members of the Islamic community.

I had the opportunity to discuss this point at length with Talha, who traces his own genealogy to the Prophet's family. According to Talha, those who do not have a deep Islamic past are much more likely to practice Hindu "customs" (*rivaj*), especially in their homes, while those who have a deep Islamic past have customs already shaped by Islam. Arabs, for instance, Talha insisted, have great ease in practicing Islam because it has seeped into their customs and therefore seeped into the habitus of their daily lives. In South Asia, he noted, because we have lived among Hindus for centuries, we have adopted many of their ways into our customs. Those who converted from Hinduism never quite eliminated Hinduism from their customs even if they accepted Islam. For the latter, living an Islamic life is always difficult, and such people are prone to "slipping" and require conscientious effort. For the former, however, Islam comes effortlessly and even unconsciously. For Talha, this meant that even though Arabs do not do all their practices (amal), they continue to live Islamic lives by habit. One can see here how an Islamic habitus about temporal depth and precedence shapes the exchange between Raheem and Mahmood.

There is also something implicit in the conversation between Raheem and Mahmood that could not openly be addressed without putting too great a strain on the relationship. This is the unspoken implication in such narratives of Islamic conversion of the historical debt of communities in relationship to one another. Those with deeper Islamic genealogies are also the ones responsible for bringing Islam to the region and bestowing Islam onto others. If Islamic habitus is something that shapes not only individual bodies but the customs and traditions of entire ethnic communities, then ethnicities themselves come to be situated in a hierarchy of purity. The fact that Islamic habitus accumulates and solidifies means it can serve to ideologically differentiate between those who have deep Islamic genealogies and those who are more recent converts to Islam, with the implication that it is the former who brought Islam to the region and bestowed it to those who are more recent converts and continue to be, in a sense, the keepers of Islam. The custom/religion distinction that underlies Islamic reform presupposes a hierarchical differentiation based on the purity of Islamic practice. Indeed, the notion of an Islamic habitus seeped into bodies, languages, and customs means that Muslims can be hierarchically differentiated based on genealogical origins and conversion histories. This framework informs a wide variety of constructions of Muslim and Islamic identity in Pakistan. Even the Deobandi ulama who emphasized deeds (*hasb*) over lineage (*nasb*) never fully rejected the importance of genealogy as an anchor to the sacred past, and thus it also shapes how they think about religious authority (Metcalf 1982).

I suggested in the previous sections that the notion of impure customs has shaped the politics of ethnicity in Pakistan and that modernists linked the acquisition of modern education to reforming one's impure and corrupted practices. Those people construed as lacking proper Islamic subjectivity thus become objects of state reform rather than subjects of the Islamic nation. It is in light of this hierarchical differentiation rooted in the custom/religion distinction that we can find why dawat has taken on significance for such a wide and diverse segment of the Pakistani population and that too with such zeal as it transforms people from objects of reform into the moral subjects of the Islamic community.

The Immediacy and Transcendence of Dawat

Tablighis understand practices that entail the commitment to the intercessionary powers of other human beings, even the Prophet, to be the primary problem associated with custom, a form of fetishism that elevates human beings to the status of God, who is the only true agent in the world. Faith, Tablighis say, is the "conviction that everything comes from Allah, and nothing comes from another" (*Allah se sab kucha hone ka yaqeen aur ghair se kuch na hone ka yaqeen*). For Tablighis, the intercessionary practices of saints represent the corruption of Islam by custom, which falsely locates agency in humans rather than God. Tablighis call for the purification of Islam and demand that Muslims build a direct relationship with God. Dawat is the sacred means for the creation of this "direct" relationship to God, and they understand this direct relationship to be the basis for their own moral transformation and for the creation of an Islamic community. I argue in this section that the moral transformation of dawat allows the Tablighi to obviate and even reverse the terms of a national hierarchy of purity and thus appeals particularly, though certainly not exclusively, to those who have been defined as low in such terms.

Take the example of Abid. Abid lives in a small, one-room flat with his mother, wife, and three children and is a gregarious person with a hearty laugh. Abid is the caretaker of a small plot of land. To be a caretaker means to watch over the plot and ensure that it is not forcefully occupied—a phenomenon called *qabza*—a common occurrence in Karachi where land is scarce and highly valuable and where powerful, politically connected land mafias have sought to acquire any available property. For many in Pakistan, qabza epitomizes the breakdown of moral life as it flags the complete rule by force of the gangster (*ghundas*), a total breakdown of law, and a blatant disregard for the well-being of others. Abid told me that he had been offered this job because people knew he was a *siyana*, a term that means being clever and intelligent but is used to mean someone who can outsmart others and preempt the ploys of others. Abid explained that this was in his nature (*fitrat*) and that, before he came to dawat, his nature was directed toward "the bad" (*burai ki taraf*), but through his participation in the Tablighi Jamaat had been diverted toward "the good" (*achai ki taraf*). He spoke with great pride about protecting the plot of land from qabza, and he attributed this quality in him to God and God's power to stave off evil.

Noticing my mild amusement at his self-description, Abid launched into a narrative about how he came to the Tablighi Jamaat:

> We did work of shipment to Dubai, me and my brother. We were shipping gold and other valuables, mostly. They call this "shipping" but actually it was smuggling.... We were of the Barelwi mentality, of the Barelwi sect. We did all the Barelwi practices like offerings to saints, processions, celebrating 12th *Rabi-ul-Awwal*, self-flagellation, roaming barefoot, basically a life of complete ignorance. Day and night absorbed in wasteful indulgence. I was always troubled, from morning to evening... troubled about money, about time, about everything. I spent all my time watching TV and films, and I was addicted to intoxicants. Then one day, as *fajr* call to prayer was occurring, I asked myself, how is it that I do not even go to pray? What is the point of this kind of life? What is the purpose that I have been sent to this world for? So, I asked Allah to put me to whatever work He desires of me.... Then, after two days, you know what happened? My feet automatically started moving and they took me to the Tablighis.... I slowly started giving *dawat*... and a revolution happened in my life. I realized that this is the truth.

One can see how effortlessly Abid moves from what he regards as the falsehood of Barelwi worship to unethical practices like smuggling and drug use. Dawat begins by purifying religious practices, and this percolates out to all aspects of life, creating a total moral transformation of the subject. Abid explained how he moved from a village in South Punjab where he and his family were committed to *pir-muridi*, the belief in the intercessionary power of that saints, and then moved to the city where he became committed to the Barelwi sect. This appealed to him, he explained, because it continued the village customs around saints, but he also felt that he was participating in more "correct" forms of worship drawn from shariat. Finally, through the force of dawat, he was pulled toward the pure, authentic (*asl*) Islam of the Prophet. Like many accounts I collected, Abid's narrative moves from the corrupted sphere of custom in the village to the pure form of religion in urban life. This reinforces the Tablighi belief that city dwellers are responsible for purifying villages of their false religious practices, captured in the oft-heard mantra "religion of the village is in the hands of the city-dwellers." (*gaon walon ka din shehr walon ke haat mein hai*).

I asked Abid to explain how he knew that his current practices were authentically Islamic given that he himself did not have the requisite education in Islamic theology to decipher the shariat, and Abid invoked the evidence of the senses:

> When one joins tabligh . . . he feels that he has become Muslim on that day, that Allah has given him this gift. He begins to experience sweet smells. He begins to fear breaking Allah's command and the Prophet's ways. Allah is correcting him, giving him guidance, he is enjoying the Prophet's ways, his love for the Prophet is growing, he is feeling a joy overcome him, joy in every practice . . . when we are giving dawat, and then it is time for namaz, and we stand for namaz and because of the vitality of dawat, a deep pleasure fills our namaz, a sweet taste . . . a feeling that Allah is with me, is watching me, is listening to me.

Abid's rich description of his bodily experience confirms how ritual practices are not just representations of an already given reality but actually shape the practitioner by cultivating Islamic virtues. When I asked Abid to explain how he knew that these practices were right, he simply invoked the evidence of the sense. He felt the presence of God in his life. The devil, he said, uses reason (aql) and argumentation to lead people astray, while faith is about feeling and realization, something one knows in the heart. It was the immediacy of religious experience in the body that demonstrated the truth of Islam. This knowledge was the effect of a "direct" relationship (*barah-e-rast*) to God. When one establishes this relationship in practice, one can feel God's presence in one's life, which is why Abid became Muslim "on that day."

Abid's account rehearses a commonly invoked contrast between a direct relationship to God as a mark of religion, on the one hand, and, on the other, the belief in the mediating power of others as a mark of custom that is a recurring feature of Tablighi discourse. Maqsood, a taxi driver and experienced Tablighi, drew this difference between false custom and genuine Islam explicitly: "Our [false] belief (aqeeda) is that of a child. If you ask a child who feeds you, the child says, 'my mother feeds me.' And if you ask him who feeds your mother, the child says, 'my father.' And who feeds your father? He will say my father's boss feeds him. And who feeds the boss, his boss. And the child will go on and on like this forever. We should be such that we know, 'Our Allah feeds us!'" The child here does not recognize his relationship with God because, in his reckoning with the world, there are multiple people standing between him and God. An adult, by contrast, is one who has the embodied and sensual knowledge that the obvious, material realities of the world are not the ultimate reality, which is less visible, and it is key to look beyond the immediate realities to the ultimate source of life. Maqsood is unequivocally stating that we must locate agency in God rather than in others, and it is only when we do this that we can fully understand our purpose in life, which is to fulfill our duties to Him and live according to His will. Maqsood is drawing a contrast between a child, who depends on the mediation of others, and an adult, who understands that he depends only on God. The implication here is that dawat grows one's faith and thus transforms one from a child who can only recognize what is immediately in front of him to an adult who understands that there is a greater, more transcendent order within which he fits and toward which he must strive. Just as one must begin as a child and only gradually become an adult, so one begins with mediation and gradually moves to a direct relationship with God, a movement that is also from dependency on other people to dependency solely on God.

Dawat is what Birgit Meyer (2006, 2011) calls a "sensational form," which she defines as "relatively fixed modes of invoking and organizing access to the transcendental" (2011, 29). Sensational forms like dawat are sacred in that they are understood by practitioners as the privileged, if not exclusive, means for creating access to transcendental power. Dawat, Tablighis say, "connects one's self to Allah's self" (*apni zat ko Allah ki zat se jor deti hai*). Dawat, then, is best understood as a ritual of transcendence, creating a direct and immediate relationship to God. Directness and immediacy with transcendental powers is a pervasive feature of modern religious and semiotic ideologies that one finds across religious movements (Engelke 2007; Eisenlohr 2011). The Tablighi Jamaat fits within this broad pattern of valuing "directness" or "immediation," and this marks the difference between true and authentic religion (din) and false customary practices. The latter is seen as a form of idolatry that misrecognizes the proper locus of agency in the world. As Webb Keane (2007) explains, "By ascribing agency to things that in truth lack it, they thereby deny, perhaps rob, the agency of those who properly possess it (whether these are humans, God, or both)" (180–81). Customary practices that erroneously attribute agency to pirs also involve a forfeiting of agency to the self as well as that of God, and thus they are seen as backward and in need of reform. Abid, for instance, explained to me that people turn to pir-muridi out of a general sense of powerlessness. People believe that their pirs will grant whatever they need and therefore are unwilling to turn to God and uninterested in performing their Islamic duties. People follow pirs, he explained, not out of love (mohabbat), an affective relationship that entails willful submission, but out of desperation: "A drowning man will even reach for a straw" (*doobte huai ko tinke ka sahara*). The effort to purify religion of custom, or rather reshape custom through religious practice, allows the Tablighi to reclaim this lost agency of the subject and to bring him into a direct relationship to God through dawat.

In the following section of the book, we will look carefully at how "directness" is materialized in the ritual practices of dawat and in the congregation life of the Tablighi Jamaat. What is crucial here to recognize is the political significance of a conception of religion organized around directness or immediacy, and the possibilities of transcendence that this affords against the cultural and historical backdrop of Pakistani nationalism that we have outlined. Tablighis identified two interrelated problems in Pakistan. First, Tablighis said that Muslims have become prone to various forms of "idol worship," in which they have elevated other people or objects to the status of God, which, as I have shown, is the central problem of custom. The second, which directly follows from this and echoes what we heard earlier from Raheem, is that Muslims have become incapable of recognizing their relationship to each other as Muslims and have become divided along lines of kinship, caste, and ethnicity, the central characteristics of the state of moral chaos (fitna). These are, for Tablighis, entangled because when one fails to establish a direct relationship to God, one also loses sight of one's transcendental relationship to other Muslims on the basis of a shared relationship to God through the Prophet. Dawat remedies both problems by establishing a direct relationship with God, and this in turn creates the basis for what Tablighis describe as a "heart-to-heart relationship" (*dil se dil ka taluq*) between Muslims. In dawat, Muslims come to stand together on "the good." In doing so, dawat creates the possibility of seeing beyond worldly powers and moving beyond worldly relationships, and thus creates the conditions for the formation of a transcendental Islamic community.

The political significance of directness must be understood against the backdrop of a hierarchically organized nationalism around religious purity and the stigma that people who are low caste, uneducated, and rural are tied to false worship and thus fail to be proper subjects of the nation and the global Islamic community. By recreating the experience of the Prophet and the Companions, dawat takes Muslims back to the "original voiced presence" of God (Messick 1992, 26), a point preceding all distinctions along genealogical lines, and creates the potential for embodying Islamic habitus in the present. This obviates the hierarchical distinctions between rural/urban, uneducated/educated, and new/old Muslims that structure Pakistani nationalism. Dawat then is best understood as a ritual of transcendence precisely because it takes one back to the original generative movement of Islam. It is through this ritual reenactment that people like Abid and Maqsood, who otherwise are defined as recipients of Islam, become conveyors (the literal meaning of the word tabligh) not only to those lower down but, crucially, even to those who, according to worldly criteria are in fact above them. In this sense, dawat carries the potential to reverse the order between givers and receivers of knowledge. By creating a direct relationship with God, dawat allows those who lack a genealogical relationship to the Islamic past to instantiate piety in the present and thus become keepers of an Islamic future.

In her work on Islamic disputation and debate in Pakistan, Naveeda Khan (2012) argues that Pakistan does not have a fixed relationship to Islam but instead is animated by a "new spirit of striving" and that this striving creates an "open future" (7). My argument here is that it is precisely the possibility of creating a direct relationship to God in dawat that creates this spirit of striving and opens the future to the possibility of radically transforming one's place in the world. As a sensational form organized around directness, dawat has a particular, though not exclusive, appeal to those defined as "low" in terms of the hierarchical structure of Pakistani nationhood. Historically, the terms of sharafat were denied not only to low-caste people but also to the merchant classes on account of their association with the pursuit of money (see Pernau 2013). It is not surprising, then, that many newly urbanized people like Abid and Maqsood

FIGURE 1. The annual congregation (ijtima) in Karachi is one of the largest with hundreds of thousands of attendees. An entire tent city stretching several kilometers is erected through voluntary labor. Karachi annual congregation, February 1, 2020. Photograph by Arsalan Khan.

FIGURE 2. Tablighis conducting ritual ablutions (wuzu) at the Karachi annual congregation, February 1, 2020. Photograph by Arsalan Khan.

or those associated with trading classes like Memons are eager to shed their association with custom, purify their practices, and aspire to become proper Islamic subjects through dawat.

The Tablighi Jamaat has seen its ranks swell in the last few decades as evidenced by the construction of large mosque complexes (markaz) in all the major cities of Pakistan and the growing attendees at the annual congregations (ijtima) that happen in the major cities, the largest one being the national congregation in Raiwind.[2] This bourgeoning interest in Islamic piety in Pakistan is not reducible to any specific caste, class, or ethnic group since practically every neighborhood of every region in the country is represented in the Tablighi

Jamaat. But, unlike many state- and corporate-driven top-down projects of Islamization that turn low-caste and working-class people into objects of reform, the emphasis Tablighis place on the ritual means for creating a direct relationship to God makes piety available to all Muslim men. This enables those from low backgrounds to obviate and even reverse the hierarchical difference between impure and pure Muslims that otherwise structures social and political life, allowing them to become moral agents of Islam and active creators of the Islamic community. The millions of Muslims in Pakistan that flock to the Tablighi Jamaat do so to realize this promise of piety.

In the next section "The Semiotics of Piety," I examine the ritual techniques and arrangements that become the basis of mediating this direct relationship to God, arguing that despite the egalitarian premise of the movement and its openness to all Muslims, these rituals create a hierarchical form of pious relationality that defines the domain of religion (cf. Janson 2014). This, I argue, is essential to understanding dawat as a mode of pious becoming, and its political significance in the context of postcolonial Pakistan as the sacred hierarchy engendered by dawat is construed as the fount for moral order in times of moral chaos.

Part 2
THE SEMIOTICS OF PIETY

3
ISLAMIC ICONICITY, MORAL RESPONSIBILITY, AND THE CREATION OF A SACRED HIERARCHY

The common point I heard throughout my research was that Islam is not understood through research (tahqiqat) but is realized only in good deeds or practice (amal). My Tablighi interlocutors invariably told me that if I truly wanted to understand dawat, I would have to abandon my research and commit myself to "doing" dawat. "Dawat will only be understood by doing" (*dawat sirf karne se samajh ai gi*), they often explained to me. Scholars of Islam have long noted the significance of "orthopraxy," or correct forms of ritual action in Islam, and the inextricable link between knowledge and practice (Watt 1998). Anthropologists Saba Mahmood (2005) and Charles Hirschkind (2006) have both stressed the link between orthopraxy and the cultivation of virtues in the Islamic tradition. Building on Foucault's notion of "technologies of the self," these scholars show that embodied practices are understood as a means for the cultivation of ethical sensibilities such as humility, patience, and pious fear, creating the virtues necessary for living an Islamic life. Tablighi ritual ideology adopts a similar perspective, claiming that "doing" dawat is the basis for becoming pious. Tablighis insist that dawat is the divinely given way to create "faith" (iman) and that faith is the condition for all other Islamic practices. For this reason, Tablighis refer to dawat as the "mother of practices" (*umm-al-amaal*) because dawat "gives birth" to faith, creating the basis for living an Islamic life.

I noted in the previous chapter that dawat should be considered a sensational form, an organized means for creating a relationship to transcendental power (Meyer 2006, 2011). Dawat is the means for creating a direct relationship to

God. This chapter examines how this relationship is materialized in the performative acts of dawat. I make three fundamental points about dawat as a ritual ideology (Robbins 2001) and ritual process (Turner 1977) in this chapter. First, I argue that dawat presupposes and naturalizes a hierarchical gender cosmology by separating the domains of religion and the world, associating men with the former valued sphere and women with the latter devalued one. In the homosocial space of the mosque, men conduct service (*khidmat*) that involves domestic tasks conventionally associated with women. In the process, men's natural inclinations are domesticated and they cultivate feminine qualities of "softness" and "openness," which Tablighis regard as the condition for the reception of faith as a gift from God. Dawat, therefore, is understood by Tablighis to be the basis of a distinct form of pious male agency. Second, I argue that dawat functions as a means of ethical self-cultivation precisely because it is a public performance. Dawat is built on a "creed paradigm" (Keane 2007) that involves mobilizing iconic resemblance with the Prophetic model. By drawing the gaze of others to the self, dawat creates a sense of moral responsibility for the ethical entailments of Islamic iconicity. It is through performance, then, that Islamic iconicity, a relationship of similarity to the Prophetic model, is transformed into Islamic indexicality, a relationship of contiguity between the self and the Prophetic model. Finally, I show that the ritual ideology that links "doing" dawat to "becoming" pious displaces and backgrounds the indeterminacy in the process of performance through a sacralization of bodies and words. This creates a social organization that takes on a hierarchical form and a model of spiritual ascent in which spiritual rank (*darja*) is indexed by the size of one's audience within the congregation.

I show in this chapter that understanding dawat as a distinct way of organizing and mediating transcendental power pushes us beyond the Foucault-inspired notions of ethical self-cultivation that have framed anthropological approaches to Islamic piety movements. Specifically, I argue that the Foucauldian concept of ethical self-cultivation has focused too much on how individuals act on themselves and therefore backgrounded the tensions that inhere in dawat as a performance. Once we recognize how dawat involves the naturalization of gender differences, the public recognition of piety, and the ideological construction and maintenance of hierarchy, we open the space to understanding how key aspects of indeterminacy like ambivalence, ambiguity, and doubt manifest in the project of pious subject formation, a theme we will take up in the following two chapters (cf. Schielke 2015).

The Prophet's Way: Orthopraxy as Gendered Ideology

Scholars of Islam have long noted the overarching importance placed on "practice" in the Islamic tradition. The renowned Islamicist Montgomery Watt (1998) attributes the Islamic emphasis on orthopraxy, or correct practice, to the proclivity in Semitic thought for the "concrete over the abstract," a position that differentiates Islam from the Christian emphasis on "orthodoxy," understood as a concern for correct theology and doctrine (168). The orthodoxy/orthopraxy is built on a Cartesian mind/body duality in which Christianity is constructed as contemplative, critical, and dynamic, while Islam is construed as mindless, repetitive, and static, a distinction that implies that Christianity encourages change and freedom of thought while Islam is stagnant and potentially tyrannical. Anthropologists have rejected the ethnocentric premises of this distinction, but they too have stressed the importance of correct practice in Islam (Antoun 1989; Eickelman 1978; Gilsenan 1982; Lambek 1993). The emphasis on orthopraxy in Islam is rooted in a conception of revelation in which sacred knowledge exists prior to and independent of human creativity and humans must constantly strive to know and embody revelation. As Michael Lambek (1993) notes, in Islam, "knowledge has external, objective substance; it can be looked up, grasped, accumulated, manipulated and made practical use of by the individual . . . what is critical for human beings is not establishing the existence of knowledge per se, but gaining and maintaining access to it" (4). In such a framework, the aim is to acquire "objective knowledge," which is, "in theory, available to everyone" (Lambek 1993, 4) and is itself free of human invention and innovation. In the Deobandi tradition, truth (*haq*) is embodied in the Quran, understood as the direct word of God transmitted without distortion to the Prophet. The Prophet is the exemplary human being (*insan al-kamil*) who was incapable of sin and was by his very nature "innocent" (*masoom*) of all sin. This means that the Prophet embodied the Quran to its fullest and lived the exemplary life to which all Muslims must strive. The Prophet's sayings and actions were documented by his Companions in hadith and transmitted through a chain (isnad) of faithful transmitters to the present day. The Quran and the hadith literature are the two principal sources of Islamic jurisprudence (fiqh), and this is the basis of Islamic law (shariat).

Tablighis, like many other Muslims, understand the Prophet's words and actions to have divine rather than human origins, and therefore the purpose for all Muslims is to replicate as closely as possible the Prophet's example (sunnat). The Prophet was a channel of God's will, and he faithfully manifests these words and actions for humanity, thus making him the exemplary human. There is no gap between what God willed and what the Prophet said and how he lived. This means that all the Prophet's actions from the everyday minutia of dress, eating, and sleeping to major decisions like how to marry, how to wage war, or how to govern reflect the perfect embodiment of God's command. It is the duty of every Muslim to emulate as closely as possible the life and actions of the Prophet. This is what Annemarie Schimmel (1992) has called "imitatio Muhammadi" (54). The significance of this impetus to replicate in one's life the Prophet's example in the Islamic tradition is captured in the following quote by the Spanish theologian Abu Muhammad Ali Ibn Hazm (d. 1069): "If someone aspires to felicity in the next world and wisdom in this, to righteousness in his conduct, to the encompassing of all good qualities, and to becoming adapted for all excellences, he should follow the example of the Prophet Muhammad and copy in practice, as much as possible, the Prophet's character and conduct" (cited in Woodward 1989, 67). Tablighis say that every action of the Prophet constitutes an Islamic practice (amal), and collectively these practices are broadly referred to as the Prophetic tradition (sunnat), which Tablighis refer to colloquially as the Prophet's way (rasool ka tariqa). According to Tablighis, all Islamic practices carry intrinsic virtues that are not immediately recognizable to human reason (aql), which is frail and cannot fully recognize truth on its own. Tablighis constantly repeat the phrase "religion is not the name of reason," meaning that one does not immediately see the benefits that come from religious practice, but because these practices are divinely inspired, they carry hidden benefits to practitioners. It is in doing the practices that one cultivates the virtues that inhere in those practices and therefore creates the capacity to live an Islamic life. Islamic practices carry God's grace (barkat). Tablighis insist that it is by molding one's life in the image of the Prophet that one draws on God's powers and creates well-being for oneself and for others.

Tablighis say that it is necessary for Muslims to acquire the requisite knowledge about how the Prophet lived to model one's own life on his life, and Tablighis understand their own congregation (*jamaat*) to be a space that provides Muslims with the requisite knowledge to live in the Prophet's way. Many described their congregation to me as a "walking madrassa" (*chalta phirta madrassa*). As one Tablighi explained, "when we were younger, we could go to a madrassa, but now we would be embarrassed sitting among children, so instead we come to the jamaat where we can learn about our religion." Acquiring religious knowledge is crucial, but Tablighis insist that this is not simply a "mental" (*zehni*) activity but an embodied and experiential one, a feature that fundamentally differentiates it from "worldly knowledge," which only requires the mind. As one Tablighi explained to me:

The feeling of joy (*lutf*), comfort (*itminan*), and peace (*sukoon*) one acquires from religious knowledge (*dini ilm*) one cannot acquire from worldly knowledge (*dunyavi ilm*). Worldly knowledge is not really knowledge at all. It is a vocation (*fan*). Think about it, yesterday it was a big deal to be a BBA. You would manage a whole factory and everyone would say 'wow, how educated he is.' Before that, it was a trend to be an engineer or a doctor. Now, everyone wants to be a computer scientist. Tomorrow, who knows what people will want, but it will be something different. Knowledge is that which is forever, the knowledge Allah has bestowed to us. The rest is just vocation. We do it because we must, but it will not mean anything in the end.

In this quotation, one can see that religious knowledge is eternal and worldly knowledge is transient. Religious knowledge, they say, will carry you from here to the afterlife, serving you for eternity, while worldly knowledge, even of the most highly valued kind, may not even serve one for a few years. More significantly, worldly knowledge is known only in the mind, but religious knowledge is felt in the body. The transcendental nature of religious knowledge stands in stark contrast to the temporal flow and flux of worldly knowledge and affairs. The former carries in it bodily pleasures in the form of joy, comfort, and peace, while the latter is a source of anguish and stress. Thus, Islamic knowledge is embodied and experiential, while worldly knowledge is mental and grasped only through reason.

The purpose of the Tablighi congregation is to acquire Islamic knowledge and to become capable of living according to Islamic precepts and in the Prophet's way. Islam must be realized in deeds or "practice" (amal), a sentiment captured in the oft-heard refrain "Muslims know but they do not do." Tablighis insist that Islamic knowledge is widely available in books, television, DVDs, and on the internet, but Muslims do not have the will or desire to perform their Islamic duties because this knowledge has not "descended into the heart" and remains only in the mind. Put differently, knowledge has not translated into "passion" (*jazba*) and "desire" (*talab*) for a closeness to God. Despite the wide availability of authentic Islamic knowledge to Muslims, they say, Muslims have never been further from the Prophet's way. The central claim of the Tablighi movement is that giving dawat to others grows one's own "faith" (iman) and solidifies "certainty" (*yaqeen*), which in turn leads one to eagerly fulfill one's religious duties. Crucially, dawat is primarily meant not for others but for the reform or "correction" (islah) of the self and only secondarily for the reform of others. I was repeatedly told that giving dawat on the virtues of a specific practice produced or "gave birth" to the desire for that specific practice. According to one Tablighi whom

I interviewed, "if you preach the merits of the mandatory prayers, you yourself will want to do your prayers, if you preach to others the merits of fasting, you too will want to do fasting. People think that one should not give dawat if one does not do oneself, but this is not right. We give dawat to others so that we realize ourselves the virtues of practice and the truth of Islam."

This transformative power of dawat on the practitioner was recounted in countless narratives. The following is one that typifies this genre:

> A young man who was clean-shaven was going to Canada for studies and he was worried about his faith, so he decided to go visit the Imam sahib to ask what he should do to not lose his faith. When he arrived at the mosque he saw the imam sitting reading the Quran. "Imam sahib, I am very worried that I will go abroad and be drawn away from religion. What should I do to protect my faith?" Without hesitation, the imam said, "spend time with Muslims and give dawat to others. Ask them to come to the mosque for prayers." The young man agreed. A few years later, after he had completed his education, he came back to his mosque and the imam was very pleased to see him. The man now had a beard, and he wore his pant legs above his ankles. His appearance was religious (*dindaar*). The imam asked him if he had remembered to do what he had asked. The young man nodded in affirmation. The imam asked, "and what happened?" The young man replied, "I felt awkward at first but because I had made a commitment, I continued to do it." "Did anyone ever come to the mosque?" asked the imam. The man replied, "no, never, but I began praying five times a day, and the rest you can see."

In these narratives, a young man, the kind most prone to losing his way, with a modest level of faith indicated by his lack of a beard and his generally "un-Islamic" demeanor, including wearing "pant-shirt" as opposed to the traditional shalwaar kameez, would be departing to a foreign, non-Muslim country where he is likely to be influenced by un-Islamic practices. The young man goes abroad and instead of coming back less pious, as one might expect, comes back a much more devout and practicing Muslim than he was before he left. This is attributed to the transformative power of dawat.

The process through which dawat grows one's faith was described as having three stages. In the first stage, one feels uncomfortable and awkward speaking the praises of God. "We live in an age," one Tablighi explained, "where we speak constantly about 'the world' and such talk flows like water but when we speak of Allah, our words get stuck in our throats. We cannot bring ourselves even to speak two words in praise of Allah." The contrast he draws is one frequently invoked in the Tablighi Jamaat between "worldly talk" (*dunyavi batein*) and "religious talk" (*dini batein*). For Tablighis, religious talk is not talk at all but a practice (amal). The Tablighi Jamaat, he explained, is where one learns to speak as a Muslim. One comes to speak about the right things and in the right manner. Through "repetition" (*takrar*), Tablighis explained, religious talk becomes habit (*adat*), and one no longer feels awkward. The "tongue opens" and the words begin to flow, Tablighis say, because when you are speaking for God, "Allah moves the tongue." Finally, when one has come to speak as a Muslim, one begins to feel the "effect" (*asr*) of this, which Tablighis understand to be "the passion of faith" (*iman ka jazba*), which comes from feeling God's presence in one's words and in one's heart. This closes the gap between knowledge and practice and translates into living an Islamic life.

Religion (din) here is understood as not only a distinct form of practice but also a set of affective qualities that sediment in the heart (Hirschkind 2006). Tablighi discourse is replete with phrases that mark the material nature of these affective virtues like pious fear, humility, and so on. Tablighis insist also that these qualities are something that a Muslim receives from God through Islamic practice. "We have entered religion, but the religion has not entered us," Tablighis often say. Similarly, Tablighis make supplications like "Allah give us the strength" and "May Allah make our practice easy" after and during all activities, suggesting that the effect of practice is a gift one acquires through dawat. When Tablighis speak about "growing" faith, they draw attention to the materiality of religion. For instance, Tablighis will frequently compare the faith of a nonpracticing Muslim to a pebble in a stream, which will be pushed in the direction that the stream flows, whereas the faith of a practicing Muslim is like a boulder that stays firm for some time but will ultimately give way and be pushed along by the stream. The faith of the Prophet's Companions (sahaba) was like a mountain. Rather than being pushed by the stream, it forced the stream to move around it, and it is the purpose of dawat to make a Muslim's faith like that of the Companions. In this way, Tablighis evoke the materiality of faith as well as its ability to grow through dawat.

The relationship that Tablighis draw between bodily discipline and piety must be understood through a broader Islamic conception of personhood. The person is comprised of three components: a "lower self" (nafs), the spirit (ruh), and reason (aql) (Kurin 1980). Spirit is understood to be a divine faculty possessed by all animate beings: angels, humans, jinns, and animals. Angels are unique because they are made of pure spirit. They are simply conduits for God's will and are incapable of breaking divine commandments. Animals also have a spirit, but their spirit is understood to be weak or relatively insignificant to their being. Animals mostly do as their base instincts tell them, thus animals are mostly lower self. Humans have both a spirit and a lower self, the former understood as the seat for animalistic desires and passions, including the passion for sex and other bodily needs. The lower self is not altogether bad; it is a necessary and even valued part of life, but it must be molded and brought in line with divine commandments (*hukm*) as they are embodied in revelation. The spirit and lower self are contrasted as high/low, right/left, and cool/hot respectively. These are also, as we will see, relations of "inner" and "outer," for the lower self is contiguous with the lower sphere of the world, while the spirit is contiguous with religion. Humans are endowed with the moral faculty of reason (aql), which is in the heart. Reason mediates between the two poles of being, spirit and lower self, angel and animal. My Tablighi interlocutors unanimously agreed that reason, by itself, would lead humans toward their base, animalistic desires. It was only through ritual practices that a person came to reason properly and was able to distinguish right from wrong, truth from falsehood, and divine commandment from the Devil's whispers. It is for this reason that what is needed is bodily discipline that keeps a person oriented toward the good.

Moral personhood, however, is also gendered in that men are considered to be more inclined toward their spirit and more capable of acquiring the requisite faith that allows them to live in terms of God's will. Gender hierarchy can be found throughout the vast anthropological literature on gender in Muslim societies and Islam (Abu Lughod 1986; Boddy 1989; Combs-Shilling 1989; Tapper 1991; Torab 2007). In her study on the relationship between Islam and gender in Turkey, Carol Delaney (1991) argues that the conception of an omnipotent male deity as the supreme creator of the universe engenders a patriarchal order centered on male creativity and female receptivity, establishing male stewardship over women. Islam, Delaney argues, conceptualizes the male/female distinction as a relationship between "seed" and "soil" in which the male seed is the active-agentive principle and female soil is the passive-receptive ground on which the male seed acts. In Sufi cosmology, this is represented as the duality between the pen and the tablet, in which the pen, construed as male, acts upon the tablet figured as female (see Murata 1992, 153–55). I am not suggesting that this male/female, active/passive, and seed/soil homology is an essential, unchanging structure of Islam, but this framework helps understand the central place of *pardah* or gender segregation in the Deobandi tradition from which the Tablighi Jamaat draws its inspiration. In this framework, women's bodies are sexually potent and incite passions in men. Moreover, women, being weaker and lacking adequate control over their bodies, are therefore seen as "open" to the advances of men. The combination of the idea that women's bodies are sexually potent and the fact that women have less capacity for self-control means that women's sexuality is disruptive to moral order, a fact captured in the widespread belief that women are a principal source of moral chaos (fitna) (Mernissi 1975; Combs-Shilling 1989; Tapper 1991; Torab 2007). The very term "chaos" also means "temptation," and it is this temptation that women create in the world that requires that they must be "closed," "hidden," and "covered."

In Tablighi discourse, the woman as temptation also stands in for the temptations of the world itself that lures men away from religion and God. One frequently heard narrative goes that on the Day of Judgment that all of humanity will be lined up, with the good people on the right and the bad on the left, and God will show to them the image of a decrepit old woman, her hair falling out, her skin decaying, her body putrefying, and God will say to the aghast and terrified witnesses, "Behold, here is 'the world' you were chasing after!" Two important points are worth noting about this narrative. The first is that temptation for the world and sexual desire for women are equated here, both of which lure a person away from God. The normative subject of such narratives is clearly, then, imagined to be male. Second, the delineation of the domains of religion and the world also associates men with the enduring significance of religion and with the spirit that passes from this world to the next, while it associates women with the decaying body that is relevant only in this life. The association of men with transcendence and women with transience is similarly manifest in kinship ideologies of patrilineal descent in which agnatic blood is the vehicle for transmitting identity across generations and the association of women as genealogical dead ends, a perspective reinforced in Islamic law (see Abu Lughod 1986).

These patriarchal assumptions inform why dawat is primarily a male activity in the Tablighi Jamaat and women's roles are circumscribed and subordinated. This is because Tablighis adhere to strict codes of gender segregation (pardah) that limit women's movement beyond the home and prohibit them from meeting nonsanctioned men (*na mehram*). As Abullah a seasoned Tablighi, explained, "Men and women are opposites, like plus and minus. They attract one another. This is very dangerous. If this happens everything falls apart and families are destroyed." The establishment of pardah is a fundamental goal of dawat and is the condition for the flourishing of Islamic virtue. While women travel on dawat tours, these tours are far less frequent than men's tours, and a woman must be accompanied by a legally sanctioned man (mehram), a brother, husband, or father. Women's tours are called *mastoorat*, a word that means "women" but the root of which also means the part of the body that must be kept hidden. While on tours women stay in the homes of a willing host rather than in the mosque, where men reside. Unlike men who travel from house to house, calling people to the mosque, women stay in place in the home of their host and other women are invited to the home for prayer and reading sessions (*taleem*). Even while on these tours, women are not allowed to give sermons either to men or to other women. Instead, a designated itinerant male gives a sermon (*bayan*) to both the women and men from behind a curtain. This establishes the essential receptivity of women relative to men. When I asked Tablighis about this, they cited the idea that Muslims must also maintain "the pardah of the voice" (*awaaz ka pardah*) by which they mean that women's voices, like their bodies, can incite male passions and therefore can be disruptive to religious practice.

The establishment of pardah is regarded by Tablighis as the basis for an Islamic moral order, and its upkeep is also one of the felicity conditions for the efficacy of dawat. For the Tablighis I came to know, living away from women in a community of men was a basis for their own reform (islah) as it established their autonomy from women. Nevertheless, dawat also involves a role reversal. While on dawat tours, Tablighis assume roles that are not expected of them at home, roles that are designated as female like cooking and cleaning. As one Tablighi explained to me, "when we are at home, our wives and mothers do everything for us. Isn't it true? You get your breakfast in the morning without any effort, eggs, paratha, and tea, whatever you want. Right? But when we are on the path of Allah, you must do everything yourself and you are responsible for others too. This work draws you near to Allah." The "work" to which he refers is formalized in the institution of "service" (khidmat). Each day on a dawat tour, a set of Tablighis are assigned the task of buying and cooking food and serving others, and generally ensuring that everyone's needs are taken care of so that they can focus on dawat. Khidmat is distributed on a rotating basis, and everyone must do it. It is considered essential work not only because it allows others to devote themselves to dawat but, crucially, also because the Tablighi doing the khidmat cultivates the virtues of humility and patience.

Khidmat entails work that is primarily "feminine," which women perform in the home but men perform in the mosque. Barbara Metcalf (1998) argues that because Tablighi men conduct activities that are traditionally associated with women, like cooking and cleaning, the Tablighi Jamaat creates more egalitarian gender relations in the home. My experience is that men are doing this work only or at least primarily in the highly ritualized and valued context of the dawat tour, while women do this same work in the mundane and less valued space of the home. Tablighis insist that khidmat produces the capacity for empathy and compassion for women, but it does not imply equality and certainly not a dismantling of gender hierarchy. Rather, as Abdullah's previous quote suggests, women and men are seen as naturally different with distinct roles. Tablighis dismiss what they regard as the "liberal" and "modern" belief that men and women can and should perform the same roles. They regard this understanding of gender as inimical to Islam as well as detrimental to women as it forces women to do work that is not in their nature (*fitrat*). As one Tablighi explained, "look, if you were an engineer and you were asked to do a doctor's work, would you be able to do it? Would it not be a burden for you? Would you not then create a loss for yourself and for others? It's the same with men and women. It's not in their 'nature' to do man's work, so asking them to be like men is wrong." Gender difference and hierarchy, then, is seen as a necessary condition for the flourishing of Islamic virtue. Rather than dismantle gender hierarchy, dawat draws a parallel between home and mosque, associating women with the former and men with the latter. The mosque is referred to as "Allah's house," and it is here that men enact the feminine role relative to a male deity. In the symbolically less valuable space of the home, women occupy the female role relative to masculine authority. Women are receptive to men in the home as men are receptive to God in the mosque. Dawat, therefore, reproduces a patriarchal structure in which men have proximity to God and thus also dominion over women.

The structure of dawat is organized around the symbolism of gestation. Dawat is frequently described as "the mother of practices" (umm-al-amaal) because it is said to "give birth" to and "grow" faith in the practitioner. Tablighis are expected to conduct one forty-day tour (chilla) each year, which Tablighis explained was the period it takes for a child to take human form in the womb. Moreover, they conduct one four-month tour, which is the equivalent of three consecutive forty-day tours, which is the point in the gestation cycle in which God blows the spirit into the child in order to create a person. When one completes the four-month tour, one acquires the higher status of "older companion" (*purana saati*) and assumes the position of instructing "new companions" (*nai saati*) in matters of ritual and ethical conduct. Many Tablighis noted that this is because older companions are more likely to have God's guidance (*hidayat*) and can instruct others without leading them astray. The procreative metaphor is key: God inseminates the heart of the Tablighi with faith and guidance, just as men inseminate women to initiate the procreative process. Through dawat, one becomes in effect a carrier of, and one might even say pregnant with, God's agency. The gendered symbolism of procreation implies that the Tablighi is pregnant with God's agency, thus invoking a husband–wife relation with God, establishing a permanent relationship of dependence on God. Through dawat, the Tablighi comes to recognize his dependence on God, and this allows him to act on the world according to the exemplary model of the Prophet and in keeping with God's command.

Dawat, then, is structured by a gender hierarchy that defines male and female roles in terms of hierarchical complementarity while also situating the Tablighi as a feminine figure in relationship to God and thus inculcating in him a form of pious male agency to act upon the world, a framework that I have called "pious masculinity" (Khan 2018). A number of gendered oppositions structure this worldview at the level of personhood (spirit/lower self), kinship (male/female and mosque/home), and knowledge (truth/falsehood), and these inform the master distinction between the domains of "religion" (din) and "the world" (dunya). These homologous symbolic oppositions undergird all Tablighi narratives. They structure the temporal contrast between the Prophet's time, the pinnacle of spirituality (*roohaniyat*) and truth, and the representative of the ideals of religion and the current fallen state of Muslims that has succumbed to the drives of the lower self and become steeped in the falsehoods of the world. The Prophet's time was one in which the Companions followed the Prophet's every word and aimed to replicate his every deed and manifest all the virtues of religion. The present, by contrast, is an age of negligence (*ghaflat*) in which Muslims have abandoned their religious duties embodied in Prophet's way for the "ways of others" (*doosron ke tariqe*). It is against this loss of faith (iman) and certainty (yaqeen) in God that dawat aims to cultivate in the Tablighi the pious male agency that allows him to act upon the world through the recognition of his dependence on God.

The argument here is that dawat naturalizes gender distinctions, affirming the roles of women and men, and their associations with the home and the mosque and religion and the world, respectively. At the same time, dawat situates men as feminine in relation to God and inculcates in them a mode of pious male agency capable of inculcating pious virtues in others. In the next section, we turn to how dawat as a ritual process transforms the here-and-now of the present to the sacred then-and-there of the Prophet's time through the mobilization of iconic signs associated with Prophetic example. Through the performance of Islamic iconicity, the Tablighi cultivates the moral responsibility to live a pious life.

Islamic Iconicity and the Cultivation of Moral Responsibility

Tablighi conceptions of dawat fit well with the descriptions of Islamic pietists in Egypt by Saba Mahmood (2005) and Charles Hirschkind (2006) who stress that ritual practice in Islam is not merely symbolic or expressive but is a disciplinary means to cultivate ethical sensibilities and selves. Ritual practices like the mandatory prayer and sermon listening cultivate morally laden affective dispositions like humility, pious fear, patience, and love, which then enable one to differentiate good from bad, right from wrong, and truth from falsehood, allowing one to live an ethical life. It is through Islamic practice that one cultivates the inner affective dispositions that propel one to live an Islamic life, and it is by living an Islamic life that one is brought back to ritual duties (Mahmood 2001). As one senior Tablighi explained to me, "the purpose of dawat is to make religion descend in the heart... we know in our minds but it has not yet descended into our hearts." Islam, he said, should "drip from the eyes" so that people can tell you are Muslim just by the way you manage your eyes. In this discourse, one finds clearly that dawat is a form of bodily discipline aimed at the cultivation of a pious self.

This perspective, however, begs the questions: why do Tablighis place so much importance on dawat rather than any number of other Islamic practices for the formation of a pious self, and why must dawat take a distinct ritual form for it to be efficacious? In other words, the question is not why Tablighis are committed to ritual orthopraxy in general but why they place distinct importance on a specific set of practices. When one poses such questions to Tablighis, they respond by explaining that God has given dawat to create faith and this is what the Prophet did to spread Islam. Tablighis say that in the earliest phases of Prophethood, even before God bestowed on him the form of the five mandatory prayers (namaz/salat), the Prophet gave dawat to others to recognize the oneness of God (*tawhid*), the fundamental article of faith. Hence, dawat is the "mother of practices" (umm-al-amaal) as it cultivates faith, and faith is the condition of all other practice. I argue that dawat functions as a mode of self-cultivation because it is a type of performance, one that draws attention to the self and thus makes one responsible to an audience for the ethical entailments of pious performance. This approach takes us beyond the notions of ethical self-cultivation that have framed Islamic piety to a recognition of piety as an intersubjective achievement, opening the path to the questions of ambivalence, ambiguity, and doubt that we take up in the following chapters.

Dawat is predicated on a ritual ideology that presupposes the transformative force of sacred words on others. The efficacy of dawat depends on three "felicity conditions" (Austin 1975). First, dawat must be conducted in a face-to-face, or as Tablighis understand it "heart-to-heart," manner and therefore requires embodied presence in the mosque. Tablighis are drawing on broader Islamic conceptions of the primacy of the human voice as the "unmediated" form of communication, unlike texts, seen as distant and mediated, or what Brinkley Messick (1992) aptly calls "recitational logocentrism." The human voice is understood to create a relationship of immediacy both between Muslims as well as with God (Eisenlohr 2010). The face-to-face encounter is seen as the basis for creating a direct relationship between the Tablighi and God that imbues words with divine power and channels that power to the addressee who is then transformed through God's agency. In Tablighi discourse, dawat "connects the self to Allah's self" and creates a "heart to heart" (dil se dil) relationship between Muslims. Second, to be efficacious, dawat must be conducted with "purity of intentions" (*ikhlas-e-niyaat*). Tablighis understand purity of intentions to be not only an inner state of sincerity but directly tied to the sacrifice (*qurbani*) of life force (*jaan*), wealth (*maal*), and time (*waqt*). For Tablighis, it is the physical hardships (*mushaqqat*) that one experiences in dawat that makes God open the heart and allow religion to settle in it. Finally, dawat is a "collective practice" (*ijtimai amal*) rather than just an "individual practice" (*infiradi amal*) and must be done with other Muslims. The importance of collective practice is fully captured in the oft-heard Tablighi maxim, "individual practice is like a speck while collective practice is a mountain." It is the collective labor of dawat that gives it its efficacy to transform the self and thus to transform the world.

Tablighis travel in groups of six to twelve to preach the merits of Islam. Each week, Tablighis conduct one preaching tour (*gasht*) in their local areas and one in another area in the city. Every month, Tablighis conduct one three-day (*sehroza*) preaching tour that takes them outside the city. Each year, Tablighis are expected to travel on a forty-day trip (chilla) that takes them to various parts of the country. Each Tablighi is expected to conduct at least one four-month dawat tour, understood as three consecutive chillas, to become what Tablighis call an "old companion" (purana saathi). This confers some authority, including the right and duty to become the leader (*amir*) of a preaching group. Dawat consists of three types of work: the tour (gasht) in which Tablighis walk around a neighborhood speaking to people, inviting them to the mosque; the "middle talk," which is conducted during the tour in which a person stays behind in the mosque, where he speaks the praises of Allah while the others are on tour; and the reconvening at the mosque for mandatory prayers followed by the sermon (bayan). Dawat tours are nestled between late-afternoon (asr) prayers and evening (maghrib) prayers and/or from evening prayers to nightly prayers (*isha*). There are a number of other pedagogical activities that serve to train new Tablighis that I will address later, but those previously mentioned are all efforts to draw non-Tablighis to the mosque to perform ritual duties and to encourage them to join in dawat, the ultimate aim of all Tablighi efforts.

The designated leader (amir) of the group (jamaat) will determine who will go on the tour (gasht), who will stay in the mosque to give the "middle talk" (*darmiani baat*), and who will give the sermon (bayan) on that day. The leader breaks the larger group into smaller units of between three and five people that will constitute the preaching group and directs them toward different locations in the neighborhood. Each group will have a "speaker" (*mutakallim*) who speaks directly to the audience. Before departing, the group will gather in a circle and one person will make supplications (*dua*) stating the intention (*niyyat*) of the group to do this in the service of God and for no other reason than to please God, establishing the sincerity of the act, much as one does in other Islamic rituals like the mandatory prayer, requesting that God help in these endeavors.

Tablighis then depart from the mosque in a single file, walking on the right side of the street, the side associated with the spirit and with the angels. The line of Tablighis displays orderliness as well as enacting the "rope of God" (*allah ki rassi*), pulling one back to the mosque. Such an enactment makes dawat tours a highly visible and marked activity, one that most Pakistani Muslims and even non-Muslims recognize, and as we will see below, this markedness is an integral part of how dawat works as a mode of ethical subject formation.

The itinerant Tablighis silently recite the third kalima or creedal statement, The Glorification: "Glory (is for) Allah. And all praises for Allah. And (there is) none worthy of worship except Allah. And Allah is the Greatest. And (there is) no power and no strength except from Allah, the Most High, the Most Great." When the group approaches a person, the speaker will initiate the dawat with the standard Muslim greeting, "*Assalamalaikum*," followed by a handshake and the exchange of a few pleasantries. The dawat frame is keyed by a deep breath and a pause followed by an explicit claim that dawat is a religious duty: "of course, you already know this, but this is our duty," thus mitigating the hierarchical implications of claiming Islamic knowledge. This is especially common when the addressee is older or a person of higher status more generally, deflecting from the charge of hubris (see Lambek 1993). If the addressee accepts the peaching frame by bowing his head in submission, then dawat will ensue. It is important to note that while many refuse to accept the frame of being the objects of preaching, few addressees are willing to break the frame once the actual act of dawat begins. Young boys often joke about how they run away when they see Tablighis approaching because they know that they will be trapped. All of this implies that many Sunni Muslims in Pakistan already recognize the moral force of dawat and the sense of moral responsibility that it can produce. It is the aim of dawat to convert this sense of moral responsibility, which Tablighis say most Muslims possess, into an active commitment to dawat.

As the speaker begins to address the listener, the others make a semicircle around him and the listener and continue to silently recite the kalima. The silent recitation of the sacred language of the kalima is meant to elicit divine power. The ordinary language is transformed through its contact with Quranic recitation in a manner that parallels how the world is being transformed by the sacred act of dawat. While the speaker is referring to the addressee, describing the importance of prayer, focused intensely on communicating his message, the others draw on God's power to make his tongue "move" and "make the heart [of the addressee] soft" so that the words will settle in his heart. The efficacy of the preaching event from the perspective of Tablighis depends on the silent recitation of the Arabic creed, which solicits God's power and transforms the interaction between the speaker and the addressee, establishing a relationship between

Muslims on the basis of a submission to God. One can think of this as linking the vertical relationship between Tablighis and God, established in the sacred language, with the horizontal relationship between the speaker and the addressee in ordinary speech (Haeri 2003).

The dawat tour ends with the call to prayer (*azaan*), and the itinerant Tablighis return to the mosque. Preparations are made for the mandatory prayer, after which one Tablighi rises to announce that there will be a sermon (bayan) after the prayers and requests that the attendees stay for the sermon. The announcement is formulaic: "Our success in both this world and in the next is in religion. To get this religion into our lives requires effort regarding this effort, Allah willing, an important talk will take place after the remaining prayers. All brothers are requested to participate. *InshAllah*, it will be very beneficial." When the mandatory prayer finishes, Tablighis quickly gather to make a semicircle around the speaker to indicate to others that the sermon is beginning, and the speaker stands and begins the sermon. The sermon deserves special treatment in this analysis as the whole dawat process, intended to draw Muslims to the mosque, culminates in this event, and it is seen as doing the real transformative work by putting passion and desire in the hearts of others as well as in the speaker himself. Seated on the floor of the mosque, Tablighis huddle closely together, bodies touching, ideally in a kneeling position or with legs crossed and with one's head down, a manner that marks one's submission to the speaker. The bayan shares features of the much more widely recognized sermon (*khutba*) before Friday prayers and draws its moral force from its similarities to other more canonical forms of devotional listening.

Tablighi ritual discourse is organized around what Tablighis call the "six points" (*che batein*). These are faith (iman), mandatory prayers (salat/namaz), knowledge and recitation (*ilm-o-zikr*), honoring of Muslims (*ikram-e-Muslim*), purity of intentions (*ikhlas-e-niyyat*), and (6) invitation of conveying (*dawat-e-tabligh*). These principles are embedded in Tablighi sermons, the middle talk, and preaching tours and shape much of everyday discourse for Tablighis. The sermon is the site for the elaboration of each of these principles. Speakers decide which of the points to stress, and each Tablighi includes his own rhetorical flourishes, creating a distinct repertoire of tropes. The purpose of the sermon is to render in dramatic form the significance of each of these points by drawing on a field of knowledge about the lives, sayings, and experiences of all the Prophets, especially the Prophet Muhammad and his Companions, Islamic scholars, Elders, and other authoritative figures of the past. This knowledge is drawn from a wide array of Islamic textual sources but, most importantly, from the *Fazail-e-Amal*, a compendium of documented sayings and stories (*qisas*) of the Prophet and Companions compiled by Maulana Muhammad Zakariyya

Khandalwi, the nephew of Muhammad Ilyas. This text serves all manner of ritual purposes including the daily reading sessions (taleem). Knowledge acquired either through reading or through listening and time spent in the Tablighi Jamaat thus creates the skillful oratory that gives the Tablighi Jamaat its distinct character. It is undoubtedly the desire to acquire the ability to speak with force and conviction that draws many Muslims to the Tablighi movement.

The primary aim of the sermon is to create in the listener a deep sense of the moral disjuncture between a pure, generative moment of Islam and the deplorable and corrupted state of Muslims in the present. Sermons invoke a corrupted and morally deficient "we" to a morally virtuous and exemplary time of the Prophet and Companions, a fallen "now" and "here" to an exalted "then" and "there," with the aim of creating a deep sense of moral responsibility for returning to the sacred then-and-there of the Prophet's time. This narrative of moral disjuncture moves from the exalted plane of religion and the purity of the spirit to the lower plane of the world and the corruptions of the lower self that have produced moral chaos (fitna). This narrative of moral disjuncture and decline outlines the need to return to the original Islam of the Prophet and the generative moment of the Islamic community through dawat.

This moral disjuncture is mapped onto spatial distinctions as well and specifically in the distinction between the purity of the world inside the mosque and the impurity of the world outside the mosque. The mosque is the space where the angels reside and where one finds peace and comfort. Because religion is absorbed through the senses, spending time in the mosque is itself purifying. Spending time outside the mosque, in the world, however, is corrupting. In sermons, as in Tablighi discourse more generally, the contrast that is drawn is usually between the mosque and the market, the former being the place of the spirit and the latter being the corruptions of the lower self: "Being in the mosque is like being in a perfume shop . . . you absorb all the smells. Isn't that different from being in a fish market? . . . The mosque is a space of angels. . . . Do you know what angel's special characteristic is? It is that they will never disobey Allah's direction. If Allah tells them to stay in prostration, they will do this for all eternity. Therefore we must spend time in the mosque, so that we can learn to obey Allah." By contrast, the market is imagined as a space that incites one's base desires for material possession and uncontrolled passions for the world. Indeed, markets are also associated with gender mixing and thus sexual desire as well as with money, a dangerous place of temptation where men can easily fall prey to the Devil. As shown in the previous quotation, one absorbs the qualities of the mosque through the senses, and it induces deep pleasure, bringing one peace and tranquility, unlike the market, which is a source of insatiable desire and thus inner chaos. It is the purpose of the sermons not only to highlight this moral disjuncture in time and space but to highlight how dawat is the solution in that it connects the Tablighi to the sacred past and keeps him inside the pure space of the mosque.

The sermon is closed by "the solicitation" (*tashkeel*), a word that literally translates as to "give shape." Tablighis insist that the tashkeel is what defines dawat as a "practice" (amal), as captured in the oft-repeated statement, "the difference between preaching (tabligh) and speech-making (*taqreer*) is tashkeel." At the end of the sermon, a Tablighi other than the one giving the sermon stands with a pen and pad and proceeds to ask who will commit to a specified period of dawat. Starting with the longest tour (seven months) to the shortest tour (three days), he invites a commitment to future dawat. This request for commitment is interlaced with exhortations and examples drawn from the life of the Prophet and his Companions or a detailing of the benefits of dawat. The present Tablighis serve as exemplars by standing and voicing their commitment to dawat, and they do this regardless of how many times they have made a commitment because "to make one's intention known is itself a meritorious deed." Newcomers will occasionally stand and register their commitment as well, which will then be tallied in the notepad. If the purpose of the sermon is to create a sense of moral disjuncture and to posit a remedy to that moral disjuncture through dawat, then the solicitation is about asking people to make a public commitment to the moral order posited in the sermon.

The ideological importance granted to the solicitation provides a key into how dawat functions as a practice of ethical cultivation. As I noted earlier, the Foucauldian models of ethical self-cultivation in the anthropology of Islam have stressed how ritual practices cultivate ethical sensibilities, but the markedness of dawat as a ritual activity makes it a public performance, one that draws the gaze of others to the self. The entire process of dawat, especially its culmination in the solicitation, bears striking resemblance to what Webb Keane (2007) has described as the "creed paradigm" (67–72). Creeds, according to Keane, are "an explicit statement of religious tenets and the norms for its verbal performance," and are crucial for proselytizing religions like Christianity and Islam because they condense complex theological arguments and give them a definite semiotic form, which allows them to circulate across many contexts. The six points function to condense the Tablighi worldview into easily learnable "objects," the structure of which can then be replicated and create a textual commonality across various sites of performance. What is crucial, Keane (2007) notes, is that creeds are not merely statements of belief but are "attached to a performative of assent," which is a public registering of one's commitment to a particular moral order (70).

The creed paradigm of Calvinist Protestants described by Keane is underpinned by the value of sincerity, and a sincere subject is one whose outer performance is aligned with his inner self, a person whose words and actions reflect an immaterial inner state, a semiotic ideology that requires perceptible semiotic forms to shed evidence of their materiality (see Engelke 2007). For Tablighis, by contrast, it is precisely the materiality of the form and specifically its memetic resemblance to the Prophetic example that makes it understood as a divinely given practice and recognizable to both Tablighis and many non-Tablighi Sunnis as an enactment of the Prophetic tradition (sunnat). The efficacy of dawat is integrally bound up with the enactment of what we can call Islamic iconicity associated with the exemplary figure of the Prophet. By enacting Islamic iconicity, one comes to embody the virtues that inhere in the Islamic signs associated with Prophetic example.

This logic is extended to all manner of bodily markers like growing beards and wearing skull caps as well as embodied practices like modes of sitting, eating, speaking, sleeping, and any number of other activities. It is evident in the pervasive discourse about the centrality of growing a beard for Muslims and how the beard functions to discipline the subject:

> The beard keeps me from all my sins. When I first kept the beard, my friends made fun of me, and said that I would drive away all the girls. I found that funny, but I soon realized that, yes, that's the whole point! A girl sees me with a beard and she thinks this person is "religious" and she is repelled. At first, I felt awkward with the beard, but every time I wanted to do something bad, I would think that people look at me and they say, this person is religious and look what he is doing, and when you know that, then you develop concern in your heart, and so you do the right thing. The beard helps me focus on good deeds, and when people see you do good deeds, then they too want to follow your example.

At the heart of this statement is the notion that signs of piety signal a public commitment and, in doing so, force one to take responsibility for one's actions. The beard communicates to others something about the inner state of the performer and thus holds the performer responsible for the ethical entailments of that performance. Being a public symbol of piety, the beard implies a claim to having the appropriate dispositions of piety and thus makes one responsible for the social expectations of that claim. The performance, then, works as a disciplinary technique because it creates a kind of communicative relationship between people about the pious interiority of the performer through Islamic iconicity.

Dawat is about demonstrating a public commitment to the moral order posited in Tablighi ideology. As Irfan, the leader of an itinerant jamaat that I was part of, frequently stated before we departed on the tour, "Now we are no longer who we were. Now we will be known as Tablighis. Now all our deeds (amal) will be scrutinized from the way we eat, to the way we sleep, how we treat each other. Now we must be meticulous in upholding these good deeds because we are now from the jamaat." In other words, it is the public stance that one takes in dawat that creates responsibility for one's words and actions. The principle of sincerity of course undergirds such performances since one must have an inner state that aligns with one's practices, and thus public performance compels one to align the inner with the outer state. By attesting to one's commitment by adopting a public stance, the gap between inner and outer is closed.

Roy Rappaport's (1999) argument that ritual creates "acceptance" and "obligation" by communicating a commitment to a shared public order is pertinent here. Drawing on Charles Peirce's (2011) tripartite typology of sign–object relations, Rappaport argues that rituals are performative acts that create the affective states they perform. According to Pierce, there are three kinds of sign–object relations: an icon, which posits a physical resemblance between the sign and the object, like the relationship between a map and a place; an index, which posits a relationship between a signifier and signified that is nonarbitrary, causal in force, and contiguous in space, like the relationship between smoke and fire; and a symbol, which posits an arbitrary and conventional relationship between sign and object, like the relationship between a word and its meaning. Rituals, Rappaport argues, create indexical links, a relationship of contiguity, between the performer and the "canonical" messages or symbols of a religious tradition: in this case Prophetic example. Moreover, rituals are autocommunicative in that "the transmitters of ritual's messages are always among their most important receivers" (Rappaport 1999, 51) and performers "transmit information concerning their current physical and psychic or social states to themselves and to other participants" (52). Rituals establish a set of conventions and imbue them with moral force. As Rappaport notes, "it is patently immoral to act incompatibly with the terms of a conventional state of affairs that one has ritually participated in bringing into being" (133). In this sense, ritual compels one to act in accordance with the moral order that is instantiated in ritual.

The performance of piety in dawat transforms iconic signs into an indexical relationship. Dawat transforms a relationship of resemblance to the Prophetic model to a relationship of contiguity with that model. Dawat brings together a dense constellation of iconic signs, drawing the attention of others to the self and thereby compelling the Tablighi to act according to the ethical presuppositions of those signs. The Tablighi becomes an icon of the Prophet, physically resembling the manner, dress, and actions of the Prophet, and this creates an Islamic habitus that is contiguous with the virtues of the Prophetic model. The enmeshing of iconicity and indexicality is a key feature of ritual, but as Christopher Ball (2014) has aptly argued, the success of ritual depends on it being seen by others as not simply a relationship of similarity (iconic) nor a conventional association (symbolic) but bearing a relationship of contiguity between sign and object (indexical). In other words, the iconic signs of dawat, such as beards, must be recognized by others as bearing a vital connection to their object, the pious interiority of the Tablighi as he identifies with Prophetic example.

Recognizing dawat as a performance aimed at creating iconic indexicality is important because it draws attention to the relational dynamics in the creation of piety. Understanding ritual practices of Islam through a Foucauldian notion of "technologies of the self" has inadvertently reproduced the notion that individuals act on themselves and thus foreclosed some of the relational work involved in creating and sustaining the pious self.[1] Critics of this approach to Islamic piety have pointed out the failure to address the plurality of Muslim voices to a single model of religious piety as well as the failure to address questions of ambivalence and ambiguity in everyday Muslim life (see Schielke 2011). The semiotic and performance approach to piety that I have adopted in this chapter retains the core insight of the anthropological work on Islamic piety movements: that Islamic pietists regard Islamic practices as a means for the cultivation of pious virtues. However, it also creates the possibility of examining all the issues of indeterminacy like ambivalence, ambiguity, and doubt that attend the pursuit of piety, themes that we will take up in subsequent chapters.

One reason why analytic approaches have erased the relational dynamics of piety is that Tablighis and other Islamic pietists, in their efforts to convince others of the benefits of ritual practice, tend to stress their inevitability and automaticity. When Tablighis compare dawat to being in a "perfume shop," they are giving dawat this aura of inevitability and automaticity. They are saying that piety seeps into the body. After all, God always rewards the sacrifices of dawat with faith. This ideological position backgrounds the indeterminacy of pious self-formation and stresses a strong indexical link between "doing" dawat and "becoming" pious, erasing the mediational process by which piety as a relationship is or is not materialized. In the final section of this chapter, I turn to how "doing" and "becoming" are linked through the sacralization of words and how this sets the terms for the creation of a sacred hierarchy that organizes the movement.

Pious Bodies, Heavy Words, and the Creation of a Sacred Hierarchy

We have seen how dawat, as a performance organized around Islamic iconicity, aims to establish a relationship of contiguity between the itinerant Tablighi and the sacred past and therefore inscribe the Tablighi with the virtues associated with Prophetic example. Piety in this sense is an intersubjective achievement, which not only aims to transform others but also transforms the Tablighi himself insofar as he becomes the primary bearer of moral responsibility. Tablighis describe the effects of dawat in terms of creating a realization or "feeling" (*ehsaas*) of one's relationship (*nisbat*) with the Prophet as well as the creation of "proximity" (qurbat) to God. Through repetition, Tablighis say, the vital relationship to Prophetic example is strengthened and one acquires the faith to live according to God's plan. This creates a system of spiritual ascent that structures what Reetz (2008) has aptly called the "faith bureaucracy" of the Tablighi Jamaat.

The Tablighi Jamaat relies on a network of small, self-constituted congregations (jamaats) in mosques throughout the country, and the mosque unit is the primary unit of dawat. Each mosque congregation is responsible for managing its own affairs, collecting its own funds, and making arrangements for dawat tours. The aim of each congregation is to grow itself in its own area and send more and more itinerant Tablighis out to conduct dawat tours throughout the country and the world. The size and reach of the mosque congregation is a source of great pride for Tablighis. To self-organize and accomplish its tasks, each congregation functions based on consultation (*mashwara*). This is a broadly democratic process in which Tablighis sit in a circle, and each individual voices his opinion on any matter of importance. Such procedures have led some scholars of the Tablighi Jamaat to regard them as fundamentally egalitarian (Janson 2014). Indeed, Tablighis adopt what one would call a form of male ontological egalitarianism in which all men are ultimately capable of piety if they perform their ritual duties and commit themselves to dawat. However, the constitutive power attributed to dawat, I argue, creates hierarchical distinctions in terms of spiritual rank (darja). This serves as the institutional basis for the movement and is central to how Tablighis conceptualize the domain of religion.

When one asks Tablighis about how precisely dawat transforms a Tablighi, one is told that the words created in dawat carry spiritual potency (*roohani quwwat*). Tablighis say that God recognizes the sacrifice (qurbani) that one makes in dawat and thus imbues words with spiritual potency. Tablighis regard dawat to be a form of sacrifice of life force (jaan), wealth (maal), and time (waqt). The Tablighi assumes the physical hardship (mushaqqat) of the journey, pays his own way, and commits his own time, all forms of wealth and power that he could put to "worldly" ends but instead devotes to God. In exchange, God grants the Tablighi a spiritual potency (*roohani quwwat*) that manifests in "heavy" words. One can think of sacrifice here as a form of "value conversion," the destruction of lower-value objects associated with the world for higher-value objects associated with religion (Munn 1986). Pregnant with divine agency, these words are uniquely capable of transforming others and transforming the self. They are said to make the hearts of people "soft" and "open," and they readily settle in the heart because they are "heavy."

Tablighis describe such words as having a life of their own. As a close interlocutor explained: "I have heard from the ulama ikraam that Allah does not even allow the words of dawat that are truthful to fall to the ground. Allah always makes these words the channel for someone's guidance." The word truthful (*haq*) here implies that these are words imbued with divine power. While one directs dawat toward a specific person, once these sacred words are released, they will circulate until they find a receptive person whose heart they will settle in and draw them to Islamic practice.

This notion of the power of pious words means that the Tablighi is only responsible for the creation of the words, not for their actual effect on the specific people to whom dawat is addressed. Tablighis draw on Surah Yasin from the Quran to claim that one's responsibility to others ends upon delivering the words of dawat: "And we are not responsible save for clear notification" (Quran 36:17). The impact of dawat on others, they insist, is always in "Allah's hands," and one's responsibility is simply in giving dawat, a perspective that shifts the focus away from the effects of dawat in its semiotic context to the process through which the words are created and delivered. If the process meets the felicity conditions of dawat, God will accept it as sacrifice and will reward the Tablighi with faith. Tablighis often say that one should conduct dawat even when there is no actual person to listen to it since even this can transform others, and it is ultimately God who is the real witness of such an act and who will reward the act. Tablighis would often conduct the middle talk in the mosque regardless of whether anyone besides the speaker was present because ultimately one is oneself the primary audience for dawat and one never knows where and to whom God will send the words.

The sacralization of pious words backgrounds the effects of dawat on others and instead refocuses emphasis on the "doing" of dawat, creating the indexical link between "doing" and "becoming" that is the hallmark of Tablighi ritual ideology. The shift away from the communicative effects on the addressee to the formal features of the ritual process sets the terms for the structure of spiritual ascent that gives institutional shape to the Tablighi Jamaat. As I noted earlier, dawat involves one weekly tour in the neighborhood and one in an adjacent neighborhood, a three-day tour (sehroza) each month that takes one outside the city, a forty-day tour (chilla) each year that will take one to specific parts of the country, a four-month tour at least once that will take one across the country, and seven-month and one-year tours that take one out of Pakistan to various parts of the world. As one moves outward from a center, one extends the circulation of one's sacred words and actions, and simultaneously rises in the ranks of the sacred hierarchy. This process was explained in one of the middle talks I recorded:

> People think that there is no solution to the world's problems. All these things you see around from floods, to target killings, to crime, to corruption, all of this hurts the religious as much as it hurts others ... But people think, "I am just one person. How can I solve the world's problems?" ... But, if you give time to the mosque, all the world's problems can be solved. There are twenty-four hours in a day. Eight of these hours are spent working, eight hours resting, and eight with family and friends. But if you give even three hours to the mosque, you will see that your life will change. You will take what you learn from the mosque to your work. You will know not to be dishonest in your dealings with others. You will bring religion to your family. You will have daily reading (taleem) in the home, and you will be able to teach your family religion, and you will be able to help your friends as well, who in turn will help their family and friends and so on ... You see if you give time to the mosque, then you can help change your family. And if you do a weekly gasht, then eventually you can bring at least your neighborhood to religion, right? And if every month you do a three-day tour (sehroza), you can change your city, and if every year you do a forty-day tour (chilla), then you can change your province, and if you do four months, then you can reach the whole country, and if you do seven months then you can reach the whole world. So if a person puts in time in the jamaat, he can bring religion to the whole world!

In this statement, each stage of dawat corresponds to a spatial area that is transformed through dawat. One begins with the mosque in one's own neighborhood, which has a transformative effect on the most intimate of relationships with kin, friends, and neighbors, and from there one moves to the level of city, province, country, and finally the entire world.

A movement outward in terms of space from local to global corresponds to a movement backward in time from the present to the past; one increases one's capacity to realize the virtues of the Prophet's time as well as a movement up in terms of proximity to God with the aim of creating a direct (*barah-e-rast*) relationship with God. It is through the moral transformation of the world that one acquires spiritual rank (*darja*). We have already noted the association Tablighis make between dawat and the phases of the child's gestation in the womb. The forty-day tour corresponds to each phase of gestation of the child, and the four-month tour, understood as three consecutive forty-day tours, corresponds to the point at which God blows the spirit in the child, thereby creating a person. In this sense, dawat is likened to a spiritual rebirth, and the congregation itself is likened to the womb within which and through which one becomes a pious Islamic subject. The four-month tour is seen as the condition for creating a stable and sturdy relationship to God and the point at which God grants a person "guidance" (hidayat). It is after the four-month tour that one goes from being a "new companion" (naya saati) to an "old companion" (purana saati), a status that gives one increasing responsibility for training new companions in ritual and ethical conduct.

As one's words become heavier, one is granted a larger audience within the Tablighi congregation. Generally, new companions only give sermons in their own local mosques and are encouraged to develop their sermon-giving skills on dawat tours where they preach primarily to non-Tablighis. Old companions, however, preach both to non-Tablighis and to fellow Tablighis in the weekly Thursday congregation in the mosque complexes of each city, and at the larger gatherings of the annual congregations. The Elders, who are the pinnacle of piety and have the heaviest words, speak from the pulpit at the annual congregations to hundreds of thousands if not millions of Tablighis. Tablighis insist that hearing these words have immense transformative power, thus it is of critical importance to attend the annual congregations. Moreover, as the exemplars of virtue, the sermons of the Elders also circulate in material media like cassettes and CDs and now increasingly on the internet. Lower-ranked Tablighis actively avoid having their voices circulate in mass media, a fact I repeatedly confronted when trying to conduct and record interviews. Tablighis explained to me that such recordings were "dangerous" because these words are not sufficiently "heavy" and therefore can lead others away from Islam. We can see, then, that lower-ranked Tablighis are pious listeners relative to higher-ranked Tablighis who are pious speakers. A movement up in the sacred hierarchy implies a relationship of directness (barah-e-rast) to Allah and less dependence on the mediation of pious others.

What we have seen in this chapter is how the metadiscourses of dawat establish dawat as an enactment of the Prophetic model. I have argued that dawat presupposes gender hierarchy and naturalizes gender difference; depends on the performance of Islamic iconicity; and, through the sacralization of words, shifts the emphasis away from the effects of the performance in semiotic context to the formal features of the ritual process, creating a sacred hierarchy that organizes the movement. The semiotic analysis developed here takes us beyond the Foucauldian approach to ethical self-cultivation that has been faulted for ignoring the relational dynamics of Islamic piety as well as the indeterminacy that characterizes Muslim life. In the next chapter, I take up the question of the relational work that is performed in the Tablighi congregation to become recognized as a pious subject, which I argue involves performative acts of submission to pious authorities and everyday forms of citationality or what I call the ethics of hierarchy. To become a pious subject in the Tablighi Jamaat is to acquire recognition from other Tablighis, particularly those with pious authority, as someone who can enact this distinct mode of pious relationality. As we will see, pious relationality structured by the ethics of hierarchy is the basis for the moral reproduction of congregational life in the Tablighi Jamaat.

4

THE ETHICS OF HIERARCHY AND THE MORAL REPRODUCTION OF CONGREGATIONAL LIFE

I began my research with the assumption that Tablighis were invested in preaching to all Muslims and that I would have little trouble getting them to discuss religious matters with me, a Muslim whom they clearly had an interest in drawing into the movement. I figured that I would become their project of dawat, and yet I found myself stifled at every turn. It was not that I could not get Tablighis to speak to me. It was that I could not get them to talk about anything beyond the virtues of dawat, which soon became predictable and repetitive. I found myself constantly trying to get beyond or behind the frame of dawat and the formulaic renderings of an Islamic life in the hope of finding what I was hoping would be data about their lives and motivations for joining the Tablighi Jamaat, but the more I sought details about their lives, the more my interlocutors insisted that what I needed was simply to listen with an open heart. When I explained to Tablighis that I was conducting research to write a book, they recoiled at the idea, insisting that dawat is a practice (amal) and not research (tahqiqat) and that Islam can only be learned by "doing" dawat. They insisted I was wasting my time because I would invariably arrive at false conclusions unless I committed myself to dawat and to the Tablighi congregation. Dawat, they say, is not about "talk" (*batein*) but is instead a deed and practice.

In the last chapter, I showed how the ritual ideology of dawat creates a link between doing dawat and becoming pious through the sacralization of words and how this gives shape to the hierarchical structure of the movement. As noted in the last chapter, Tablighis insist that dawat is a "collective practice" (ijtimai amal) rather than an "individual practice" (infiradi amal), and this means that it must be conducted in a specific manner with other Tablighis in the congregation (jamaat). In this chapter, I draw on my own experience of being a novice in the congregation to examine how one comes to be recognized by other Tablighis as a pious subject, as someone committed to the Tablighi movement. I argue that beyond simply performing the formal ritual genres of the Tablighi Jamaat, one must learn to inhabit what I call the ethics of hierarchy, a form of relational ethics that involves performative acts of submission in pious listening and discursive acts of citation that recognize the virtuous qualities of pious authorities. It is by enacting the ethics of hierarchy that one comes to be seen as an "acted upon" self and thus capable of spreading Islamic virtue.

Enacted in pious companionship (sohbat) in the congregation, the ethics of hierarchy manages the central tension in dawat, the fact that dawat is meant to replicate Prophetic example and that each iteration of dawat has the potential to create change. This means that the assumption of pious authority can easily lead someone to elaborate on the tradition in ways that depart from the original Islam of the Prophet, a problem captured in the obsessive concern Tablighis have with innovation (biddat). The problem is not only theological, however, but also organizational. Tablighi concern about dangers of "talk" indexes a tension within the movement. The growth of the Tablighi Jamaat depends on inculcating in practitioners the desire to become pious authorities and to model one's life on the pious Elders of the movement, but this can create an overzealous assumption of pious authority that creates tensions and conflicts and thus fissures in and dispersal of the congregation. I argue that the ethics of hierarchy regulates the assumption of pious authority by emphasizing the levels of piety that stand between the Tablighi and the Elders of the movement. This in turn creates a temporal structure for pious becoming that recognizes the slow cultivation of pious virtues and defers the realization of piety to the future (Kloos 2018). The ethics of hierarchy, then, is both a relational structure in that it involves accepting the authority of pious others and a temporal frame in that it encourages patience in the realization of pious authority. Combined, these features manage the fissures and dispersal of the congregation latent in dawat. The ethics of hierarchy, therefore, serves as the basis for the moral reproduction of congregational life.

Pious Listening and the Problem of Talk

> The philosopher Plato was very clever, he said, the cleverest of men. Plato had decided that he wanted to live forever and he planned to cheat death. Plato knew that Allah had determined the precise time that every

person would die, and it was precisely at this time the Angel of Death comes to take your soul. Plato pleaded with Allah to tell him when he would die, and Allah knowing Plato's intentions, decided he would make an example out of him for all of humanity. Knowing the exact moment of his death, Plato devised a mischievous plan. He would spend the rest of his life crafting a series of statues that were perfect replicas of himself, so perfect there was no way for a human being to tell which was Plato and which was the statue. He knew that if he could fool the Angel of Death even for a split second, the time of his death would pass and he would have defeated death and would become immortal. Plato lined up all the statues in a single file in a giant room and awaited the Angel of Death. When he heard the Angel of Death approaching, Plato stood perfectly still among the statues. The Angel of Death came into the room and there seeing Plato's mischief said, "You are very clever Plato, but you have forgotten one thing!" To this, Plato, in a panic, blurts out, "What?" And the Angel of Death says, "This. Now come with me!"

This was a story told to me by a Tablighi about the essential problem of life. This is an account of extreme hubris of believing that one can "reason" one's way out of death. Plato represents all those who think they can live outside of God's plan. As Tablighis often say, "in the end, we are all caught" (*akhir mein sab ki pakar ho jati hai*). But this is not only a story of hubris. It is also a story about the tongue. Known for his ability to spin tales, the philosopher represents all those who tell stories that lead them to unduly believe in their own power and forget that they exist in God's plan and at the mercy of God's power. The tongue comes to represent the surplus human agency that must be regulated. The belief in your own agency and the failure to recognize God's agency is the central problem that Tablighis confront. Faith, after all, as Tablighis regularly say, is the "knowledge that everything comes from God and nothing comes from another." It is the tongue that gets Plato into trouble. The tongue itself is a dangerous thing, and "controlling the tongue" (*zabaan pei qabu rakhna*) is needed to stay within God's plan. The tongue simultaneously has the power to draw people to Islam, but it can also lead a person to imagine himself, like Plato, to be so powerful as to be outside of God's reach. Indeed, as I will show in this section, this is a danger inherent in dawat, and it is the key to understanding the importance that Tablighis place on submission to pious authorities in acts of pious listening and pious companionship.

I have already outlined some of the key features of Islam as a knowledge system, but they are worth repeating here. In the Deobandi tradition, the Quran is the direct word of God in its absolute perfection. As Niloofer Haeri (2003) notes, the truth-value of this word is carried in the very form of the sacred language, Arabic, and because form cannot be translated, it is therefore "untranslatable." (13) All renditions of the sacred language in ordinary language are "interpretations." Unlike the sacred language, interpretations are humanly authored and therefore subject to human frailty. In Tablighi discourse, although this is hardly peculiar to Tablighis, Muslims must strive to emulate the example of the Prophet who embodied and transmitted Islamic knowledge in its total perfection. The conception of knowledge as total and perfect means that its transmission is always fraught with the danger that one will create innovation (biddat), understood as a departure from the original meaning. In a rich historical account of Islamic textual knowledge in Yemen, Brinkley Messick cogently argues that the transcription of Islamic knowledge in texts raised deep concerns about the transmission of authentic knowledge. On the one hand, Messick argues that texts were understood as the necessary means of preservation of Islam, without which Islamic knowledge could not be transmitted across time and space. On the other hand, however, the very process of transcribing knowledge also elicits desires for invention or what Messick (1993) calls the "temptation of the pen" (211). The Devil's efforts to draw Muslims away from proper Islam means that transcription and writing are dangerous endeavors as texts can become the vehicle for the spread of falsehood (*batil*) and pull Muslims away from the truth (haq), a truth understood to be embodied in the perfection of the Quran. This means that only men of impeccable moral character should transcribe the tradition because only such morally exemplary men can faithfully resist the desire to create innovations.

What Messick outlines in relation to textuality applies also to oral discourse, at least in the Tablighi Jamaat. I found that at every turn, Tablighis stressed the importance of controlling the tongue and referred repeatedly to the threat posed by the "temptation of the tongue" (*zabaan ka fitna*). The word *fitna* here once again means both "temptation" and "chaos." Like all other temptations, falling prey to the temptations of the tongue also signals the dominance of the lower self over the spirit and a lack of cultivated faith. This reflects a deep tension within the very process of dawat. On the one hand, dawat is the means for the cultivation and spreading of faith, but as a practice that involves learning to become a skilled speaker, it can also lead a person to believe they are in possession of a power that belongs only to God. Tablighis repeatedly explained to me that while giving bayans was very good at inducing the passions of Islam, bayans could also incite the passions of the lower self, induce "hubris" (*takabbur*), and create the desire to manipulate religion for one's ends. Tablighis often noted that the "heat" of passions created from the dawat tours could easily lead one to the temptations of the tongue. This is why there is so much emphasis on other forms of work in

Tablighi Jamaat, such as khidmat, that inculcate humility to cut against the hubris that can be born of the process of preaching and especially in giving sermons to crowds of people.

Tablighis are preoccupied with the problem of "talk" because all acts of transmission risk elaboration on the original sources and therefore carry the threat of "innovation" (biddat). Tablighis insist that dawat is a form of "repetition" (takrar) and that it is not meant to introduce anything new. This sentiment is captured in the oft-heard statement "the difference between tabligh (conveying) and taqreer (giving a speech) is takrar (repetition)." When conducted properly, dawat should only recreate authorized Islamic knowledge. But, if dawat is an explicit and self-conscious process of producing Islamic iconicity, how can Tablighis be sure that they are not in fact the ones creating the gap between truth (haq) and falsehood (batil) and falling prey to the temptations of the tongue?[1]

This is the central tension for Tablighis, and it is what inspires their immense investment in congregational life. It is only through participation in congregational life that one comes to live as the Prophet and Companions did, and it is the relationships cultivated in this space that keep one on the path of God and allow one to draw others to the movement. This emphasis on the disciplining function of "collectiveness" (*ijtimaiyat*) is manifest in the oft-heard claim that a lone person is open to the ploys and temptations of the Devil, and that one should always be in the presence of pious others to guard against the Devil's whispers. Hence, Tablighis while on dawat tours are strongly discouraged from leaving the mosque on their own because then they will be seduced by un-Islamic activities. It is the presence of pious others that keeps one from straying from the path of Islam. Tablighis, then, see "proper" Islamic virtue as a product of pious companionship and believe that it is by crafting the ethical relationships within the congregation that Islam remains anchored to the sacred past.

The problem of innovation associated with the tongue, which is the problem of surplus agency, must be consistently offset through an emphasis on pious listening and pious companionship. Tablighis insist that sacred knowledge requires the cultivation of appropriate ethical and affective relationships between Muslims, relationships that are modeled on the Companions and the Prophet. This means that they are relationships structured by a hierarchy that situates Tablighis as pious listeners to those who have more Islamic knowledge and authority. "The Prophet's every word and every movement became the Companions' faith," one Tablighi explained in a sermon. "When a word left the Prophet's mouth, it would enter straight into a Companion's heart . . . because their love (mohabbat) for the Prophet was so intense." Tablighis always stressed this relationship of love between the Prophet and the Companions as one of directness. The relationship of love involved total submission to every word that left the

Prophet's mouth, which means the word went straight to their heart. The Companions felt no need to evaluate for themselves what the Prophet was saying and doing for they had "certainty" (yaqeen) that whatever he was doing came directly from God, and thus this was a transmission unmediated by the trickery of reason. It is because of this love for the Prophet that they would do anything he called on them to do, and much of Tablighi discourse is about detailing the sacrifices of the Companions. "Remember, the Sahaba were only special because of their faith," he continued. "Allah is connected to practice, not the Companions. Be like them and fill your heart with the love of the Prophet."

The Companions are the model for emulation for Tablighis and for what we can call pious listening. One of the central texts of the Tablighi Jamaat is the "Lives of the Companions" (Hayat-us-Sahaba), a compendium about the hardships the Companions endured and how they addressed the issues of their times. The Companions assumed these hardships because of their unwavering and robust faith and love for the Prophet. Narratives about the Companions serve to instruct the audience about how to create the proper mode of receptivity, and specifically how to cultivate what Charles Hirsckind (2006) calls an "ethics of listening." Hirsckind shows how in the Islamic tradition, listening, far from being a condition of passive reception, is an active process of sedimenting faith in the body. "Make your whole body an ear," Tablighis would frequently say. By invoking the relationship between the Prophet and the Companions, the speaker also draws a parallel between himself and the Prophet, on the one hand, and between the audience and the Companions, on the other. These metacommunicative statements instruct the listeners on how they should be relating to the words of dawat. It tells them that they should be listening to the sermon with total submission, just as the Companions listened to the Prophet. Explicit directives to the audience like "listen with your eyes!" or "make your body an ear!" pepper the sermons. I was told repeatedly by Tablighis that what I needed to do to understand dawat was listen from the heart, not from the mind, and emulate the Companions, and only then will "religion descend into the heart." These repeated injunctions instruct practitioners on the adoption of a stance of pious submission in relation to pious authority.

The emphasis on the faithful replication of tradition is certainly not unique to Tablighis and is found across traditionalist Islamic groups and actors, but the continuous entextualization, decontextualization, and recontextualization of discourse in dawat means that the movement itself is pregnant with the potential for creating intertextual gaps or changes in the meaning of the terms as they are produced and reproduced across contexts. These intertextual gaps must be minimized to establish and maintain traditional authority (Bauman and Briggs 1990; Briggs and Bauman 1992). It is the potential changes in the meaning of terms in dawat that augurs the threat of "innovation" (biddat). The emphasis on the ethics of listening involves a shared commitment to the preservation of tradition and to the management of the problem of creativity and invention that inheres in dawat, hence the suspicion of speech.[2] The power of speech to produce innovation, falsehood, and spread waywardness (*gumrahi*) is expressed by the fact that a person stands before God on the Day of Judgment without a tongue and will speak directly from the heart, revealing his deeds without any linguistic mediation, in other words without the capacity to lie or distort the truth, without any possibility for misrepresentation, and with a perfect alignment between the inner self and outer performance. This suspicion of language is found in recurring stories that depict and valorize the "mute" (*goonga*) as the paragon of piety. Take, for instance, a version of a story I was told:

> A mute was traveling in a jamaat to Sri Lanka. He was sitting next to a European foreigner. He kept looking at the foreigner and the foreigner was confused by this behavior. Suddenly he began crying. Shaken by this, the foreigner asked another companion why he was crying. The companion who understood him well explained to the foreigner that he is very sad because he thinks you are very beautiful. The foreigner responded, "why should that make him sad?" The companion explained that he is sad because he does not want to see someone as beautiful as you suffer in the afterlife. The European was very moved by the power of the mute Tablighi's tears and said he would go to the mosque when he returned to his country.

The moral of the story is that pious virtue is not the same as verbal dexterity but a product of one's sincere love for the Prophet and commitment to God. One cannot gauge genuine piety from the capacity for discursive production as language itself is suspect, and indeed it is tied less to one's faith than it is to reason.

The suspicion of language extends also to other bodily signs like beards and skullcaps, which, while necessary for cultivating virtue, are not seen as sufficient. This is captured in a familiar Tablighi account: a pious Elder in a town who is dying asks that only someone who has never missed the optional *tahajjud* prayers, prayed between the nightly (isha) and morning prayers (fajr) should lead his funerary prayers. When the Elder dies, a pious person is solicited from the town, and, to everyone's surprise, the only person to come forward is a clean-shaven young man wearing "pant-shirt," someone who displays no evidence of piety. Such possibilities of surprise flag the fact that Islamic iconicity, verbal or physical, does not always imply indexical relations with the piety that they represent. This invokes another common theme in the Tablighi Jamaat, the problem of the hypocrite (*munafiq*). The hypocrite is someone who appears for all intents and purposes as a pious person but has no faith. The hypocrite, Tablighis often say, is destined for the "deepest pits of hell."

In the previous chapter, I noted that the performance of Islamic iconicity was the key to cultivating a pious self. I argued that Tablighi ritual ideology displaces the indeterminacy of this process and instead emphasizes the automaticity and inevitability of "doing" dawat and "becoming" pious, like how "perfume in a perfume shop" seeps into the body. However, here we can see that Tablighis recognize that the pious surfaces of Islamic iconicity do not guarantee pious interiorities and that such gaps between outer performances and inner selves persist and are even dangerously manifest in the figure of the hypocrite (munafiq). The indeterminate relationship between the surfaces of pious language and bodily signs and the interiorities of Muslims means that one must commit to pious companionship (sohbat) in the congregation. It ensures that congregational life is the fundamental condition of dawat as it disciplines the Tablighi, turning him into an "acted upon" self, and allows him to spread Islamic virtue without innovation.

Pious Companionship (Sohbat) as a Discipline of Presence

When Tablighi Elders like Hazrat would walk through the grand mosque, a hushed reverence would envelop the onlookers. Tablighis would cease whatever chatter they were engaged in and gaze upon Hazrat solemnly. As many noted, even to gaze upon those who are "Allah's people" (*Allah walei*) was a religious practice because this was how the Companions gazed upon the Prophet. Through gazing upon the Prophet, the Companions absorbed piety through the senses. In his capacity as a Chishti sheikh, Hazrat would often sit in the front of a room in his spiritual house while his disciples observed him, a process that could go on for an hour or more. A similar process would occur, often, after sermons. The Tablighi Jamaat draws on this Sufi model of companionship (sohbat), but, while Islamic authority in the Sufi model is centered exclusively around the sheikh, in the Tablighi Jamaat, it is distributed through the congregation (Metcalf 2003). While this tendency to gaze upon the sacred was most pronounced in the relationship with the Elders, hints of it could also be seen in the relationship with other Tablighis deemed of high spiritual rank. I found it difficult to square this reality of Tablighis' everyday practice, built as it was on the mediation of pious others, with the claim that dawat entailed a direct relationship between a worshiper and God. In other words, why did Tablighi ideals of immediacy necessitate these relationships with pious others? Why was immediacy so clearly mediated by pious others, and how, as a sensational form, did dawat remain a channel for divine presence?

I was not the only person who noticed the tension between the emphasis on directness and the importance of the Elders. I routinely encountered Sunni Muslims who asked Tablighis why dawat must take this form and why it was not sufficient to simply go to the mosque and do one's obligatory ritual practices like the mandatory Islamic prayer (namaaz/salat). Other denominations like the Ahl-e-Hadith as well as many modernist Muslims who stress a direct relationship to God also accused Tablighis of treating their Elders with the same reverence that one finds in the pir-murid system of Sufism. As one critic explained to me, "Tablighis are creating another 'sect' (*firka*) around their Elders." Such criticism suggested that the reverence for the Elders was a form of idolatry (shirk), and commitments to their own forms created the fragmentation of Islamic community. Tablighis responded to such criticism with the claim that the Elders were their teachers who were telling them only what was in the Quran, Prophetic tradition, and Islamic law and were a "channel" (*zariya*) for God's will because they were embodying Prophetic example. Tablighis explicitly rejected the association of this with Sufi notions of intercession (tawassul) and argued that it was therefore not a violation of the commitment to directness. Nevertheless, the importance placed on the emulation of pious Elders and authorities sometimes made the difference difficult to discern in social life, and Tablighis had to regularly navigate such criticisms from Salafis and modernists.

Abid's description of the importance of the Elders should make clear what I mean when I speak about the mediation of pious others:

> People say that the sheikh's sohbat or Allah's people put focus [*tawajjo*] in the heart. I heard these things about pir-muridi but only in tabligh did I see such pir-muridi and what focus actually is, and who a sheikh actually is. And really, our sheikh [Hazrat] was this. May Allah fill his grave with light. He was that person . . . when I wanted to do sin, the thought of my sheikh would come to me, so because of his grace and his sobhat, Allah would save me from sin . . . it is a strange power. The focus that they say a sheikh brings, that focus was there, so being in the company of Allah's people brings benefits. Sitting with our Elders is the same. They just say that in this place there is a congregation . . . and *MashAllah* people come . . . so this is it. It is all their work, their focus, their sacrifice, and it is because of this that Allah saves us [from sin]. . . . It makes it easy for us. They pray for those who are their lovers, just as the Prophet did for the Companions . . . and like the relationship of the Prophet with the Companions, the Prophet's sohbat

made the Companions the Companions . . . it was the Prophet's love and care. . . . The Companions did not even let the Prophet's saliva fall to the ground. . . . That is how much love they had for the Prophet. This is how our Elders are too. When something bad enters our heart, we become scared that we might be caught [by them] because there is this quality in them. We can see it.

Abid's quotation stresses that the relationship with pious others like one's sheikh and the Tablighi Elders is what keeps one away from sin and focused on the "the good." It is the presence of these pious others that create the pious dispositions that allow one to live an Islamic life. This description of the creation and sustenance of Islamic piety depends on being "acted upon" by pious others (cf. Mahmood 2005; see Mittermeier 2011).

The religious framework represented in Abid's description is modeled on what Brian Silverstein (2011) in his study of Naqshbandi Sufis in Turkey aptly describes as an "ethic of companionship" (143). Silverstein analyzes the Islamic notion of companionship or *sohbet* (sohbat in Urdu), which has the same root as the word for Companion (sahabi) of the Prophet. For the Naqshbandi Sufis in Silverstein's work, spiritual realization or the cultivation of ethical dispositions requires mystical techniques that involve "companionship" with the sheikh. "For the proper formation of character," he writes, "one should always be in the company of 'good people,' defined as those who seek the approval of God, and only God, and are not led astray by popular fashion, prestige or power" (Silverstein 2011, 144). Similarly, Brannon Ingram (2018) has shown how in the Deobandi tradition, sohbat is the mechanism to ensure that the Islamic tradition spreads without losing its link to the authority of the ulama. In the Tablighi Jamaat, sohbat is the social and discursive space in which one acquires ethical sensibilities and dispositions that orient one toward pious action. It is the submission to pious authority and especially to the authority of the Elders of the movement that disciplines the religious passions and gives them the proper shape, creating someone who is not only themselves capable of living in terms of divine commandments but also able to spread Islamic virtue to others without leading them astray.

We can see in Abid's description that staying on the path of piety requires the presence of Elders in one's life, and we can see here that the gaze of the Elders is what does the work of disciplining the subject. Tablighis often compare dawat to the process of creating a glass vase that needs heating first and then must be cooled before being molded into shape. When an individual ventures out to preach on his own, he can easily become enamored by his own authority and fall prey to self-worship and thus create innovations (biddat), novel forms that depart from the original Islam of the Prophet. This danger even attends practices that are themselves modeled on the Prophet's example. For instance, Tablighis say that giving sermons (bayan) is an important act of piety and a craft that one must develop, but that the sermon can also be dangerous because it has the potential to create hubris (takabbur) that in turn can lead one astray. Sermons create passions in the Tablighi, a necessary condition for a pious life, but these passions must be molded into shape through pious companionship. Pious companionship cools this passion, giving it shape and making it sturdy and stable. It is the practice of submission in the space of the congregation that keeps a Tablighi on the path and allows him to remain a vehicle for pious virtue. By cooling the passions and molding them into shape, pious companionship is a condition for the effective transmission of Islamic truth, knowledge, and affect. The emphasis on pious companionship is key to how Tablighis draw the distinction between the domains of "religion" and "the world." The domain of religion is structured by a semiotic ideology that stresses the creation of a direct relationship with God, a position found commonly across the Abrahamic religions and modern religious ideologies, but pious companionship is what Silverstein (2011) has called disciplines of presence and is understood by Tablighis as the basis for maintaining a direct connection to God through the pious Elders of the Tablighi Jamaat.

For this reason, Tablighis place such an enormous emphasis on the Thursday evening congregations (shab-e-jumma), where the pious Elders speak from the pulpit, as this is seen as an immensely potent place to accrue religious merit and acquire pious virtue. Every Thursday evening, thousands if not tens of thousands of Tablighis flow through the many gates of the Madni Masjid. Every Thursday evening, I would accompany my Tablighi friends to the Madni Masjid shortly before evening prayers and stay till the afternoon prayers on Friday afternoon. The Madni Masjid is a massive space that stretches for several blocks, with six large gates, that can contain tens of thousands of worshipers. Built in the early 1990s, the Madni Masjid was designed to accommodate a rapidly growing population of Tablighis. The Madni Masjid partially replaced the other grand mosque complex in Karachi, the Makki Masjid which is considerably smaller than the Madni Masjid but continues to be the main administrative center of the Tablighi Jamaat in Karachi and is a space where the old companions have regular meetings. The Madni Masjid is, however, the single unifying space where the entire body of Tablighis in Karachi congregates.

The thousands of motorcycles, cars, and buses that line the exterior of the mosque complex reveal the staggering popularity of the Tablighi Jamaat in Karachi. It is difficult not to be overwhelmed by the sight of these tens of thousands of worshippers flowing into the Madni Masjid. Thursday evening, or what is

FIGURE 3. The main gate of the Madni Masjid (markaz) in Federal B Area, Karachi. Photograph by Arsalan Khan.

called "the night of Friday" (shab-e-jummah), is understood as a "big night," a night designated for worship. Tablighis worship late into the night and then sleep on the marble floors of the vast open mosque courtyard, after which they wake up early to pray and listen to sermons before they return home to prepare for Friday prayers in their neighborhood mosques. Shab-e-jummah is an especially meritorious time. The Prophet, they frequently noted, usually spent all of Thursday night in worship. Many Tablighis insist that God accepts all prayers in the period between Thursday night and Friday afternoon prayers. Others suggest that one can expiate all sins if one worships through the night. Tablighis also stress the importance of praying in large congregations with other pious Muslims. They claim that God grants the religious merit (*sawab*) earned by the most pious in a congregation to the entire congregation, and since the Elders of the Tablighi Jamaat are so immensely pious, shab-e-jummah is an unparalleled opportunity to achieve religious merit and cultivate pious sensibilities.

Each Tablighi comes prepared to spend the night, bringing his own sleeping mat, blanket, and pillow. Tablighis sit with their respective mosque congregations (jamaat) in areas that have been roughly designated by the Elders according

FIGURE 4. Motorcycles lining the external wall of the Madni Masjid. Photograph by Arsalan Khan.

to the location of their mosque in the city. One's identity is directly connected to the mosque to which one belongs, and this becomes most evident at dinner. Everyone contributes to their mosque fund for dinner, and each mosque congregation makes its own arrangements, bringing food, plates, some silverware, though most food is eaten with hands, a tea kettle, and a long eating mat (*dastarwkhwan*) around which all the members of the congregation sit to eat. The dinner makes clear that one's primary unit of relationship is one's local mosque. Shab-e-jummah was extremely important for most of the Tablighis I knew, and they would try their best not to miss it. It was important for a Tablighi to be seen by others since it revealed one's commitment to dawat and showed

FIGURE 5. The courtyard of the Madni Masjid as Tablighis begin arriving for the shab-e-jummah congregation. Photograph by Arsalan Khan.

one's willingness to sacrifice for it. Not being seen, on the other hand, meant that one failed to recognize the value of the congregation. When someone missed shab-e-jummah once, he became the subject of mild and friendly teasing, which could be a source of embarrassment, but when someone missed shab-e-jummah more than twice or more in a row without a legitimate reason, he started becoming a source of concern for other Tablighis in his mosque. This meant that some effort had to be exerted on them to draw them back, and many of my Tablighi friends did not want to be seen as someone who needed others to draw them to the mosque. In other words, one's status in the mosque congregation was intimately bound up with one's presence at shab-e-jummah.

The shab-e-jummah seemed to be an ideal place for research as it allowed me to move between mosque units with which I had become acquainted and to talk to Tablighis beyond these specific mosques. However, it was precisely at shab-e-jummah that my awkward position as a researcher in the Tablighi Jamaat became evident. What was at stake in this was brought to my attention one hot and humid August evening. I was sitting with a few younger Tablighis after dinner. The conversation was banal. Usman, a polite and soft-spoken young man in his early twenties was describing to me how some customers at his phone shop

FIGURE 6. Local Tablighis bring food from home for the night, while itinerant Tablighis staying at the Madni Masjid bring with them needed food, utensils, and instruments for cooking. Photograph by Arsalan Khan.

in the Electronics Market come in to trade their phones for new ones almost every month, and how phones had become an obsession for young people. In the middle of the conversation, a young boy came to Usman and told him that Yusaf bhai (bhai being the title for older brother) was calling him. Usman promptly went over and kneeled next to him. Yusaf bhai was a slender man with small features and a large forehead. He was very well respected in the Al-Aqsa Mosque and would often be invited to the quarters of the Elders. He was widely considered an exemplary Tablighi, who possessed an unusual level of piety and faithfulness. Yusaf bhai had recently returned from a seven-month tour, considered the second highest level of commitment after the one-year tour, which took him to numerous countries in Africa. He and I had met briefly at the annual congregation in Raiwind from which he departed on his extended tour. It was clear over those few days that Yusaf bhai was a pivotal person inside the Al-Aqsa Mosque, and he in many ways acted as a representative of their mosque at the national congregation. Since his return a few months earlier, he and I had become loosely acquainted. It was apparent even in our few conversations that Yusaf bhai found my presence at Al-Aqsa to be rather odd and even unsettling, and I suspect that he had consulted others about what exactly I was doing there. He was always polite and would often greet me, but the sense he left me with was that he did not feel like I should be there. He understood that Hazrat had wanted me around, and of course, the mosque was a place where all were welcome, so it seemed he could not really express his discomfort with my presence. I was always worried that Yusaf bhai would create barriers to my research and possibly even have me excluded from mosque activities, though I had trouble imagining how exactly he would do that without violating the sanctity of the mosque space and without potentially insulting Hazrat. As I walked over to Yusaf bhai, though, these were the thoughts that raced through my mind.

"Come, come, Arsalan. Please sit down," Yusaf bhai said. "Assalamalaikum, Yusaf bhai. How are you?" "*Waleikum asalaam*, well by Allah's grace. *MashAllah*, I'm very pleased to see you've been coming to shab-e-jumma regularly." I nodded. "It's nice," I said. "I get to meet new people and get to talk to people, and it helps me better understand what dawat is about. I am learning a great deal." Yusaf bhai smiled and nodded. "Dawat is our purpose in life," he said, and "shab-e-jummah is a very 'spiritual space' [*roohani mahol*]. Just being here helps one become a better Muslim." I nodded in affirmation. "Islam is absorbed by the senses, so just being here helps one absorb religion, but then it must descend into the heart." Yusaf bhai went on to explain that even though it is a powerful space, I should not just come here and expect it to transform me automatically. One must put in the effort (*mehnat*) to acquire the results, he explained. Again, I nodded in affirmation to things that I had heard frequently. "Without doubt," I said. The issue is, he noted, hinting at my research, that Islam is not a "bookish religion" (*kitabi mazhab*) but a "religion of practice" (*amali mazhab*). Religion does not settle in your heart only by reading and writing about Islam, and it certainly does not settle in your heart just by talking about Islam. Yusaf bhai launched into a story about a professor he encountered who was very knowledgeable about Islam. This professor, he explained, knew the Quran inside out, and one could ask him anything about what was in the Quran and he would tell you exactly which book (*sipara*) it was in. It was hard to believe that this man had so much knowledge (ilm) because he did not do any of his practices (amaal). "See, we know this in our minds [zehn] but it has not descended into the heart." Yusaf bhai, then, described how even though this professor had all the knowledge in the world, he was always "troubled" (*pareshan*) and never had any "peace" (*sukoon*). He was always running around seeking new knowledge, which is why he seemed to know so much, but this knowledge was "empty." It did not have God's grace (barakat), and so it never satisfied his yearning to know and just made him more and more troubled. Yusaf bhai explained that when one is troubled, one becomes incapable of living one's life in a religious way (*dini tariqe se*). One is pulled in every direction, and this leads one into despondency and away from God. "Do you understand, Arsalan?" I nodded in affirmation. After explaining this, Yusaf bhai, as if speaking to a child, said I was now free to go back to the others. I arose and departed.

On the surface what Yusaf bhai was saying was that dawat is an orthopraxy and embodied process and that Islam is absorbed through the senses and not simply a set of doctrines or rules to be grasped by the mind. There seemed nothing new here as I had been hearing this from the day I began my research. However, by this time, I had been participating in the necessary embodied activities of pious listening and spending considerable time in the mosque and in companionship with Tablighis. I had on numerous occasions been invited into the quarters of the Elders to be given instruction by them and had spent considerable time in Hazrat's chambers with him and with many prominent Tablighis that were closely tied to him. I had been doing dawat, listening to sermons, and engaging in pious companionship in the congregation. Why was this still not sufficient for me to acquire faith and pious virtue? Why, according to Yusaf bhai, was I still the wayward professor?

I decided to consult others about it to see if they could help me understand. I asked my friend Shahzaib. Shahzaib and I had gone on a ten-day preaching tour together that took us from Karachi to Multan and from there to the three-day national congregation (ijtima) in Raiwind. This was also Shahzaib's first preaching tour, and although he only intended to do a ten-day tour (ashira), the others had managed to convince him to complete a forty-day tour (chilla) with them. Since then, Shahzaib had become an active presence in the Al-Aqsa Mosque, and we had become friends. Like me, he was in his early thirties, and he had gone to college in North Carolina. He spoke English fluently and was eager to speak to me in English because he did not have many opportunities with his fellow Tablighis. He saw our relationship as an opportunity to talk to me about his life before dawat for which he clearly had fond memories. He had given up many of his friendships along the way, and, like with many Tablighis I met, there was a sense of loss, and this weighed heavily on him. This gave us a strong basis for building a friendship.

When I told Shahzaib what Yusaf bhai had said, he emphatically agreed. "Don't take it the wrong way, Arsalan. Yusaf bhai is only showing concern (*fikr*) for you." Shahzaib noted that Yusaf bhai was only trying to guide me to the right path and this was his duty. I asked him what he thought Yusaf bhai was trying to communicate to me, and Shahzaib explained that Yusaf bhai knows that you have been coming to the mosque and Hazrat's khanqa for some time now, and he just wants to help you "come to religion in the proper manner" (*din pei sahi tarah ajao*). Shahzaib noted that while I was spending time in the mosque and in Hazrat's khanqa, it was not having the "effect" (asr) on me that one would expect. What Shahzaib said next made this abundantly clear. "Look, you and I have been coming to the mosque for around the same time, but you are distracted by your research, which is why dawat is not having the right effect on you." This was a more honest answer than I would've received from other Tablighis, who generally refrain from directly commenting on another person's faith, which they say is "hidden" from view and knowable only to God, but Shahzaib felt we were close enough for this level of honesty. When I asked Shahzaib why he thinks that this space has not had the proper effect on me, he explained that while I come to the mosque and the spiritual house and have made friendships, my research is always dragging me "here and there." "You are not settled in the 'daily ties' [rozana ka jor] of our mosque or of your own mosque," Shahzaib said. "This means that although you come to the mosque, and you even do some practices, you are not following the Prophet's way [tariqa]."

In Shahzaib's explanations, the efficacy of Islamic practice was far from automatic, and my prolonged presence in the congregation and even doing the ritual practices was far from sufficient. I had spent a considerable amount of time in mosques doing precisely what Tablighis were doing. As a Muslim, and someone who had spent much of his life praying in mosques, I had few qualms about conducting the mandatory prayers. Like Tablighis, I regularly listened to sermons, both the ones that were given at Al-Aqsa and at Madni Masjid, and I even devoted a considerable amount of time to listening to the sermons of the Elders that circulated on CD. When asked to, I even actively participated in the preaching itself, and while I was not exceptionally skilled at it, I surely was not the least skilled either. Over time, I had learned how to speak about the content of these sermons in ways comparable to many Tablighis. Tablighis were invested in acquiring this knowledge as a guide for how they should live their lives, so this was a valuable trait for them. I began to ask what exactly it was about my practice that failed to create faith. Why the failure of embodiment if I spent so much time in the mosque engaged in what Tablighis said were legitimate forms of practice that were designed to cultivate faith? What was implied here was not just that I was not conducting the rituals of dawat in the proper way, which surely it seemed I was, but that my relationships inside the congregation were not shaping me into a pious subject. I was still not properly inhabiting the pious relationality of the congregation.

When Tablighis invoke the refrain "religion is on the tongue, but it has not descended into the heart," they are referring to a general problem that there are many overtly religious people who have not actually cultivated virtuous dispositions and who do not act in a virtuous manner. Many new adherents who find their way into the Tablighi congregation are quite zealous, and Tablighis see this passion as both necessary in that it keeps people focused on the congregation but also disruptive in that such people can also try to acquire too much power and influence in the movement that others do not believe reflects their level of piety. Shahzaib's claim that I was not embodying the virtues because my practice was "here and there" and because I was not part of the "daily ties" of any mosque points to how one must learn to inhabit the correct form of pious relationality.

My presence in the company of the Elders of the congregation was a source of great consternation as it suggested I could acquire this power without the requisite sacrifice of life force, wealth, and time that generates faith. My subject position as a guest in the mosque congregation also kept me from performing the necessary labor and committing the resources that facilitate the reproduction and growth of the mosque congregation. Tablighis, therefore, routinely advised me to start in the mosque in my neighborhood rather than being attached to the Al-Aqsa Mosque. They insisted that I would learn to do this work properly. As Yusaf bhai was saying, I was not adopting the stance of a humble novice, a new companion, and a pious listener. My connection to Hazrat, my presence in the quarters of the Elders, and my connection to people higher up in the sacred hierarchy of the Tablighi Jamaat were seen by others as premature and did not reflect my commitment to the congregation or the sacrifices of life force, wealth, and time, and so even pious companionship with Hazrat was not going to have the correct effect on me. I was not conforming to the correct process of ascending the sacred hierarchy of the movement.

Tablighis draw on the broad principles of Deobandi Islam, including notions of orthopraxy and notions of pious companionship (sohbat), but they also define these in specific ways that are about the moral reproduction of the Tablighi Jamaat. My experience of failing to be recognized as a pious subject, despite my efforts to be a pious listener and commit to pious companionship, reveals how the broad commitments to orthopraxy and pious companionship drawn from the Deobandi tradition take a specific institutional form in the Tablighi Jamaat. The Tablighi refrain that preaching (tabligh) is not the same as giving speeches (taqreer) and that "religion is only on the tongue but not in the heart" implies that many people can speak and present themselves in a manner that evidences piety but are lacking in the faith of a truly pious person (*dindar*). It is pious companionship that offsets this tendency, cooling the passions, cultivating the virtues, and molding the Tablighi into shape, but pious companionship is not just about physical presence with pious authorities like the Elders, and Islamic piety is not something absorbed through osmosis. Instead, Tablighis' concepts of sohbat require the sacrifices of dawat, participation in the daily ties of the mosque, and a recognition of one's place in the sacred hierarchy of the movement.

The Citationality of Piety and the Temporality of Pious Becoming

It became clear to me that Yusaf bhai's consternation around me was not only that I had not committed myself to the daily ties of the mosque but also that I had failed to adopt a stance of pious listening toward him. Indeed, I came to understand that he and many other Tablighis saw me as a harbinger of hubris and an agent of disruption. Along with doing my ritualized practices, I spent considerable time trying to elicit information from my Tablighi interlocutors about their ideas and understandings of dawat as well as their lives. In my ethnographic approach, I did not distinguish between the ranks of Tablighis and treated them all as equal representatives of the movement, equally capable of speaking about their own experiences in dawat. Many Tablighis, as I noted earlier, would turn me away when I asked them questions about dawat or they would direct me to the Elders who they said were authorized to speak about such matters. Very few Tablighis were open to being recorded because they worried that recordings could include falsehoods that would then circulate and lead others astray. The fact that I aimed to turn my knowledge into a book that would circulate widely meant that I could easily spread falsehood and waywardness and draw Muslims away from Islam. All of this was captured in Yusaf bhai's claim that Islam is not a "bookish religion." Indeed, I was seen by many Tablighis as harboring the capacity to undermine their piety by transforming them into authoritative speakers, thus auguring the problem of talk.

The notion that Muslims were too willful and self-centered and that they failed to listen and take instruction was, for Tablighis, a pervasive and foundational problem in modernity for which pious listening was the remedy. The unauthorized and self-authorized assumption of authority in the world threatens how Tablighis define faith as "the certainty that everything comes from God and nothing comes from another" (*Allah se sab kuch hone ka yaqeen aur doosron se kuch na hone ka yaqeen*). My presence in the congregation thus provoked fears of hubris and talk because I went around the congregation trying to encourage people to represent themselves and their understanding of dawat. I learned though that while I might have provoked this problem, it permeated the movement and had to be assiduously managed. Let's return to the example of my friend Shahzaib. Shahzaib and I had gone on our first preaching tour together, which took us from Karachi to Multan and to the national congregation in Raiwind over the course of ten days. While I went from there to Lahore and ultimately back to Karachi, Shahzaib went along to complete his first forty-day tour (chilla). Shahzaib came from a family that was deeply involved in the Tablighi congregation. His father, who was an old companion, had encouraged him to go on the forty-day tour, and Shahzaib had several cousins who were very active in the movement. Shahzaib told me he felt he should pursue dawat to uphold the values of his family and to make his father happy. More significantly, though, as he repeatedly expressed to me, he wanted to be "close" to Hazrat. Shahzaib's desire to please Hazrat clearly preceded his participation in dawat and instead came from the general respect and admiration for Hazrat that Shahzaib had acquired from his family and broader social milieu. Shahzaib told me how much he wished Hazrat would look at him the way he looks at Talha, like a son, and he was clear that his participation in dawat was to please Hazrat.

It became clear to me that many Tablighis in his mosque congregation did not view Shahzaib as a particularly model Tablighi. In generally hushed tones, several Tablighis had told me that Shahzaib lacked "control over his tongue" and "didn't know when to talk and when to listen." Indeed, these were the kinds of comments that one heard often about many people in the congregation, especially those who had a newly found passion for dawat. The hubris (takabbur) and selfishness (khudgarzi) of such novices was a common enough aspect of Tablighi discourse even if it was not done openly. People attributed some of this to the fact that Shahzaib was from a wealthy family. His family owned a successful textile factory, which meant that he was wealthier than many of the others in the Al-Aqsa congregation, and he had studied textile design in the Unites States as well. Some Tablighis thought that this continued his attachment to the world. Over the two years of my research, however, I began to witness a shift in Shahzaib's attitudes toward others in the mosque. He assumed increasing responsibility inside the mosque, such as committing himself to "service" (khidmat) at shab-e-jumma and devoting time to help organize mosque activities. Furthermore, the more involved he became in mosque activities, the more he came to speak about the virtues of other Tablighis, often elaborating on the positive qualities (*sifaat*) of others. On one occasion at the mosque, Shahzaib, without any prompting and while gazing longingly at Yusaf bhai, said, "You know what Yusaf bhai told me? He said the Elders don't want to be Elders. Nobody who is eager to be an Elder should ever be one since it comes with so much responsibility. Yusaf bhai is very faithful and knowledgeable. One can learn so much by spending time with him." Yusaf bhai was clearly encouraging him not to be so eager in his pursuit of authority in the congregation. On another occasion, Shahzaib cataloged the different qualities of various members of the congregation like their "softness of temperament" (*narm mizaaj*) or their "cheerful temperament" (*khush mizaaj*) or their "concern" (fikr) for others, and so on. This shift in Shahzaib was not lost on other Tablighis, who increasingly started seeing him in a more positive light. Shahzaib was demonstrating the virtue of pious listening through recognition of those above him in the sacred hierarchy of the congregation.

What became evident to me from Shahzaib's example and from my own failings as a Tablighi is a broad ethical commitment to the mediation of pious others. When Shahzaib began dawat, he wanted a direct relationship to Hazrat, a relationship that he was eager to acquire and for which he felt competitive toward others. In one instance recounted to me by another Tablighi, Shahzaib had dismissed a fellow Tablighi for not knowing enough of the content of the Fazail-e-Amal, thereby suggesting hubris in his textual knowledge but failing to understand how to relate to others. Such acts are seen as highly disruptive of the social relationship within the mosque and threaten to undermine the unity of the congregation. Gradually, Shahzaib desisted from this desire to connect directly to Hazrat, and his sense of competition diminished. He came to see the value of all the levels of piety that stood between him and Hazrat. Increasingly, the congregation came to resemble the tiered structure of relations of the Companions with the Prophet who all had different roles, statuses, and qualities. This subtle shift marked Shahzaib's shift from "worldliness" to piety in the eyes of other Tablighis in the congregation. Shahzaib had learned to "control his tongue" and had stopped claiming authority that others had not yet granted to him. The direct and individuated relationship Shahzaib sought with Hazrat gave way to collectivism (ijtimaiyat) and a broader sense of pious mediation within congregational life. This transition from wordliness to piety, hubris to humility, and selfishness to collectiveness meant that Shahzaib had truly become a pious listener and companion.

The notions of pious listening and companionship take on concrete, material form in citationality. Shahzaib's references to pious others in the congregation are the informal manifestation of the more citational practices that one hears in the formal genre of sermons and in other speech genres. Sermons are replete with references to hadith that document the sayings of the Prophet and accounts of the Companions, ulama, pious Elders of the past, and current Tablighi Elders. To become a citation in the formal genres of the Tablighi Jamaat is to become consecrated as a religious authority. The historian Barbara Metcalf (1993) aptly notes that the primary aim of a Tablighi is to become a "living hadith," someone who embodies the virtues of the Prophet as they have been documented in the hadith literature. What I am describing can be thought of an enactment of the hadith as a relational paradigm. Every hadith carries a chain of transmission (isnad), a series of moral persons who faithfully transmitted the knowledge carried by the hadith. When one invokes a hadith, one cites the requisite authorities on whom the hadith relies, and when one explains a hadith or paraphrases it, one makes note that it is an inference (*mafhoom*) of the meaning and not the original so as to indicate to the listener that it there may be a gap between the explanation and the original. Similarly, the Tablighi must acknowledge the chain of linkages between himself and the authoritative sources and must cite the exemplary qualities of others on whom any claim to knowledge rests, perpetually pointing to the gap in knowledge and piety between pious authorities and the self. In acknowledging this gap, the Tablighi is deferring to pious authority and thus enacting humility. When Shahzaib came to acknowledge the levels of piety between himself and Hazrat, he was disavowing his own agency and identifying the qualities of pious others that must be emulated on the path to piety.

Citationality is key to the rich tapestry of discourse that mediates and materializes piety as an ethical relationship in the Tablighi Jamaat. It is how the "doing" of piety is made manifest beyond the preaching tour and even beyond the physical presence in the mosque. Unlike formal genres of speech like the sermons, pious citationality cuts through everyday discourses and becomes the mark of a pious subject. The pious subject must routinely perform acts of humility, disavow one's own agency, and acknowledge the authority of pious others. It is this citationality in discourse that creates an iconic-indexical link in everyday life between the "here-and-now" and the sacred "then-and-there" of the Prophet's time. Crucially, it is also citational practice that gives material shape to the aspirational nature of the pursuit of piety (cf. Khan 2012). As Constantine Nakassis (2016) argues in the context of the study of branding, a citation involves placing something in brackets such that one maintains a relationship to it without assuming an identity with it. Just as the sacred past does not have an identity with the present but is something toward which one must constantly strive, so citational practices acknowledge the gap between oneself and pious others and construing them as an ideal toward which to strive.

The citationality of piety gives flesh to the two key virtues of Islamic piety in the Tablighi Jamaat; it manifests humility (*khushu*) in that it recognizes the importance of others above oneself in a hierarchy and it materializes patience (*sabr*) in that it turns pious others into a model to realize in the future. Shahzaib's shift from worldliness to piety is instructive because he was originally assuming pious authority that he did yet have and was too eager to connect himself to Hazrat's authority and therefore failing to manifest patience. His ability to recognize the virtues of others and temper his eagerness for ascending the sacred hierarchy of the movement came to be recognized by others as the mark of a pious subject. Years later, Tablighis from his mosque congregation would jokingly tell me how Shahzaib has now become a pious Elder (*buzurg*), suggesting in humorous fashion that he in fact was on the path of piety now. And what, after all, is a pious Elder if not someone who never wanted to be a pious Elder in the first place but always deferred to others?

In the last chapter, I noted how despite the egalitarian premise of the Tablighi Jamaat, the claim that all Muslim men can and should participate in dawat and that piety is something realizable by all, the ritual ideology of dawat structures the Tablighi Jamaat around a sacred hierarchy and promises the Tablighi a path of ascending this sacred hierarchy. What we see in Shahzaib's example is how becoming a pious subject involves committing to a hierarchical form of pious relationality that regulates the eagerness to claim pious authority and attach oneself to the pious Elders of the movement, slowing one's ascent up the sacred hierarchy, engendering a temporality of pious becoming that defers the realization of piety to the future.

The Ethics of Hierarchy and the Moral Reproduction of Congregational Life

Much has been made in the anthropology of Islam and Muslim life of a tension between the study of Islamic piety and "everyday" Muslim life, but Islamic piety is itself an everyday form of ethics (Fadil and Fernando 2015; Deeb 2015). What we have seen in the example in the previous section is that ritualized forms of dawat and performative acts of listening must also translate into more mundane forms of speech and action to be recognized by others as a pious subject. The broad tradition of Deobandi Islam that emphasizes orthopraxy as a mode of self-cultivation takes on an "everyday" form in pious relationality, and the ethics of hierarchy is an "ordinary ethics" (Lambek 2010) in the Tablighi Jamaat. My inability to enact pious relationality in the mosque congregation meant that I lacked both humility and patience. I encapsulated the menacing figure of "talk" because I did not understand when to speak and when not to speak and I was aiming to make substantial claims about Islam and dawat in a book that would surely lead others astray. Moreover, I was promoting such impious behavior among fellow Tablighis by asking them to assume pious authority, which they consistently refused and deferred to those whom they saw as more authoritative than themselves. Shahzaib, by contrast, learned that he must recognize and emulate the authority of pious others around him and committed himself to the daily ties of the mosque, and thus he was seen by others in the congregation as having realized the core aspects of being a pious companion.

The pious relationality that I have outlined is structured by what I have called the ethics of hierarchy (Khan 2016). This is a mode of relating to pious others in ritualized acts of listening to sermons and in the disciplines of the presence of pious companionship, and it must be translated into the more mundane work of congregational life, including the performing of menial tasks, and in the everyday citationality of piety. The ethics of hierarchy links the ritual and formal genres of the Tablighi Jamaat with mundane discourse and actions and everyday relationality that shape life in the congregation. Indeed, it is in these practices of relationality that Tablighis find the iconic-indexical signs of religion and manifestations of the Prophet's way that they do not see in other Islamic movements in Pakistan. The ethics of hierarchy reproduces the relations between the Companions, each with their own proximity to the Prophet. The Tablighi Jamaat, thus, takes on the image of a graded sacred hierarchy in which one must adopt one's place.

The problem of talk that I represented and Shahzaib had overcome is not only a theological problem in the Tablighi Jamaat but also an organizational one. The exemplary figures of the movement are seen as those who started a mosque congregation in their own neighborhoods and built the mosque congregation up through sacrifice and effort. The Tablighis of the Al-Aqsa Mosque would say with no small measure of pride that when Hazrat began preaching here many decades ago, there was not a single Tablighi, and now this is one of the biggest and most active congregations in all of Pakistan. The model for pious becoming, the Elders, created their reputation by growing their mosque congregations and then becoming citational figures in the informal discourse and ultimately the formal genres of the Tablighi Jamaat. It is not hard to see, however, that in such circumstances where acquiring pious authority is the aim of the Tablighi, many overzealous people will try to assume this authority without having performed the necessary work and without being recognized as such by others. Some will do this, as in the example of Shahzaib, by trying to create a direct connection to the pious Elders and bypassing other pious authorities in their mosque. This is a common enough problem that it must be managed consistently. The guards with sticks who manage the flow of people in and out of the chambers of the pious Elders at the Tablighi markaz is a glaring manifestation of a broader problem of regulation of "directness" with the pious Elders. The overzealous desire to acquire pious authority inside the mosque can lead to conflicts and the splintering and dispersal of the congregation, a perennial problem in the movement. The ethics of hierarchy functions to regulate this tendency by creating a sense that one must slow one's process of ascent up the hierarchy and through the recognition of the levels of pious authorities between the individual and the pious Elders and by creating a sense that one must slow one's process of ascent up the sacred hierarchy. It is by inhabiting the ethics of hierarchy that one is recognized as a pious subject and an agent of moral reproduction.

We have seen in this section how the domain of religion is constituted in dawat and in sohbat and how the ritual genres of the Tablighi Jamaat are translated into everyday practices of pious relationality structured by the ethics of hierarchy. Dawat is a ritual of transcendence that allows a Tablighi to become a pious authority, but this leads to competition and thus potentially to the fragmentation and dispersal of the movement. The discourses about the problem of talk that I have described index the threat of fragmentation of the congregation that looms large within the movement. The ethics of hierarchy can be understood, then, as a reflexive technique for managing a central tension within the movement (cf Kloos 2018). To acquire the aptitudes and sensibilities of the ethics of hierarchy is to become an agent of moral reproduction of the Tablighi congregation.

In the next section of the book, "The Promise of Piety," we turn to how Tablighis draw on the ethics of hierarchy to reconfigure relationality beyond the congregation with the aim of constituting an Islamic moral order that Tablighis believe provides a remedy to the moral chaos (fitna) that afflicts life in postcolonial Pakistan. We will see how the ethics of hierarchy that manages the internal problems of dawat also serves as a basis for reconfiguring relationality in spheres of kinship and politics and becomes the basis for creating an Islamic moral order.

Part 3
THE PROMISE OF PIETY

5

CERTAIN FAITH, THE PIOUS HOME, AND THE PATH TO AN ISLAMIC FUTURE

Umer and I first met during our trip from Karachi to Multan to the national congregation in Raiwind in 2010. He was a close friend of Talha's and a faithful follower of Hazrat who was always available for service (khidmat) at Hazrat's spiritual house. A jocular young man in his late twenties, he had recently begun buying and selling cars, and he was in the process of acquiring space in his friend's car showroom. He was also a very capable cricketer who had briefly played in the club circuit, which is a level below national cricket, and he knew many of Pakistan's national cricketers as friends. To differentiate him from the many Tablighis named Umer, the name of the Prophet's Companion and second Caliph of Islam, in the Tablighi Jamaat, he was referred to as "Umer cricketer." Besides being a capable cricketer, Umer was also a remarkably adept Tablighi. He drew on a wide repertoire of Islamic textual sources to establish his rhetorical authority in dawat. He often quoted Urdu poetry and even included a few Persian couplets. He evoked sharp contrasts between religion and the world, painting the image of a corrupted and fallen world that had to be redeemed by infusing it with the spirit of Islam. "When mosques are populated," Umer often retorted, "our prisons and mental asylums are empty. But, when mosques are empty, our prisons and mental asylums are full."

Umer's charisma and his ability to connect with young people was truly remarkable. I witnessed this myself as we walked together through a boys' high school giving dawat to young students who were mesmerized by his rhetorical acumen and his ability to connect Islam to their lives. They were also quite riveted by the stories he told about his adventures with cricketers. Umer frequently pointed out how many of the cricketers of the national team were affiliated with the Tablighi Jamaat, suggesting that they, too, might get the opportunity to meet them. That Umer frequently brought up his own stories with national cricketers was a running joke among his Tablighi friends, but everyone agreed that, even as there was something a little self-serving about these stories, they were a great asset as they drew others to the movement. That day, we collected five to ten students to come back to the mosque for prayers and to listen to the sermon, an achievement by all standards, and one that everyone acknowledged.

In our interactions, Umer vacillated between an earnest and serious desire to instruct me and, on the other, a joking relationship in which he mocked me for being too far from Islam. I found this vacillation both entertaining and interesting. Umer spoke very little English, less I would say than many other middle-class Pakistanis. He would speak to me in a deliberately exaggerated English accent, stressing the foreignness of English and mocking me for being "too English." I enjoyed this joking enough that I responded in kind with an accented English, and we would carry on, sometimes to the amusement of others, in an entirely unintelligible language, marked by its utter foreignness. Umer had an inviting sense of humor and would frame Tablighi concepts as jokes. "Pass 'the world' over here," he said, pointing to his phone, an object seen as a perpetual distraction from religious devotion. He would also try hard to put me on the spot by drawing scrutiny toward me, "Arsalan could do so much for the religion if only he would try," and, on another occasion, "Arsalan, you are too full of 'the world.' It is in your bones!" More than once, he turned to other Tablighis and said, "Let him be. No point talking to him. He is a gone case," suggesting that I would never come to religion properly. Humor was an important way to develop camaraderie and bring some much-needed levity to what was often a physically and emotionally taxing experience of travel and pious devotion, the strain of which sometimes grew into tensions and conflicts within the itinerant group. The highlight of our trip was probably Umer and I playing cricket in the courtyard of the mosque, and to my amusement, others joined in, including the imam of the mosque. Umer was especially gifted at making the congregation a space of comfort and creating "connection" (jor) between Tablighis, an immensely important quality that other Tablighis acknowledged.

Yet, for all of his jovial and lighthearted banter and his skills at bringing people together, Umer would often seem to go into a deep and solemn state that was so marked by its seriousness that even in a context of assiduous worship was noticeable to others. For hours, Umer would commit himself to the reading and recitation of the Quran, during which he would not speak to anyone. In one of these bouts of serious devotion, Umer turned to me and said, "you know, Arsalan, I only make these jokes so time passes quickly and to make things easier on myself and on others. Every night I pray and ask Allah to give me more faith, so I can spend my time in practice, but it is difficult." On another occasion, Umer explained to me how faith is fickle. "One minute it is here," he said raising his hands above his head, "and the other minute is way down here," reaching for the floor. Indeed, I had come to see that Umer, for all his charisma and all his ability to draw others to Islam, was frequently racked by anxiety and doubt about his own faith.

I found Umer's vacillation between play and humor, on the one hand, and seriousness and earnestness, on the other, to be so sudden and dramatic that I asked others if this was common for people in the Tablighi Jamaat. Others recognized that this happens sometimes since regardless of how devoted one is one can always have doubts about one's own faith. The best person to turn to about this was Talha who had been on a dawat with Umer several times and knew him well. Talha said that Umer has the tendency to become "dried out" (*khushka*). Talha explained to me that when one is out on "the path of God," one should focus intensely on one's practice, but going from one "extreme" [in English] to another is not good, and one needs to have "balance" [in English]. It was odd to hear someone who was himself so intensely focused on dawat suggesting the need for balance. But Talha's point was not that there could ever be too much practice. The goal of dawat was, after all, to make one's "whole life" a practice in the image of the Prophet. Rather, his point was that the movement from one extreme to another indexed an underlying problem. The notion of being "dried out" implied a faith that is hard and brittle and thus easy to break rather than soft and supple and adaptable to multiple scenarios and contexts.

What could possibly be the problem with Umer's practice? He was, after all, an old companion who had done the four-month tour, regularly attended Thursday night congregations, committed time to his own mosque, and was a regular at Hazrat's spiritual house. He was also an extraordinarily adept Tablighi who was effective at drawing others into the movement, and unlike Shahzaib in the previous chapter, was recognized by others for his commitment to both his own mosque congregation and Hazrat's spiritual house. Umer was a model Tablighi, as far as I could tell, and yet, he too seemed to fail to realize the ideals of piety that are said to spring from dawat. My initial reaction to the issue was to assume that Umer's problem was idiosyncratic, but the more time I spent around other Tablighis, the more I could see that Umer's deep anxieties, his lack of certainty, and his doubt were a recurring theme in the Tablighi congregation. Indeed, the earnestness and seriousness of devotion itself indexed the precarious nature of divine presence in everyday life. And, while divine presence is difficult for all Tablighis to secure, I realized that this affliction did not affect everyone equally. While Umer seemed to be fulfilling the conditions for the efficacy of dawat, it became apparent to me that there were aspects of his life beyond the space of the Tablighi congregation that were an obstacle to the process of pious becoming.

Mathijs Pelkmans (2017) argues that Tablighis in Kyrgyzstan are afflicted by what he calls "fragile conviction." Pelkmans shows that Tablighis recognize that the feeling of piety and conviction is intense during dawat tours but wanes in between tours as one returns to everyday life. This is another reason why Tablighis place so much emphasis on pious companionship and the importance of the daily ties of the mosque, which keep one on the path of piety. In the last chapter, I argued that to be recognized as a pious subject by other Tablighis, one must learn to enact pious relationality in congregational life. In this chapter, I focus on how interactions with non-Tablighis and the effort to reconfigure relationality beyond the congregation can become a source of doubt and uncertainty in the Tablighi. Regardless of how zealous a Tablighi is in the mosque, he does not spend all his time among Tablighis. He also must live in a world suffused with other people and practices, some of which contradict pious pursuits, and these people and practices threaten the faith that he engenders in dawat. In general, Tablighis respond to this threat by enclosing their lives from the impious and working as much as possible to remain within the religious space (*dini mahol*). But there are spaces beyond the mosque and the Tablighi congregation that affect the Tablighi. Specifically, I argue that it is the space of the home (*ghar ka mahol*) that must be refashioned in terms of pious ideals since it is one's most intimate relationships that determine one's ability to live in pious terms. To acquire "certain faith" (yaqeen), one must draw one's kin into the movement, but kin often reject dawat, and this can place great strain on one's relationships.

I argue that "certain faith" requires subsuming paternal authority in the home within the pious authority of the Elders in the mosque, creating a pious family in which authority flows from mosque to home, religious authority to paternal authority, and ultimately from fathers to sons. Those Tablighis who are not able to establish a pious home and for whom there is tension between the mosque and home, I argue, are most afflicted with doubt and certainty about faith and thus experience becoming what Talha described as "dried out." The ability to create a pious home is not realized by all, but the story does not simply end there. Instead, we must attend to how Tablighis respond to this condition. I argue that the ethics of hierarchy manages the problem of radical doubt by recognizing the limits of pious agency, valorizing individual striving, and thus pushing the realization of piety into the future (Kloos 2018). This management of doubt has a stabilizing effect in that those who are not able to establish a pious home can nevertheless imagine doing so in the future. Moreover, the management of doubt allows Tablighis to accept in their lives relationships that do not conform to pious ideals and thus live in a world of religious and cultural difference. This, I argue, allows the Tablighi Jamaat to absorb people from diverse backgrounds in terms of caste, class, and ethnicity and also enables the movement to sustain itself in diverse religious and cultural contexts. The management of doubt through the ethics of hierarchy, therefore, is a key aspect of the growth of the movement.

Pious Masculinity and the Model of an Islamic Home

"How can these feet that cannot take you from the home to the mosque when the azaan calls take you from this world to the next?" Tablighis often ask. "When one starts to give dawat, one's feet automatically move, and you find your way to the mosque." The hardship (mushaqqat) of dawat makes the routine fulfillment of Islamic duties like the mandatory prayer seem easy. Leaving the comfort of the home is crucial for the development of a pious habitus, but this is also an Achilles heel for Tablighis. The single most common charge against them is that they abandon their families and especially their wives and kids for long periods of time. As an elderly and seemingly devout man in the mosque once scoffed, "these people do not feel any shame leaving women and their elders at home to fend for themselves." Many non-Tablighis of all sects and denominations see dawat as an escape from responsibilities, a childish desire to travel and have fun, and a forsaking of male duties to protect and care for one's family. For many non-Tablighi Muslims, abandoning one's primary responsibility to family means that one is not fulfilling one's Islamic duties and thus not being a good Muslim.

This is a charge that Tablighis take seriously. Tablighis respond to this by saying that while the Quran says one must care for one's family, dawat is the "greater practice" (*afzal amal*). More importantly, however, Tablighis claim that because dawat is God's work, it brings spiritual and material well-being to their families. This perspective was reinforced through stories, both mundane and miraculous, about the benefits of dawat to the moral and economic well-being of the family. Such stories often went that a particular Tablighi leaves his family for dawat only to discover that some great tragedy has befallen them. Rather than turn back, the Tablighi places his faith in God. Despite the opprobrium he receives at the hands of the wider public, his faith compels him to continue on the path of God. When he returns home, he finds that God has intervened to secure the welfare of his family.

This expression of deep faith in God draws its inspiration from the paradigm of Ibrahim (Abraham) and his wife Hajra (Hagar). In the account from the

Quran, God commands Ibrahim to leave his wife Hajra and infant son Ismail helpless in the desert near Mecca. In the desert, Hajra and Ismail are without water and suffering from thirst. In desperation, Hajra searches for help at the hill of al-Marwa and when she doesn't find any, she runs frantically to the hill of al-Safa. When she doesn't find any water or assistance there, she makes her way back to al-Marwa and continues going back and forth between the two hills. After seven trips between the hills, the Angel Jibreel (Gabriel) appears. The Angel Jibreel stamps his feet on the ground and water gushes out. This becomes the well of Zamzam, around which develops the original community of Muslims. Muslims reenact this event by walking back and forth between the hill of al-Marwa and al-Safa during the annual Hajj pilgrimage, and Muslims throughout the world consider the water that flows from the well of Zamzam to be sacred.

Tablighi accounts of leaving one's family because of God's command directly or indirectly evoke this model of faith. Like Ibrahim, they leave their families as God commanded of the Prophet Ibrahim and all the Prophets who follow him. The paradigm of Ibrahim's sacrifice also has another dimension that is relevant to Tablighi ideas about dawat. When the well of Zamzam springs up, other tribes of the region come to Hajra to request that they allow them to stay, to which she agrees. This is the origin of Mecca, and it is in this community, brought into being through the miraculous intervention of God, that Ibrahim's son Ismail would marry and give birth to a line of Prophets. It is from this line that the Prophet Muhammad would be born. The story of Ibrahim's sacrifice and Hajra's prayers, then, is the tale of the birth of the Islamic community. The sacrifice of Ibrahim and Hajra an act of pure faith, is then the fount—materialized in the well of Zamzam—for the creation of the Islamic community. Like Ibrahim, Tablighis imagine themselves to be leaving their families to ensure God's intervention in the world, and this is understood as a fount for the Islamic community.

Tablighis draw on this paradigm to claim that it is dawat that will ultimately offset the gravest threat to the Islamic community: the moral dissolution of the family, which is the surest sign of the state of moral chaos (fitna). When one asks Tablighis to give examples of the corruption of the world, they refer to the degeneration of kin relationships: parents are not fulfilling the needs of their children, brothers fight with one another over property, husbands divorce wives over minor infractions, wives have no regard for their husband's needs, children abandon their elderly parents, and so on. As one Tablighis asked rhetorically, "when there is no peace inside the home, how can there be calm in the world outside?" Stories about husbands beating their wives or brothers usurping the property of another brother cut through both everyday discourse and provide much of the content for sermons. In one sermon, Hazrat explained that there are only a few sins for which one is punished in this life, rather than in the Hereafter. These include dishonoring the Prophet, bothering a pious Helper of God (Allah ka wali), and disrespecting one's parents. "One should not even say 'ufh' to one's parents," Hazrat explained, voicing the sound one makes when one is frustrated and dissatisfied. "When parents ask you to do something, you should consider this a gift from Allah." In this statement, the Prophet, those close to God and parents occupy similar structural positions as objects of respect and veneration. Just as one should occupy a position as a pious listener in relation to the Elders of the movement and through the Elders to the Prophet, one should assiduously listen to the demands of one's parents. Similarly, just as the Prophet cared for his followers, one must care and show tenderness and kindness (shafqat) to those who are younger and weaker, including children and women. On another occasion, Hazrat decried how men go home and their wives and children are terrified as if a "wolf has come home." Hazrat explained that every time the Prophet came home, it felt like "the first day of spring." In countless sermons, I heard the Elders and older companions implore their fellow Tablighis to be kind to their wives and children and respectful toward their parents. This sentiment is captured in the oft-heard refrain "respect one's elders, and care for the young." Being ethical here entails recognizing one's place in a hierarchy and meeting the obligations that pertain to one's station. Hierarchy here is organized around two axes: age and gender. The young and women must show respect to elders and men, while elders and men must show care for the young and women.

Dawat inculcates in Tablighis the ability to be receptive to those above in a hierarchy, including God, religious authorities, and parents, and care for those below in a hierarchy like wives, younger siblings, and children. Once again, we can see how the ethics of hierarchy is understood to offset the gravest threat to the Islamic community: the fissures and fragmentation within the family characteristic of the state of moral chaos (fitna). Tablighis say that it is only through dawat that the moral decay and dissolution in the home can be forestalled. The reason that dawat engenders moral relations is because of its disciplinary power. Tablighis say that by disciplining the lower self, dawat allows a person to live on ethical terms with one's family and to both garner respect and show care and kindness. As noted in Chapter 3, the ritual ideology of dawat is structured by gendered symbolism that gives the Tablighi qualities that are mostly associated with femininity. Dawat creates an open and soft heart in which religion can settle. This in turn creates a "softness of temperament" (narm mizaaj), which makes one care for the well-being of others, and a "coolness of temperament" (*thanda mizaaj*), which allows one to regulate and control one's emotions. The symbols of openness, softness, and coolness are qualities of the spirit, as opposed to closedness, hardness, and hotness, which are associated with the lower self. These are also gendered symbols in that women's bodies are naturally seen to be open and soft, hence the need to "cover" women. Men's bodies, by contrast, are seen as closed and hard and characterized by a surplus of agency. Dawat appropriates qualities naturally associated with women, "cooling" their passions and taming their surplus agency. I have referred to the construction of this idea of the male with feminine-coded virtues as pious masculinity (Khan 2018). The pious male becomes capable of enacting the ethics of hierarchy as he simultaneously acquires the capacity to submit to those above himself, such as parents, religious authorities, and God, and exhibit the capacity to care for dependents like younger siblings, women, and children. Tablighis see the constitution of a pious male subject as the gift of faith that God gives, which is critical to the preservation of the Islamic home and therefore the basis for the moral reproduction of the Islamic community.

By embodying these virtuous qualities, one becomes an example (*misaal*) for others. Hence, just as a Tablighi is a conduit for divine words, a Tablighi becomes a conduit for morally laden affective dispositions that draws one's kin to Islamic practice. The importance of establishing a pious home was stressed in sermons as well as elaborated in my many conversations. Abdullah a follower of Hazrat and a regular at Hazrat's spiritual house, described to me how his participation in dawat transformed his family. According to Abdullah:

> I was the first in my family who committed to tabligh. Now, Alhamdulillah, many people have committed. Allah has taken much work from us. Many family members have done three days (sehroza), forty days (chilla), four months (chaar mahine). Alhamdulillah, women have started doing pardah. You came to my house that day. Did you not see how there is a religious environment in my house? You saw an environment of pardah. You did not see any women come in front of you. It was not like this before. Now, Alhamdulillah, the whole family is like this. Even in family parties it is like this, ladies separate and gents separate, and in the ladies section, there will be ladies waitresses, not men. They feel good about this too, especially the ones who do pardah, otherwise they feel in a lot of pain if a man comes in. So closeness to Allah takes work.

In this quote, Abdullah stresses the rise of Islamic practice in his family, with the stress on dawat for men and pardah for women. He claims that it spread from his immediate home of his father and brothers to his extended kin of uncles and cousins. The implementation of pardah has now extended across the family and family events such as weddings. When I asked Abdullah if he encountered any resistance from his family, he explained that in the beginning there were many who were against dawat. He said that his own father was opposed to him going on dawat, but now he thinks that Tablighis are "ideal people." "My father now says [to others], 'I have become too old to go but please take my children.' By Allah's grace, he is happy when we go, he prays for us, he tells us to pray for him, and he worries if we don't go."

I asked Abdullah why he thinks people like his father were initially opposed to dawat. He explained:

> They think that he is not a person who does work. They think that "the world" is everything. They think that if we don't work, how will we eat. They have forgotten that when you are born, you do not do any work. For twenty years, a person is mostly studying and does not really do any work. Who is feeding a person for those twenty years? Allah is feeding you! Who puts love in the hearts of mothers and fathers? Allah puts love in their hearts. Who puts the passion in parents' hearts that they must nurture their child, that one must care for the child, buy the child's clothes, feed the child? Who puts this love in their hearts? Allah puts it in their hearts. If that same Allah takes away that love, then one is tested. If a person stays on the religious path, then Allah leaves love in their hearts.

In this quotation, Abdullah notes that it is God who puts love in the hearts of parents, which sustains a child into adulthood, but God only keeps that love in the hearts of kin if they are fulfilling their duties. According to Abdullah, his father's transformation from being opposed to dawat, to recognizing its virtues, to becoming a strong proponent of dawat is made possible because the effort of dawat solicits God's support and God puts love in people's hearts. Indeed, in the same way that a Tablighi acquires the ability to differentiate right from wrong through dawat, one's kin also come to realize the virtues of dawat and come to live in Islamic terms. "If you walk with the love of the Prophet's way in your heart, Allah will Himself put love in the hearts of others." Such a statement makes clear that genuine practice plants the seed of desire and affect in others.

We can see that what Tablighis anticipate is the flow of virtue from the mosque to the home. The "home" is construed here as a kind of liminal space between religion and the world, a space that can pull one toward the mosque or toward the world. It is a necessary task of the Tablighi to connect the home to the mosque. For one to be able to consistently commit to dawat, one must transform one's home into a pious Islamic home. Ideally, the Tablighi becomes a conduit for faith that will reconstitute kin relations and bring them in line with Prophetic ideals. For Tablighis, this transformation of the home will address the deep visions and conflicts that structure the home. As one Tablighi, explained to me, dawat allows one to transcend the seemingly intractable problems of kinship:

> You know, the mosque is like a store. You have to go to the store and pay to acquire what you need. Similarly, you have to give energy, wealth, and time [*jaan/maal/waqt*] to the mosque to receive Allah's grace. . . . When you have Allah with you, and your wife asks you to go out for shopping, but your mother wants you to stay home, then you are able to make both of them happy, but when you don't have Allah on your side, then you can even give whatever they want, and they will still be fighting!

This quotation draws on a widely recognized and richly dramatized contradiction in South Asian, especially North Indian, kinship between mother-in-law (*saas*) and daughter-in-law (*bahu*). In a virilocal family arrangement in which the wife moves into her husband's house and is expected to carry a great deal of the burden of domestic work, many daughters-in-law find themselves at odds with their mothers-in-law and try to draw their husbands away from the husband's parents' house to constitute a separate home, creating a tension with the husband's family. I heard a range of such examples that focused on a wide variety of conflicts between husbands and wives, fathers and sons, and brothers and cousins. In these narratives, one is given the image of a Tablighi traveling from mosque to mosque, further and further afield from one's home, purifying one's own heart and acquiring Islamic virtues, only to return to one's home to be able to gift these virtues to one's kin, who then find themselves doing practice, realizing their respective rights and responsibilities, and reordering their relations with one another in light of Islamic teachings and Prophetic ideals.

In Tablighi narratives of moral transformation, the self is transformed in dawat, and then the most immediate effect is on those closest to oneself and with whom one lives. From there, Islamic virtue will spread to friends, neighbors, and the community more broadly. But, just as a person must be willing to be "acted upon," kin must also be willing to submit to the demands of piety. The story of Ibrahim and Hajra is a paradigm. Hajra gives her consent to Ibrahim as an act of faith in God. Hajra stands in here not only for a woman's faith but for the receptivity of the home itself. Such models of pious becoming, as we should recognize now, do not in fact unfold as Tablighi narratives would have it. We must then ask, what happens when one's kin reject the gift of piety that one brings from the mosque?

The Problem of Doubt: The Disjuncture of Home and Mosque

The Tablighi Jamaat's annual congregation (ijitma) in Raiwind, Pakistan, is one of the largest gatherings of Muslims anywhere in the world with hundreds of thousands, if not millions, of attendees. The congregation is hosted in a massive tent city that stretches for several square kilometers and is thickly populated. Men from across Pakistan, old and young, rich and poor, and from every conceivable ethnic and linguistic community attend the annual congregation. The congregation begins on a Thursday, just like the shab-e-jumma, and ends on Sunday morning after the collective prayer given by one of the pious Elders, which is said to be especially transformative. Tablighis spend three days giving and listening to sermons and conducting daily Islamic prayer and practices at the annual congregation. Just like the Thursday congregation, the annual congregation is organized into localities, cities, and regions. One stays in the space allotted to one's neighborhood mosque and is surrounded by mosques from one's own locale. The annual congregation is like the weekly Thursday congregation except at a massive scale and is where the dense networks of relationships that cut across mosques and localities and sometimes even across cities and regions become apparent.

We arrived at the annual congregation in Raiwind after a ten-day tour. Our itinerant congregation was composed of members of two separate mosque congregations, and, when we arrived, the travelers all dispersed to their respective local mosques. Talha went to the quarters of the Elders, where he stayed to tend to Hazrat's needs. I stayed with the congregation of the Al-Aqsa Mosque, and Umer returned to his own mosque congregation. On numerous occasions over the course of the three days, I had asked Umer to take me to his mosque introduce me to fellow Tablighis in his congregation. On the evening of the third and final day of the annual congregation, I pestered him a few more times, and he finally took me to the section apportioned to his neighborhood. As we arrived, Umer immediately suggested that we go for a walk around the area, to which I agreed. At the time, I did not think anything of Umer's eagerness to leave the space of his mosque, but in retrospect, after repeated attempts to become acquainted with them over the course of my fieldwork, I can say that he was reluctant to let me become too familiar with his mosque congregation. As we walked away from the tent, a short, rotund man in his early fifties greeted Umer warmly. Umer introduced him as Imaad bhai and referred to him as the amir of his congregation. Imaad bhai requested that we sit down, and we did. Umer sat in a kneeling position with his head bowed down in a way that marked his deference to Imaad bhai, making himself available to the instructional mode of dawat that was to follow. Umer told me that Imaad bhai had been one of the first Tablighis to give him dawat and bring him to "Allah's path."

Imaad bhai began with a narrative about Umer's transformation. Umer was quite "spoiled" (*bigra hua*) when he had first started dawat and didn't listen to anyone, he explained. He always wanted things to be "his way." Gradually this began to change as Umer started coming to the mosque more frequently. Imaad bhai proceeded to explain how difficult the process was for Umer. Sometimes he would come to the mosque every day, he explained, and spend all day in practice, but then you would not see him in the mosque for several weeks. We were always worried about him, Imaad bhai explained. He did this for a long time before he settled into the daily ties. Umer's gaze remained fixed on the ground and quiet. Not only was Umer making himself available to listen, but he had entirely placed his own narrative in the hands of Imaad bhai without any interruption. As Imaad bhai told Umer's story, Umer would nod in affirmation. Imaad bhai then said, "See, nobody knows what a person is going through . . . what sacrifices a person has made." Imaad bhai's usage of the term "sacrifice" here was a reference to the standard sacrifices of life force, wealth, and time that are involved in all dawat, but I could sense that within this generic narrative of sacrifice, he was pointing to something more particular about Umer's emotional struggles that kept him from consistent participation in congregational life.

The more time I spent among Tablighis, the more it became apparent to me that the struggles Tablighis faced extended well beyond the commitment of life force, time, and resources and were also deep emotional struggles with loss. It was this sense of loss that gave the term "sacrifice" (qurbani) such moral weight in Imaad bhai's account, the very transformation of one's life and one's relationships that took a deep emotional toll on so many Tablighis. If dawat "connects one's self to Allah's self," as Tablighis say, then it also does so by disrupting or at least transforming one's most intimate relationships, especially those with one's own kin. Tablighis insist that commitment to dawat leads God to put faith in one's heart, and yet there seemed to be so many for whom dawat was itself a source of great strife with their families, whether with fathers, brothers, sisters, or even more broadly with uncles, aunts, and cousins. Indeed, one encounters people in Pakistan regularly who have drifted or become estranged from a family member because of their commitment to Islamic piety or found their own families distancing themselves from them. As we will see below, this is a key problem that the Tablighi Jamaat must manage in order to sustain itself and grow in a diverse religious and cultural context like Pakistan.

This experience weighed heavily on many Tablighis that I encountered, and I came to recognize a structural sense of loss that permeated the movement. This sense of loss is most pronounced in those who experience the most dramatic ruptures with their past life and so is not shared evenly across the movement. For some Tablighis, participation in dawat was an extension of their family traditions, as we saw with Shahzaib in the previous chapter, and thus is expected, while for others it is considered anywhere from a mild nuisance to something to which they are adamantly opposed. Some people simply reject dawat because they regard it as an unnecessary or useless practice and, thus, the stereotypes encountered in the previous section that the Tablighi is someone who does not work and that dawat is a form of enjoyment (tafreeh) and an escape from one's responsibilities. Others have an even more adamant ideological opposition to dawat. I came to learn that Umer's family was of the Barelwi denomination and that dawat disrupted his most valued social relationships. His reluctance to introduce me to his mosque congregation, I suspect, was because he did not have any kinship ties within his mosque congregation. Umer's uncertainty and doubt about his own faith, I argue, was precisely because his commitment to dawat was rejected by his family. It was the rupture between the home and the mosque that created in him the profound experience of doubt and uncertainty about his faith.

The experience of loss so common in the movement did not surprise me. As I explained in the introduction, my friend Talha had rather abruptly severed his ties with his friends, including me, when he joined the Tablighi movement. The experience of seeing such a close friend remove himself from his social network was surely one of the reasons I became interested in the Tablighi Jamaat. The intensity of the commitment that it can inspire and the willingness to transform one's social life is a central dimension of the Tablighi Jamaat. A few friends had reached out to him but to no avail. Occasionally some mutual friend or another would run into him somewhere and try to arrange for us all to hang out, but these meetings never materialized. It was clear that Talha was keen on cutting off his old ties to build a new social network inside the Tablighi Jamaat with people whom he deemed to be living within the parameters of Islam. This is, after all, simply an extension of the principle of sohbat, to surround oneself with good Muslims and distance oneself from those who might draw one away from Islam. Talha's story represents a common example of the need to fortify piety by disassociating from friends and turning the Tablighi Jamaat into his primary social network. Talha had to create a rupture between his past and his present, disassociating himself from friends who had been very dear to him for a very long time, and this loss weighed heavily on him. When I asked Talha why he had disconnected from his friends, he explained that it was all very difficult for him, losing his friends, but he stated unequivocally that our way of life was "way outside of Islam."

In contrast to Talha, there are Tablighis who do not have to take such drastic measures. Their friends, like them, already abided by most of the strictures of Deobandi Islam, even if they were not committed to dawat. For instance, many of the Tablighis I met at the Al-Aqsa Mosque clearly had a line of continuity between their present and past lives. These Tablighis adjust their friendships such that they remain inside the "boundaries" (*hudood*) of Islam. Mostly it means that they had to avoid certain kinds of male humor of the explicitly sexual variety, and they had to adjust their language such that they were not using foul language. This meant that they often found themselves trying to police the behavior of their friends, and, when this was not possible, they would have to disengage from such spaces. One Tablighi explained to me that he stopped playing cricket with his group of friends because that space invariably brought out un-Islamic language and behavior. Once again, these are behaviors that manifest unruly male agency and an absence of pious self-control.

The idea that one must enclose oneself from one's impious relations and spaces to realize a moral transformation was widely recognized as an essential feature of the pious life. Tablighi discourse on sacrifice indexes the sense of loss and strain of such enclosures of piety, but the intensity of this enclosure is not felt equally and is meant to become easy over time as one's faith is solidified. Talha's commitment to dawat came with relative ease because he had many cousins on both his maternal and paternal sides who were Tablighis, and he even reconnected with an old childhood friend who had joined the movement independently of him, so he was able to build an alternative network to our group of friends. While his brother and father were not actively involved in the movement, his father had come to see the importance of dawat over time and became involved more directly in the mosque congregation even if he did not go on dawat tours. Talha's mother was modestly committed to pardah (gender segregation), the strictures of which were much looser before Talha became a Tablighi. Talha's younger brother never joined the movement and often invoked the same discourse that dawat is unnecessary and distracts from one's responsibilities. This remained a source of contention in the household, but eventually they established an understanding that involved less and less interference in each other's life. When I first met Talha's brother, after many years, I asked him why he was not involved in dawat. He snidely remarked, "some people have to live in this world too!" However, as time passed, he became more amenable to dawat and recognized its value in the world. He did not live up to the high standards Talha had wanted, but he did pray, and the more I met him, the more favorable had become his understanding of dawat.

Talha's friend's network, by contrast, was made up of people who were not particularly committed to Islamic practice, or as he put it, "way outside of Islam," but his family was already committed to the strictures of Deobandi Islam. Talha told to me how when he was out at a party and mixing freely with women in his teens, he never felt that what he was doing was right and he always thought about how if his family knew what he was doing, they would have been very disappointed. In many ways, he would narrate that past as one in which he experienced a constant rupture between the world of his home and the world outside with his friends. The home is framed in Talha's narratives as the "inside" and the authentic locus of his spiritual self, while his friends' network is framed as the "outside" that is in tension with this inner self.¹ It was when he joined the Tablighi Jamaat, he said, that he found that inside and outside were finally in harmony.

In many ways, Umer represented the opposite pole of the movement to that of Talha. Umer came to the Tablighi Jamaat through his friends' network, friends he had made through the domestic cricket circuit. Unlike Talha, who had to disconnect from his friends, it was Umer's primary network of friends he had developed through years of playing cricket that was instrumental in drawing him to dawat. But, his family, and especially his father, strongly disproved of his participation in the Tablighi Jamaat. Umer's family was of the Barelwi denomination. As I noted in chapter 2, Barelwis remain committed to the lineage of saints and believe in the intercessionary powers of saints and the Prophet. In Deobandi tradition, the belief in the intercessionary powers of saints is regarded as a form of idolatry (shirk) and thus at odds with establishing a direct relationship to God. One Tablighi described Barelwis as being *deihati*, a term that literally means "rural" but also carries the connotations of being simpletons who are easily manipulated by false religious leaders. The contrast between a scripturally grounded "urban" Pakistan and a "rural" religiosity, understood as idolatry, of saint worship was, as I noted earlier, a common theme in the Tablighi Jamaat. Barelwi religiosity as "rural" carried with it the connotation that their religiosity was anchored in false and corrupted forms of religiosity associated with "custom," and potentially with Hinduism, with the implication that they are not proper Muslims.

Umer's inner conflict was tied directly to the rupture between home and mosque. While conducting dawat in the same students' dormitory mentioned earlier, Umer and I stumbled upon a young Barelwi teacher who was a resident assistant there. The young teacher, a thin man with a dark complexion and a short beard, invited us into his room to "discuss" religion. Umer began to give dawat with his usual flair. Within a minute of the dawat, the young teacher abruptly interrupted him. "This is all fine. This is all fine," the teacher said. Umer was forced to pause. "How it is possible that the Prophet did not have knowledge of the unseen (*ghaib*) when the Quran explicitly says so?" The teacher was invoking a central theological disagreement between Barelwis and Deobandis, with the former insisting that God had granted the Prophet knowledge of the unseen, something in keeping with his status as a being who partakes in God's essence, which in turn has implications for whether the Prophet can intercede on one's behalf by moving between these realms. Umer quietly listened as the teacher made his case. When the man finished, Umer responded by positing the conventional Tablighi response to sectarian division, which is that these are debates between the ulama and that we need to focus on what is common between Muslims. The man agreed that there was much in common, after which we exchanged pleasantries and departed.

When I asked Umer what the teacher was referring to, he sidelined the question by saying that there are some differences but did not elaborate. It was not long after this that Umer became "dried up" (khushka), spending hours in recitation and stricken by anxiety. I would not have thought that there was any connection between this event and his subsequent behavior if it were not for the fact that it arose whenever Deobandi and Barelwi disagreements surfaced. Once, during the same trip, we sat around the mosque courtyard about fifteen minutes or so before the evening prayers (asr) when the sounds of a distant *naat*, devotional songs in praise of God, became audible. Tablighis see naat as acceptable under limited circumstances if they do not invoke the intercessionary powers of the Prophet. One Tablighi joked that Barelwis confuse "music" for worship (*ibaadat*), and they all asked God to give them guidance. Umer was notably silent through all of this, his head bowed in a worshiping position, his lips moving in scriptural recitation.

Another incident confirms this. It was *Eid-e-Milad-un-Nabi,* the day of the Prophet's birth, a day that Barelwis celebrate by hanging green tinted lights on streets and on houses and gates and distribute food, hold processions, and recite naat. Deobandis consider the commemoration of the Prophet's birth a form of innovation (biddat) that can lead to the worship of the Prophet (see Tareen 2020). I sat with Umer and Abdullah and asked them why they think Deobandis are opposed to the celebration of Eid-e-Milad-un-Nabi. Abdullah went on to explain that in Islam we do not celebrate birthdays and that this is a Western custom. He said that one should only remember the day of death. Some ulama, he noted, say that 12 *Rabi-ul-Awwal*, the day of the Islamic calendar on which Eid-e-Milad-un-Nabi falls, is the day of the Prophet's "return" (*visaal*) and should be remembered as a somber occasion, not a celebratory one. "But maybe it's still acceptable because it reminds people of the Prophet," Umer murmured. It was apparent that Umer was sidelining the deeper theological disagreements and trying to fold the Barelwi and Sufi-inspired celebration into a Deobandi framework. Abdullah glanced at me, and both of us could sense Umer's concern and contrition. "Allah knows best. May He give us all guidance," Abdullah said in a sympathetic tone. Umer's uncertainty and ambivalence stood in marked contrast to the certainty and authority expressed by Abdullah even though both shared the same status as old companions. Umer was asking a question that he had to ponder himself. He was trying to find the basis for mediating between the teachings of the Elders and the Deobandi ulama and the voice of his own family.

The contrast between Talha and Umer, then, is striking because Talha could discard his friendships, and, by discarding these friendships, he could eliminate the voices that intruded, asked questions, and raised doubts. In other words, becoming a proper listener in the Tablighi Jamaat entails not only embodying the right voices but also discarding the wrong ones, voices that pull one away from dawat. Talha was able to purify the self and fully submit to the teachings of the Tablighi Jamaat. Anchored in kinship ties that he could not discard without rupturing his own self, Umar consistently tried to find the "common ground" between Tablighis and Barelwi versions of scriptural truth. Umer experienced a radical disjuncture between the space of the home and the space of the mosque with the former always intruding into the latter. He thus felt a tension within himself that he experienced as a problem of pious receptivity and a crisis of faith. The rejection of dawat and Deobandi Islam more generally by his kin was a great source of concern and contrition for Umer, who was always trying to find ways to bring them to a better understanding, but his failure to do so generated anxieties, doubts, and deep sadness in him. This experience of rupture between mosque and home was experienced as the precarious presence of faith in his life.

The Habitus of Certain Faith and the Making of an Islamic Home

Irfan was the amir of the traveling congregation that I accompanied from Karachi through Multan to the national congregation. Many of us jokingly continued to call him *amir sahib* from then onwards. A short, pudgy, and affable young man in his late twenties, he had a warm and hearty laugh and a high-pitched voice and spoke, as many Memons are stereotypically thought to, very fast. He was exceedingly polite, always taking great pains to welcome me and make sure that I was doing well. Irfan was a permanent fixture in the evenings at Hazrat's spiritual house, where he always conducted service (khidmat) responsibilities like serving food and caring for the needs of visitors. Irfan was seen by many to be a model Tablighi, not only willing to sacrifice but also exceedingly humble in his demeanor, only assuming a position of authority relative to others when it was demanded of him. He always situated himself as a pious listener relative to those more experienced than him. Irfan seemed to embody what Shahzaib had described to me as the most virtuous quality of the Elders, that they were so pious that they did not seek any recognition at all. If Umer represented one end of the spectrum of people who break from their family traditions to recreate themselves as Tablighis, Irfan represents precisely the opposite situation. Irfan's father, Basharat bhai, was one of Hazrat's primary and oldest caretakers. He had been involved in the life of the spiritual house since its founding in the mid-1990s. Irfan's paternal uncle was the amir of the Al-Aqsa congregation, and his youngest uncle was involved in the Al-Aqsa Mosque committee, where he could advocate for Tablighis. All three brothers lived together in a three-story house in which each brother occupied one floor located a few streets from the mosque and spiritual house. All their children had some formal education in Islam, whether they were studying to be an alim (scholar) or *mufti* (jurist), and many were hafiz-e-Quran, those who have the entire Quran memorized. Irfan was also a hafiz. Along with this training in Islam, the entire family was deeply involved in the life of the mosque and Hazrat's spiritual house. They also frequently hosted naat recitations on their roof. In other words, the Basharat family was a model pious family and at the center of the Islamic life of the Al-Aqsa congregation.

I asked Irfan on several occasions to help me with research, and, like others, he said that I just needed to keep coming to the mosque and spiritual house and I would learn all that I needed to learn. I insisted though that he let me interview him and that it would help the process along, and he agreed, but he kept putting it off until shortly before it was time for me to leave for the United States. I suspect that he, like others, thought that if I got my interview, I would stop coming to the mosque and thus it was incumbent on him to allow me first to learn dawat properly. A week before I was ready to leave, and two years into our regular meetings at the mosque and spiritual house, I managed to sit down with Irfan for the interview. Irfan explained to me how his family all came to the Tablighi Jamaat. Irfan explained that his paternal uncle, who is younger than his father, drew his father to dawat, and together, they brought their father to dawat as well. Irfan remarked, "When we were born, Alhamdulillah, there was already religion in our whole generation." Irfan's narrative was one I had heard many times before, a story of how one person's religious awakening spread to all the members of his family, and then all subsequent generations were born inside a "religious space" (dini mahol). I asked Irfan what the difference is between people like him who are born into a religious environment as opposed to those who must create it themselves:

> Those who come to religion on their own, who start from zero, they are more important to Allah. Those in my category have less importance because they have always been in that environment, but those who are zero, they have nothing, and they suddenly come in religion, they understand the value of religion. This is why if you see Muslims abroad . . . those Muslims are such that you will say, "this is a Muslim" . . . because

this person has lifted himself from the step of zero and brought himself to religion. He has borne the cost. People like us have been Muslim since childhood, we've been in tabligh since childhood, so we do not see its value ... it is all we know.

In this quotation, Irfan is rehearsing the pervasive idea in the movement that God rewards those who make sacrifices for him. Muslims living abroad, by which he means those living in un-Islamic environments, remain Muslim through their sacrifice and determination, and for this God rewards them. Note that in Irfan's remarks, the person who gives great sacrifice is not only important to God but also recognizes the value of religion in a distinct, conscious way. Such reflexive awareness, like that of Umer, is highly valued because it indexes struggle and sacrifice, and so people like this are considered an ideal.

Paradoxically, however, while those like Umer are highly valued, they are not in a position that is easy to sustain. Irfan explained that while those who have grown up in a religious space might not see its value, they are habituated to living their lives in religious terms. "While we might not always see its importance, there is the benefit that if a person has lived in this environment from the beginning, it's easier for him to keep walking in this path. This is why people who have completely changed are fewer than those who come from homes where there is already religion." In other words, growing up in an Islamic environment means that one is habituated to Islam enough that one does not even need to make a conscious effort. While Tablighis celebrate those who have come to Islam through their own volition and personal sacrifice, the aim of the Tablighi is ultimately to create a space (mahol) in which being religious (dindaar) becomes easy and unconscious, a matter of habit. It is in this second sense that those, like Irfan, who have been raised in what Tablighis deem a religious space (dini mahol) are the end point in the process of pious becoming.

There is something undeniably practical about the ideal of a pious family in a movement built on voluntary labor. The division of labor inside Irfan's family allowed one brother to devote time to Hazrat's spiritual house, another brother to give time to the mosque, and still the youngest brother to care for the family's business and property, and these tasks could be rotated between them without creating too much strain on the family's ability to fulfill their worldly expectations. Tensions can mount in families if one sibling is seen as failing to meet their obligations to the family and, as we saw in Abdullah's narrative, can be perceived as someone who fails to work. In Irfan's family, the brothers and their children all invested a considerable amount of time and resources in the day-to-day functioning of the mosque. At major Tablighi events like shab-e-jumma and especially at the annual congregations, the labor of the brothers and their many children becomes evident. At the annual congregation, Irfan, who doesn't have brothers, and his many cousins contribute a great deal to the organization of the trip. Many mosques in Karachi are clustered around a few key families, many of which entail three generations of Tablighis. It makes sense, then, that Tablighis seek to draw in their brothers and cousins to dawat and create their own Tablighi families.

The heart of the Tablighi ideal of an Islamic family is the hierarchical relations between genders, and this is understood to be the quintessential mark of piety. Tablighis insist that the most essential aspect of an ideal Islamic moral order is the maintenance of gender segregation or pardah. In chapter 3, we explored how the naturalization of gender difference and hierarchy is the premise of the entire framework of Tablighi piety. Women occupy the world of the inside (home), while men occupy the world of the outside (mosque and work). In Tablighi narratives, women are often cast as the central problem that men need to overcome to realize pious virtues and are thus cast as the temptations of the world. Just as a person must reshape his lower self, similarly the creation of a spiritual home requires the establishment of a gender hierarchy in the home, which entails the subordination of women to men, mother to father, wife to husband, and sister to brother. As Pelkmans's (2017) ethnography on Tablighis in Kyrgyzstan shows, men's commitment to dawat can wane and wax depending on how their wives respond to it. If we think back to the story of Abraham and Hajra, it is women's willful acts of faith and submission to pious male authority that is the fount for Islamic virtue. Securing women's commitment is therefore a key part of the process of establishing a pious Islamic home.

Women's commitment to dawat is explicitly manifest in their participation in the mastoorat tours discussed in chapter 3, and indeed this might be the most fully realized form of the pious Islamic home. However, even when sisters and wives do not directly participate in Tablighi activity, women's acceptance of pious male authority and thus the proper ordering of the home is manifest in the mosque in the form of food. There is a strong commitment to bringing home-cooked food to shab-e-jumma, and this food, made in the space of domestic life, is seen as pure. At shab-e-jumma, each Tablighi brings with him food, which he contributes to his mosque congregation. Tablighis insist that this food should be from the home and strongly discourage buying food from the market, except for the *roti* (bread), which is best eaten fresh. The food of the home is described as having divine grace (barkat) that gives it a fullness that is not there in food bought from the store. Sharing food from various homes creates commensality and connection (jor) between the congregants. In this sense, the women's labor comes to embody their consent and their active commitment and becomes the foundation for the creation of Islamic community. The presence of male kin inside the congregation, then, not only stands for male commitment to dawat but also evidences female commitment and the proper ordering of the home. In this, we can see the total realization of the model of pious kinship (see Thomas, Malik and Wellman 2017).

When Umer described to me how faith is fickle, sometimes powerful but sometimes weak and fleeting, he was directing my attention to the very erratic involvement of people in the Tablighi Jamaat. Some Tablighis were intensely committed to dawat for short periods of time, ranging from a few days to a year, and then would gradually slip away, never to return. Others drifted in and out of the movement but never seemed able to commit fully to dawat. Still others, like Umer, remained within the fold of the Tablighi Jamaat for long periods of time, but they were profoundly troubled by what they saw as the fleeting nature of their own faith. Tablighis would certainly agree, and many did, that firm and continuous commitment—understood as certain faith—largely depended on the support or, better still, active participation of one's kin. One finds, then, a range of Tablighis from those who are alone in the movement, like Umer, to those who have patchy and loose kin networks but some support from their kin, like Talha, to those, like Irfan, who are what are often referred to as "familial" Tablighis (*khandani*), who have been Tablighis for multiple generations and have entirely grown up in the world of the Tablighi Jamaat. The creation of certain faith requires that one move from being an individual to a familial Tablighi.

Recuperating Piety: The Limits of Pious Agency and the Path to an Islamic Future

We saw in the previous chapter that pious becoming depends on companionship with pious others and the enactment of pious relationality around what I called the ethics of hierarchy. This model of pious becoming requires, I argued, the ability to be a pious listener in relation to those who are deemed more pious than oneself in a sacred hierarchy. What we see here is that certain faith depends not only on living within the space of the Tablighi congregation but, crucially, also on establishing a semiotic and interdiscursive link between the mosque and the home. Such material links take semiotic form in performative genres like the reading sessions (taleem), which one is expected to perform once daily in the mosque and once in the home. These performances connect the pious authority of the mosque to the kinship authority of the home in a hierarchical arrangement in which virtue is seen as flowing from the former to the latter. The receptivity of the pious home is manifest in the presence of men from the family in the daily mosque activities and the movement of food from the home to the mosque and, thus, indexes an acceptance that the relationality of the home must be reconfigured according to the pious authority of the Elders of the congregation.

The distinction between Umer, an individual Tablighi, and Irfan, a familial Tablighi, is registered as a distinction between uncertain and certain faith. While both Umer and Irfan were able to perform the ethics of hierarchy in the mosque, only one was able to carry this into the home and thus embody certain faith. For Umer, the ethics of hierarchy ran against the kinship ideals of a diligent and dutiful son. He found himself having to defy his own father's authority to be a pious subject. The tension between the voice of the Elders and the voice of his father was registered as the uncertain presence of faith in his life, which he tried to remedy in intense bouts of ritual observance. By contrast, Irfan's father was a pious listener to the Tablighi Elders, and therefore Irfan could simultaneously be a dutiful son and a pious listener to the Elders. Indeed, being a dutiful son was consistent with being a pious listener to the Elders.

The purpose of dawat is to constitute piety as the "paramount value" of social life, or that value that is the encompassing one in relation to others (Dumont 1980). This requires establishing a single line of authoritative transmission from God to pious authorities to father to son. This means that certain faith depends on the subordination and subsumption of paternal authority within the authority of the Elders, the home to the mosque. The words of the Elders are heavy with divine agency and therefore must be the guiding force for life. The disruption of this line of authoritative transmission engenders religious doubt. In recent years, anthropologists working on Muslim societies have stressed the importance of ambivalence, skepticism, and doubt in Muslim social life (Khan 2012; Marsden 2005; Schielke 2009, 2015; Pelkmans 2017). Critiquing the "piety turn" in the anthropology of Islam, Samuli Schielke (2015) argues that an approach that treats the goal of Muslim life to be the perfection of piety fails to acknowledge the multiple "moral registers" that shape "everyday" life for Muslims. What I have shown in this chapter though is that the problem is not an inevitable product of the interaction of distinct "moral registers" in "everyday" life. Rather, doubt here is a structural problem generated by a demand integral to the framework of Islamic piety to create a single, authoritative line of religious transmission and an effort to subsume other forms of relationality into a single moral framework. If Tablighis have what Pelkmans (2017) calls "fragile conviction," it is because tension arises when that project of subsuming other forms of relationality fails, especially when these forms of relationality are understood to be definitive of the self. Doubt arises most forcefully when there is a rupture between religious and kinship authority, a problem that can arise when efforts are made to establish a transcendental Islamic community above and beyond kinship ties (see, for instance, Shryock 1997). Understanding that religious doubt arises from these structural tensions rather than assuming that it is simply an intrinsic feature of "everyday" life helps us better account for how such tensions are reckoned with and managed.

Despite Umer's zealous participation in congregational life, certain faith remained elusive to him because he experienced what Webb Keane (2016) calls "the inner clash of ethical voices," a conflict between the voice of the pious others of the congregation and the voice of his kin, particularly his father, and he was unable to "attune" these voices into a single framework (143). The demand to create a pious Islamic home reveals the limits on the efficacy of pious agency to transform others and the impact that this can have on the Tablighi himself. However, as Kloos (2018) argues, we must also consider how people and movements respond to moral failure in the process of pious becoming. Indeed, Umer remained a committed Tablighi despite his struggles with doubt. In the valorization of Umer's striving by both Imaad bhai and Irfan, we can see the contours of how doubt is managed in the Tablighi Jamaat. Tablighis place the highest value on the struggles and sacrifices made to remain on the path of piety. This valorization of the individual striving for piety is central to Tablighi narratives. In doing so, someone like Umer is constantly reminded of the value that he has in the eyes of God. Moreover, as noted in chapter 3, the sacralization of words of dawat means that a Tablighi's responsibility ends with the delivering of the message. Tablighis are encouraged to be an example (misaal) for one's kin but also defer to the ultimate authority of God. The notion that dawat is principally about the transformation or reform (islah) of the self and that it is God who will transform others means that the Tablighi must recognize the limits of his own pious agency. After all, ultimate agency rests not with any human but instead with God. The valorization of individual striving and the deferment of agency to God reflexively reframes the struggles with doubt as a sacrifice and thus as a valued stage on the path to certain faith. By valorizing individual striving and recognizing the limits of one's pious agency, the Tablighi can maintain the possibility of creating a pious Islamic home in the future through God's agency.

The Tablighi Jamaat's aim is to draw Muslims from across caste, class, and ethnic lines to create a universal Islamic community. As I mentioned in chapter 2, dawat enables those who are otherwise defined as "low" in terms of the caste, class, and ethnic hierarchies that structure Pakistani nationalism to reinvent themselves as the proper subjects of Islam. Low-caste and working-class people in Pakistan are some of the most likely to have kinship structures and values that do not conform to the terms of pious relationality, but examples in this chapter show that all kinds of Tablighis are faced with tensions that arise within their families when they commit to dawat. How could an Islamic movement that draws people from such diverse caste, class, and ethnic backgrounds hold together if it failed to attend to and manage conflicts with intimate others like kin? The valorization of individual striving and the deferment to God's agency serves as a recuperative frame that affirms the value of striving for the Tablighi but also allows him to accept that his kin are not necessarily going to be drawn or at least not drawn immediately to dawat. It, therefore, serves to recuperate piety as it alleviates the doubt one experiences while also encouraging a stance of acceptance toward kin who have not committed to and accepted dawat, thus encouraging the maintenance of harmonious relations in the home.

The Tablighi Jamaat is a universal movement that aims to incorporate people from all kinds of backgrounds and a transnational movement that aims to embed itself in diverse social and political contexts. The valorization of striving places stress on the Tablighi to persist in being a model for others, and the acceptance of the limits of pious agency entails a recognition that one cannot transform everyone and insulate oneself from the world. It tells the Tablighi that he must accept that some of his most important social relationships will not be transformed, at least not in the present, but that one must continue to strive to live by Prophetic example and continue to be a model for others. In this way, the Tablighi accepts that even as the present is imperfectly pious, he remains on the path to an Islamic future.

6
PIOUS SOVEREIGNTY IN TIMES OF MORAL CHAOS

The question of whether dawat is a mandatory practice emerged throughout my fieldwork. Many Muslims respectfully and reverentially decline the Tablighi invitation to the mosque. Some treat such requests with indifference and even mild amusement. Young boys would often run when they saw Tablighis approaching, and the Tablighis would in turn laugh. Indeed, there was often, at least in the more intimate sphere of the neighborhood, a playfulness about many of these interactions when they built on the presumption of a shared commitment to the tenets of Deobandi or broadly reformist Islam. Conflicts tended to emerge along denominational lines, as we saw in the previous chapter, or between more liberal-minded Muslims who were angered at the presumption of religious authority by the Tablighi. Occasionally, however, one would find someone who attended the same mosque and was clearly a committed and practicing Sunni Muslim, but was adamant that the Tablighi form of dawat was not only unnecessary but beyond the pale of Islam.

One incident stands out in my mind. Before dusk prayers, I went to buy a soft drink from one of the general stores built into the ground floor of the Al-Aqsa Mosque. The shopkeeper, a middle-aged man with a long beard, told me that he had seen me come to the mosque many times and asked me if I live in the area. I responded that I do not live in the area, but I have friends who live in this area who are involved in tabligh, and I come here to listen to sermons and participate in other activities. He noted that he had seen me with Tablighis. I noted that his beard betrays that he is "religious" (dindaar), and I asked him if he was involved in dawat, to which he responded in a harsh and dismissive tone, "no!"

I asked if there was a reason, and he explained to me that there is no Islamic basis for this dawat. Nowhere in the Quran or Prophetic tradition, he said, is it stated that Muslims must do this. I said that Tablighis say that this is what the Prophet and all other prophets in the past have done and that Muslims must do whatever the Prophet did, and the storekeeper was irritated, even angered. "No, this is all innovation!" he said, implying that the Prophet never did or said to do dawat in this way. The Tablighi Elders, he explained, have just made this up, and their followers just do whatever they tell them without verifying anything for themselves. "They do not use their own reason [aql]!" Noting his irritation and knowing the sensitivity of such topics, and the fact that prayer time was approaching, I chose not to pursue the conversation any further. Later, I asked a fellow Tablighi about his adamant rejection of dawat, and he told me that the shopkeeper belonged to the Islamist political party, the Jamaat-e-Islami.

We have already explored the sectarian tension between Sunni denominations, Deobandi and Barelwi, in the previous chapter. In this chapter, I focus on how Tablighis drawing the boundaries of religion around their conception of pious relationality also serves as a basis for critiquing the entanglement of Islam with modernist institutions. I focus primarily on the tensions between Tablighis and modernist Islamists who aim to create an Islamic society through the Islamic state and increasingly through a range of modern institutions like corporations, NGOs, and new educational institutions. While Tablighis often acknowledge the shared doctrinal commitments with many Islamists, they nevertheless insist that Islamist activities do not conform to the Prophet's way and are therefore incapable of spreading Islamic virtues. Some Tablighis took an even harsher stance to say that Islamist activities were inimical to the Prophet's ways, destructive of pious virtue, and therefore themselves a source of moral chaos. "Stay away from these organizations [*tanzeem*]! They have nothing to do with Islam," Tablighis often proclaimed. Similarly, Islamists, as the previous conversation attests, also believed that the Tablighi form of dawat is "innovation," a product of the teachings of Tablighi Elders, which they failed to verify through their own reason. Tablighis and Islamists agreed that what was needed was a return to the original sources, but Islamists insisted that the path to this was through individual reason, which Tablighis fail to apply. In other words, Islamists regard the Tablighi conception of dawat to be an obstacle to creating an Islamic state and see their commitment to the sacred hierarchy of their Elders to be a forfeiture of reason. Tablighis, in turn, insist that the Prophet's way is the sacred means for spreading Islamic virtue and creating an Islamic community.

Barbara Metcalf (2004) argues that the Tablighi Jamaat is an "apolitical, quietist movement" because it shuns formal engagement with politics and instead focuses on the reform of the individual (266). In his rich study of the historical emergence of the Deobandi tradition, Brannon Ingram (2018) shows how the Deobandi tradition represents a "revival from below" or what he describes as a "bottom up reform largely invisible relative to the top-down reform of Islamist political projects" (18). Ingram's argument, like my own, focuses on the place of sohbat as a framework for crafting pious subjectivities and shows how this becomes the basis for the development of the role of the ulama in public life and the spread of an Islamic tradition. Ingram shows that in the 1920s and 1930s, key Deobandi luminaries like Ashraf Ali Thanwi opposed Muslim involvement in mass politics, which they saw as a source of "crisis" (fitna), and most notably rejected the mobilization of Muslims in the Khilafat Movement (1919–1924) as well as taking direct action against the British. In Pakistan, state-driven Islamization has incorporated Deobandi ulama, who have found themselves not only at the helm of major political parties like Maulana Fazlur Rahman's Jamaat-e-Ulama-e-Islam (JUI) but integrally bound up with the workings of the state and corporations. While Tablighis express immense respect for the Deobandi ulama, they maintain a deep ambivalence toward much of this activity and an oppositional stance toward what they call *politiks*.[1]

This chapter focuses on the Tablighi commitment to maintaining the division between religion and the world and between dawat and politiks as an oppositional stance to the Islamization of public life through the arms of modernist institutions of the state and corporations. I show that the division that Tablighis draw between religion and the world and dawat and politiks is underpinned by distinct concerns about the maintenance of pious relationality and the moral reproduction of the Islamic community. While dawat, as we have seen, produces a pious masculine subject who accepts the authority of pious others and recognizes the limits of his pious agency, politiks creates the exact opposite: a self characterized by unruly agency, one that fails to respect authority and also aims to push Islam on to others by force. This destroys Islamic virtue and undermines the creation of an Islamic community. Politiks is, therefore, construed as a worship of the self (*khudparasti*) and a quintessential source of moral chaos. The Tablighi stance on politiks takes shape against the backdrop of political fragmentation and violence along both ethnic and sectarian lines that characterizes life in postcolonial Pakistan. I argue that Islamization in Pakistan has been paradoxical in that the entanglement of Islam with modernist institutions of the state and corporations has created intense competition over Islamic authority, which in turn has created a pervasive sense that it has become emptied of ethical substance. In the division Tablighis draw between religion and the world, dawat and politiks, Tablighis aim to reimbue Islamic authority with a moral force that they believe can transcend the political fragmentation and violence that characterizes life in postcolonial Pakistan.

Politiks as the Worship of the Self: The Problem of Surplus Agency

The Tablighi concern about Islamism was forcefully brought to my attention one evening at the weekly Thursday congregation. Three Tablighi friends were discussing a mutual acquaintance of theirs, a young man in his early twenties who, although not a regular Tablighi, occasionally stayed after prayers to listen to sermons and participate in other mosque activities. He had potential, they insisted, because of his "passion" for Islam. But, when he suddenly stopped participating in mosque activities, they became concerned about his well-being and began seeking him out. They inquired with his family members where he had gone, and they were told that he is busy with his studies, which keeps him busy. For reasons I was not privy to, they arrived at the conclusion that he stopped his limited participation in the congregation because he had joined an Islamist political party at his university. They all agreed that they should try to intervene, but they were worried that their intervention would drive him further away from religion. They agreed that they would pray to God on his behalf and that after the Friday prayers they would conduct a "special visit" (*khasoosi gasht*), a form of visitation that involves drawing Tablighis who were drifting away from dawat back to the congregation. I asked why they were so worried about him if they believed he was pursuing his passion for Islam in other ways, and one of them promptly explained, "he has passion, but he is very far from practice!" Such undisciplined passion was a dangerous thing.

I had the opportunity to discuss the tension between Tablighis and Islamists with a few Islamist political party workers as well. In an interview with a representative of the Islamist political party Jamaat-ud-Dawa about their participation in rehabilitation efforts for the victims of the catastrophic floods in July 2010 that devastated large swaths of the country and left millions of people displaced. After the interview, I asked the representative what he thought about the religious work of the Tablighi Jamaat, and he responded, "we don't have any issue with them on religious grounds, but I don't understand why they don't get involved in politics. Sometimes you must do some things for yourself." This is characteristic of Islamist critiques of Tablighi forms of dawat, which they believe rely only on God to do what they themselves should be doing. For Islamists, even if Tablighis root themselves in correct doctrinal principles, a fact he was noting when he said we agree with them on "religious grounds," but the exclusive commitment to dawat was not grounded in reason. The Tablighis' stance against politiks made little sense if the purpose was to create an Islamic society, which required means other than dawat. In an interview I conducted with another Islamist party member, this time of the Jamaat-e-Islami party, he explained the position more comprehensively: "Pakistan is full of problems and these Tablighis only want to preach about religion. Religion is right in its own place, but we need an Islamic "system" (*nizam*) here to fix our problems, and that requires getting people involved in politics. People must take responsibility. They cannot leave everything to Allah." He then proceeded to explain that politics is also a "religious practice" if it is being done in "defense of Islam." What mattered for this Islamist party representative was not how it was being conducted but the "intentions" (*niyyat*) behind it and its ultimate effect in creating a more Islamic society. This was the kind of instrumental reasoning that Tablighis, in their commitment to the Prophet's way, found anathema to Islam.

When I told a long-time Tablighi about the Islamist statements, he proclaimed definitively, "They have no faith! . . . They want to do this on their own. They don't understand that only Allah can fix these problems and the only way to bring Allah to our aid is through dawat." *Politiks* was unauthorized by the authoritative textual sources, a point Tablighis made frequently, and they also argued that the Islamist perspective evidenced a lack of faith in God's power and the false belief in one's own agency. The notion that Muslims must solicit God's aid in securing whatever they hoped to secure is central to Tablighi definitions of faith (*iman*) and is captured in the first and most significant of the Tablighi Jamaat's six principles (*chei batein*): the article of faith, which declares that Muslims must have "certainty that everything comes from Allah and nothing comes from another" (*Allah ki zat se sab kuch hone ka yaqeen, ghair ki zaat se kuch na hone ka yaqeen*). This is the principle on which Tablighis reject theological commitments of intercession (*tawassul*) in both Sufi and Barelwi forms. But, here we see that it also serves as a critique of the modernist assumption of a belief in one's own agency. It is the failure of Islamists to have faith in God's agency and their belief in the agency of the self or that of some others, like their political leaders, that demonstrates their lack of faith in God.

The most common accusation Tablighis lodge against Islamists is that of hubris (*takabbur*), arguing that by locating agency in their own self rather than God, Islamists conflate the issue for source and signifier for signified, falling prey to the worship of the self. Tablighis claim that this worship of the self inheres in Islamist political praxis and is not only ineffective but also dangerous. Maqsood, a taxi driver and long-time Tablighi, was forceful in highlighting this danger:

> I knew this young man who was part of some party, and he would go off to these rallies each day, and sometimes, like us, he would even go to the villages, not for dawat of course, but he said he was going for Islam, but you know, he would come back and he would fight with his family, with his wife and beat his children also, even his parents, and

> he never had any peace at home. His neighbors were also all wary of him. Everyone said that he was an angry person and had hardness of temperament ... he has passion for Islam, but he is home fighting with his parents and wife. His passion is just his "lower self" speaking, and this is what gives birth to anger and aggression in him. How is someone like this going to bring others to Islam? When we come back home from dawat, we come back with a sense of peace. It creates softness of temperament and makes us feel calm and cool ... dawat awakens your spirit and brings Allah's support.

Because it fails to take proper ritual form, Islamism is not only inefficacious but also threatens to invert the Islamic moral order by producing undisciplined subjects who claim to represent Islam. In this narrative, the lower self is the one "speaking" and producing passions and dispositions that are precisely the opposite of those induced by dawat. Contrasts of high/low, soft/hard, and cold/hot are all inverted, the former being subordinated to the latter. This inversion of piety creates a person who is incapable of caring for those below (wife and children) and respecting those above (parents), that is, a person who fails to understand and disregards his place in a hierarchical order. The worship of the self disrupts harmonious relations in the family, between families (neighbors), and in the Islamic community more generally, creating the conditions for moral chaos (fitna).

The space that most fully embodies moral chaos is the political rally that Islamists hold in the streets. As Maqsood explained, "these rallies people are sitting in the street. They are listening to their leaders and these leaders are saying this party ate this much money and that party is eating that much money. They are not focused on stories of the Prophet or the Companions. Faith is not created in such spaces." Indeed, the contrast here between the mosque and political rally is a direct analogue to the contrast between dawat and politiks, and if there is one thing that defines the latter it is the problem of talk. "When people listen to such speeches from their leaders they are themselves enraged and they go out and they tell others and those others tell others and so a fire spreads." If dawat is the basis for "positive value" creation, the creation of pious words and actions that draw Muslims to Islam, politiks is a fount for "negative value" creation (Munn 1986; see also Graeber 2001, 83–84). Dawat produces a subject with a disciplined self, whose spirit speaks through them, and who has a "cool" temperament. Such a person is characterized by humility (khushu) and pious fear (*khauf*), and these qualities allow him to recognize his place in an Islamic hierarchy. Politiks, by contrast, produces undisciplined subjects characterized by arrogance (takabbur), whose lower selves speak through them and who either commit themselves to false authorities like their political leaders or locate authority only in themselves. They are incapable of recognizing legitimate forms of authority and thus spreading Islamic virtue. Such people are not only themselves "far from Islam" but also lead others away from Islam.

The sharp contrast that Tablighis draw between themselves and Islamists frames the Tablighi commitment to dawat against state driven Islamization in Pakistan. Tablighis insist that the state is not the means through which Islamic virtue can be spread because, as one Tablighi explained, "the government cannot put love in people's hearts. Only Allah can put love in people's hearts." The government, he said, is "the greatest idol" (*sab se bara buth*) because it makes people think that Islam is being spread but it in fact does nothing to create Muslims who can live by God's will. Tablighis are not opposed to the Islamic state in principle, but they insisted that only dawat could ultimately bring about such a state. In this sense, Tablighis recognize "the state" to be an "effect" of definite forms of practice (Mitchell 2006). An Islamic state can only be born of Islamic practice. An Islamic state created through Islamic practice would become a conduit for God's will, but insofar as the Islamic state was created through the false attribution of agency to someone other than God, it would fail to produce pious Muslims, and like other idols, would ultimately lead Muslims away from Islam. Because this critique is centered on forms of agency, it is not exclusively limited to statist Islamism either. It applies equally to other modern institutions like banks and NGOs, which Tablighis understand as embodying the same false attribution of agency to the self. The proliferation of idols is, then, a fundamental problem of modernity.

Islamic Governmentality and the Crisis of Moral Reproduction

The sharp boundary Tablighis draw between dawat as the basis for moral order and politiks as a quintessential source of moral chaos is underpinned by distinct moral concerns about how self-authorized, individuated knowledge creates an unruly form of agency that tears apart the Islamic community. Understanding the political significance of the Tablighi stance on politiks requires taking a deeper look at the entanglement of Islam with state sovereignty in Pakistan and especially against the backdrop of state-driven Islamization and the fragmentation of Pakistani social and political life. As noted earlier, Pakistani nationalism was structured by a broad distinction between high-caste Muslims (ashraf) who claimed deep Islamic genealogies and low-caste Muslims (ajlaf) understood to be recent converts and lacking Islamic pedigree. From the 1950s to the 1970s, the state and particularly the army and civil bureaucracy drew on this distinction between high and low culture to pursue a project of authoritarian modernization (Verkaaik 2004). Authoritarian modernization created a backlash from ethnolinguistic movements that demanded democratization and devolution of authority to the provinces, most notably the Bengali nationalist movement in East Pakistan (now Bangladesh). As Pakistan transitioned to democracy after the secession of Bangladesh in 1971, ethnolinguistic identity came to be central to the national imaginary. Democracy and the decentralization of power from the federal center to provinces were coupled with a shift from Urdu and modernist Islam to regional languages and the growing importance of Sufi imagery, poetry, ritual forms, and religious spaces like saint shrines. The period, as Oskar Verkaaik (2004) argues, linked national belonging to ethnolinguistic and territorial identity and challenged the cosmopolitanism of ashraf classes.

In urban areas, Islamist political parties like the Jamaat-e-Islami had long claimed that the Pakistani state should move in the direction of becoming a genuine Islamic state based on Islamic law (shariat). They mobilized to compel state authorities to institutionalize and enforce Islamic injunctions to create an Islamic society. The shift to ethnolinguistic identity and Sufism invigorated an Islamist backlash that viewed it as a direct threat to their vision of an Islamic society and state. When General Zia-ul-Haq (1977–1988) overthrew the democratic government of Zulfiqar Ali Bhutto in a military coup, he adopted the Order of the Prophet (*Nizam-e-Mustafa*) platform of the Islamist-led Pakistan National Alliance, an alliance of opposition parties to the Bhutto government. While Islam had been acknowledged as the state religion since the Constitution of 1956, Islamization under Zia formalized the link between Islam and state sovereignty by establishing the Federal Shariat Court and elaborating the central place of Islamic law. These changes have left a lasting impact on Pakistani society, especially in terms of their negative consequences for women and religious minorities. For instance, the notorious Hudood Ordinances enacted in 1979 include laws that criminalize and decree severe punishments for adultery and extramarital sexual relations (*zina*). Ordinance XX passed in 1984 declared that the Ahmadiyya sect, an Islamic revival and reform movement that the state had previously declared non-Muslim, was now barred from claiming a Muslim identity and using Islamic symbols, thereby criminalizing their religious practice. The most lasting legacy of Islamization has been the increasing sectarianization of social life, the rise of militant Sunni and Shia organizations, and the proliferation of attacks against Muslim and non-Muslim minorities (Zaman 1998).

The pendulum swing between state authoritarianism, centralization, and Islamization, on the one hand, and democratization, provincialization, and ethnicization, on the other, provides a broad frame for understanding the intersecting forms of violence in urban Pakistan. The reestablishment of democracy in 1988 unleashed both sectarian and ethnolinguistic violence. Karachi was awash with violence in the 1990s, and it is not surprising that violence has been the focus of most anthropological and sociological accounts of Karachi (Ring 2006; Verkaaik 2004; Gayer 2014). Violence, of course, takes many forms and has many sources and certainly cannot be reduced to a single cause, but the perennial fragmentation along ethnic and sectarian lines that characterizes Karachi can be productively understood by examining the transformation of masculinity in Pakistan. In a rich ethnographic account of Karachi centered on Muhajirs, Urdu-speaking Muslim migrants from north and west India, Oskaar Verkaaik (2004) shows that Muhajir values had shifted from ashraf values of gentility and propriety (*adab*) to an emphasis on physicality, strength, and competitive street humor. Much like the Hindu nationalists in India described by Thomas Blom Hansen (1996), Muhajirs were seen "feminine" and "weak" relative to other ethnic communities like Pathans. Violence became a means for "recuperating masculinity" from their ethnic others. Performances of violence were also integral to the demands for recognition from the state. In a rich study of Islam and state sovereignty, Shenila Khoja-Moolji (2021) argues that the Pakistani state, particularly the Pakistani military, performs "Islamo-masculinity" in its claims to be defenders of the nation by constructing itself in the role of father that protects the women and children of the nation. Khoja-Moolji shows, however, that this role is contested by other forces like the Pakistani Taliban that reject the state's performance of sovereign authority by drawing an alternative relationship between Islam, masculinity, and state sovereignty. In Pakistan, an entire field of actors has emerged that both draws on and contests the sovereignty of the state, a theme we will return to in the next chapter.

For the Tablighis I came to know, Karachi's crisis—evidenced by both quotidian and dramatic forms of violence and by deep ethnolinguistic and sectarian divisions—was among the clearest signs that Muslims had abandoned Islam and had fallen into a state of moral chaos (fitna). Tablighis frequently noted the problems associated with male violence across the domestic and political realms as well as across the religious/secular divide, for instance in ethnic and Islamist political parties. They attributed this violence to the hardening and closing of men's hearts and said that this has created an unbridled drive for wealth and power. Tablighis invoke what Thomas Blom Hansen (1999) describes in the context of India as a sense of the "pleabeianization" of politics in that it has become dominated by those who lack control over their lower selves. One can see this discourse in the routine invocation in Tablighi discourse of the figure of the gangster (ghunda), a person whose power is based on brute force, fear, and coercion. In Tablighi narratives, the gangster, who is an object of fear and a source of mayhem in the neighborhood comes to the mosque to listen to a sermon and is radically transformed. God opens and softens his heart, allowing religion to settle in it. This creates in him a "cool" temperament that allows him to channel his natural tendencies like strength and courage toward the good. He is then able to draw his followers away from illicit activities toward moral ones, which radically transforms the neighborhood. Such narratives serve to underscore the claim that Islam is the solution to all the problems that afflict Muslims, especially violence and insecurity.

Politiks is a great source of moral chaos because it encourages men to act as willful agents in ways that violate the ethical parameters of Islam, parameters that require recognizing one's place in a kinship and religious hierarchy, hence the claim that politiks is the "worship of the self." This has unleashed an uncontrollable desire for wealth and power without any regard for the well-being of others, including even one's own family. Those with wealth and power, Tablighis say, treat those below them with harshness (*sakhti*), and those without power and wealth will resort to any means to acquire it. Moreover, politiks, according to Tablighis, leads to a situation in which each person claims for himself the mantle of Islam, which leads to intense contestation about who is the bearer of true Islam. It is this fragmentation of religious authority that Tablighis see as contributing rather than ameliorating the pervasiveness of moral chaos and disorder, and it is precisely this fragmentation that has become the source of deep consternation for Tablighis.

Tablighis insist that even legitimate religious authorities like the ulama are being drawn into politiks, and, as such, they are being drawn away from Islam. The ulama, too, they insist must do the work of dawat to become pious Muslims. Competing claims to Islamic authority indexes the state of impiety, and conflict is seen as a clear sign that Islam is being peddled by forces that are not genuinely Islamic. As one Tablighi informant noted, "there is now a pir (Sufi spiritual leader) under every rock and an alim (religious scholar) in every shop, but you'll never see them at the mosque!" Tablighis regard this cacophony of voices claiming the mantle of Islam as being in many ways an effect of new information technologies, which is why they repeatedly insist that only the human voice can communicate Islam. But the technologies themselves, for Tablighis, embody the worship of the self, an ethic in which every individual, regardless of the state of their spirituality, comes to speak on behalf of Islam. One can see the dangers of talk that we addressed in chapter 3 as a product of the use of new information and communication technologies. As with orthodox movements in other parts of the world, the usage of communication technologies is seen as a threat to the interiority of the pious subject (Fader 2017). Tablighis see the proliferation of Islamic authorities and the mass mediation of Islam as entangled problems because they result in people whose lower selves are not disciplined speaking for Islam. As such voices proliferate, Islam becomes unhinged from its traditional moorings, creating "innovations" (biddat) or accretions and changes to the original Islam of the Prophet, hence making it more and more difficult to draw God's power to one's aid. Contestation of Islamic authority, then, is bound up with the spread of false Islam and claims to Islamic authority have themselves become a principal source of moral chaos.

The Tablighi Jamaat is only one in a dizzying field of Islamic forces shaping Pakistan's public sphere today. The Islamization of public life pursued by the state and specifically the martial regime of General Zia-ul-Haq (1977–1988) cultivated a climate in which countless Islamic revivalist currents, including militant ones, thrived. The loosening of government regulations on private media and the general liberalization of the economy since the early 2000s has created the space for the rise of many popular televangelists, radio broadcasters, new educational institutions, online communities, companies, and organizations that claim the mantle of Islamic legitimacy. Facilitated by new information technologies, this flurry of Islamic revivalist activity has meant that the Islamic public sphere is increasingly experiencing what Eickelman and Piscatori (1996) have called the "fragmentation of authority" in which traditional religious authorities like the ulama and prominent Sufi sheikhs now share space with a host of other contenders. Tablighis regard this fragmentation of authority as symptomatic of moral chaos.

Postcolonial scholars of South Asia have long pointed to the role of state governmentality in reifying caste, ethnic, and religious identities, which then become the basis for political conflict (Dirks 2001; Breckenridge and Van der Veer 1993; Mahmood 2016). The effort of the Pakistani state to define Islam as the pivotal object of national culture and identity has led to reification of both ethnic and sectarian identities. A centralized state controlled primarily by the army that is invested in Islam as a unifying and centralizing ideology has therefore intensified the politics of representation along both ethnic and sectarian lines. As Saba Mahmood (2016) argues in the context of Egypt, interventions into the sphere of religion can essentialize and reify religious identities and narrow the space for religious dialogue and engagement. Similarly in Pakistan, state Islamization has created a space of intense competition over the mantle of Islam. It would then not be inaccurate to say that what Tablighis recognize about politiks as a source of political fragmentation are the essentializing and reifying dimensions of Islamic governmentality and the fierce and violent contestation for Islamic authority that has become central to public and political life in Pakistan.

The political fragmentation of national life has engendered a deep and widespread sense of crisis that Tablighis frame in the idiom of moral chaos. But the sharp boundary that Tablighis draw between religion and the world and dawat and politiks does not mean that Tablighis restrict themselves to the formal processes of dawat alone. Rather, dawat engenders an alternative form of sovereign intervention into the world.

Pious Mediation and the Moral Regeneration of Islamic Life

We saw in previous chapters how Tablighis understand pious companionship and how this is structured by an ethics of hierarchy as a necessary means to cool the passions and mold faith into proper shape by regulating the lower self. For Abid, whom we met in chapters 2 and 4, it was the continuous presence of Hazrat in his life that kept him from all bad activities. "Whenever I think of doing something bad, I ask myself, what would Hazrat think, and it keeps me from all bad activities. It is our relation (nisbat) to our Elders that keeps us on the right path." Abid explained that when he was involved in smuggling, he knew that what he was doing in life was wrong, but it was only forging relations in the Tablighi Jamaat and ultimately his relationship with Hazrat that compelled him to change his life. He decided that he, too, wanted to be a force for good in the world. Hazrat provided a model for him, and what stood out to Abid about Hazrat was not only Hazrat's ritual devotion but, along with that, his capacity for dealing with others in a just manner.

One of the central roles that Hazrat performed at his spiritual house was addressing people's problems and particularly mediating conflicts (*sulha karana*). Every day, Hazrat's many followers, who were spread out across the city and even various parts of the country, would bring people to consult Hazrat on how to deal with a family or community conflict in the hope of finding a solution to the problem and some basis for reconciliation. These problems ranged from interpersonal conflicts over differing interpretations of religious duties to the most recalcitrant and divisive problems over money and property. In cases of money and property, the various stakeholders would otherwise have to go to courts for a solution, but many sought Hazrat's counsel because they wanted to avoid the courts, which they believed were not good at meting out justice and also produced bitter acrimony between parties. Unsurprisingly many of these conflicts were between family members who did not want to escalate by taking their issues to the courts and who wanted to find a basis for reconciliation. Finding a pious mediator like Hazrat was seen by many as a more effective way to address conflicts while preserving kinship relations.

The Tablighi Jamaat generates Islamic authority and places it in the hands of an ever-expanding sphere of people. Indeed, one of the implicit although never fully stated aims of the Tablighi Jamaat is to transform the mosque into a site of pious mediation such that people can bring their grievances and concerns to be addressed. As one Tablighi explained to me, "the mosque was once a major institution for Muslims and people spent time there and came to find solutions to their problems but now it is seen as just seen as only a space for the mandatory prayers." Tablighis often nostalgically yearn for times when the mosque served as a vital community institution and a place where big decisions were made on behalf of the community. Islamic authority, Tablighis often lament, no longer carries the moral weight that it once did. Religion, Tablighis say, is made of five spheres including customs and habits (*muashirat*), creed (*aqida*), interpersonal dealings (*muamilat*), morality (*akhlaq*), and worship (*ibadat*), but today it has been mostly reduced only to a focus on worship. One of the central aims of dawat is to imbue Islamic authority with moral weight, to make it a part of the lives of Muslims in all spheres of life, and to turn the mosque into a site for the exercise of sovereign authority.

Once, as Abid and I were sitting in the mosque, a young man came and kneeled next to him. The young man glanced at me and hesitated a bit, but then gradually eased into a narrative about his brother. He said that his younger brother has stopped giving money to his home, even though his family is struggling because his father is ill and has not been able to work. The entire responsibility for the parents, he said, is now on his shoulders, as his other brother is jobless. With two young children of his own, this had created a deep strain in his own marital life, with his wife being perpetually angry at him, his parents, and his brothers. Abid told the young man that he should first pray to God to give him guidance (hidayat) and to open and connect their hearts. But, he also told him that he would be happy to discuss the matter with both of them if that is what he would like. The young man, to my knowledge, never brought his brother in to see Abid, but it was clear that Abid could serve the function of pious mediation if it was needed. If this pious mediation failed, Abid would surely have taken the young man to Hazrat for a more powerful form of pious intervention.

While conflicts among kin are the primary site for pious mediation, conflicts in the larger community also occasionally are brought to Tablighis. Take the example of a Tablighi named Asghar. Asghar had been a committed Tablighi since the late 1980s and so was an experienced Tablighi and the head (amir) of his local congregation. Unlike Abid, who was a migrant from rural Punjab, Asghar grew up in Karachi and was from a middle-class, educated Urdu-speaking family. Like many Urdu-speaking people in Karachi, Asghar's family was closely tied to the Jamaat-e-Islami political party in the 1970s. But, in the 1990s, as he was coming of age, he found his way into the Tablighi Jamaat. When I visited Asghar, he asked me to accompany him to the local mosque. Asghar was there to mediate a conflict between two young men from the community who had been involved in a business transaction involving joint investment in a rikshaw. The rikshaw had been involved in an accident while one of the boys was driving it that left it considerably damaged, creating a conflict over how much responsibility there was for its repair and who would pay. Rather than involve the police, which they felt could cost the family more as the police may extract a bribe and could even lead to the loss of the vehicle, the families of the boys sought the council of Asghar, who was well known in the area as someone who could fairly adjudicate the matter. Asghar convened the two boys' families in the mosque to discuss the loss of property. Asghar began the pious mediation with the invocation that as Muslims, they are connected through their relation to the Prophet and thus should try to find a common ground. He asked the boys why they embarked on a joint venture, while emphasizing their deep emotional connection by pointing to the importance of friendship and how much the Prophet valued friendship. The goal of this was to stress the sense of moral relatedness between the two. In the end, the young men decided that they would simply split the cost of the repairs. Whether kinship or friendship, the purpose of pious mediation is to stress the relationship between people by invoking Prophetic example, the pious Companions, or other examples of exalted Muslims from the past to affirm their mutual obligation to one another as Muslim brothers.

Dawat confers Islamic authority on Tablighis who are trained in the virtues, and there is a general acceptance that they can address kinship and communal conflicts. A person like Abid from a humble, rural, working-class background can go from being a petty smuggler to someone with the moral wherewithal to intervene in sensitive matters of family life. Similarly, Asghar developed a reputation in his neighborhood for being a pious person who could resolve communal conflicts. The Tablighi becomes capable of regenerating moral relationships and restoring moral order even beyond the congregation. If Abid and Asghar can resolve small-scale local conflicts, the Elders of the Tablighi Jamaat are widely acknowledged both within the movement and beyond as being capable of mediating much greater issues like ethnic and sectarian conflicts. Pious mediation is a form of sovereign intervention that can regenerate moral relationships of kinship and community.

Pious mediation is not formalized or even officially acknowledged by Tablighis, and Tablighis often insist that their only role is to perform dawat. This erasure from explicit discourse is important because Tablighis want to restrict such moral intervention to those who are capable of performing it. They certainly do not want new companions to assume the role of communal authorities. One can see why this would be a serious threat to the integrity of the movement. If people do not abide by the limits of their capacities, then they can easily undermine the moral authority of the Tablighi Jamaat. As we saw in chapter 4, the tendency to be overzealous in one's pursuit of pious authority is regulated by the ethics of hierarchy. In chapter 5, we also saw how pious masculinity is involved recognizing the limits of pious agency to create a harmonious home. Here, we see similarly that pious authority involves a self-limiting form of power that allows the Tablighi to conduct himself with a keen eye toward fairness and justice. The emphasis on deference to authority limits the assumption of this authority. Tablighis often refuse to perform such roles, just as they refuse to assume authority over theological matters and encourage people to seek the guidance of the pious Elders. The steady flow of non-Tablighis brought by their local Tablighis to the quarters of the Elders at the Tablighi markaz attests to the potency of the ethics of hierarchy as a mechanism for regulating the exercise of pious authority. It is precisely this self-limiting form of power that Tablighis see as a solution to the unruly agency of politiks and the basis for the moral regeneration of Islamic life.

Pious Authority and the Paradox of Islamization

When I would visit Abid to discuss dawat, he would invariably take me to a nearby juice house where he insisted on buying me juice. Despite my considerably higher socioeconomic status and my repeated protests, Abid said this was all part of his duty (*farz*). One of the six principles (che batein) of the Tablighi Jamaat is the principle of "honoring of Muslims" (*ikram-e-Muslim*). This is a broad ethics of care that encompasses all manner of large and small acts of kindness directed toward fellow Muslims, a general commitment to helping other Muslims in times of need. But one of its key manifestations is the voluntary giving of small gifts, usually of food and drink, to fellow Tablighis in the congregation. Such gifts go above and beyond the mandatory contribution to the congregation each individual is obligated to give, and these voluntary gifts are seen as the basis for a heightened sense of connection between Tablighis and belonging in the congregation. The gifts are usually small gestures like buying the mosque or itinerant congregation sweets that do not come out of the general budget to which all participants have contributed. They are efforts to show that Tablighis are connected to each other in relations of mutuality that exceed the otherwise meticulous calculation of contributions required for participation in the life of the congregation. Abid's refusal to let me buy him a juice, however, implied that I was not part of those relations of mutuality that are part of the congregation and remained a "guest." "Arsalan, this is Allah's work and our purpose in life. We must sacrifice for Allah. I am giving you dawat, so I cannot take anything in return from you." Dawat, in other words, was about satisfying God and could not be for any material gain. To benefit from dawat would be to undermine its efficacy. Abid explained that there is a big difference between practices done for God and those for worldly rewards, those done for religious merit (sawab) and those done for self-interest (*mafaad*). This, he explained, is the main difference between dawat in the Tablighi Jamaat and other Islamic groups that claim to be doing similar work for God.

In his classic work *The Gift*, Marcel Mauss argues that gifts in traditional societies are means through which to establish and continue relations of moral obligation. Gifts carry the spirit of the giver and thus demand reciprocity. In "gift economies," there is no distinction between altruism and interest because gifts simultaneously advance one's own interests and create relations of reciprocity that are necessary for social and economic reproduction. As Carrier (1995) argues, in gift economies, people cannot conceive of any act as being purely self-interested or purely altruistic in nature. In commodity or market logic, by contrast, objects are alienable, not tied to the identities of those who are exchanging them, and they do not create relations of mutual obligation. Carrier argues that it is only in contexts in which commodity logic is ascendant that people come to imagine an act being purely self-interested or purely altruistic and they come to reconceptualize the gift as something freely given and disinterested, a pure gift, something that is understood as distinct from and radically at odds with self-interest. Abid's claim above and refusal to accept a return gift from me invokes the division between a pure gift as the mark of religion, something done for God with no material reward, and worldly pursuits characterized by self-interest.

The logic of the pure gift, I want to argue, anchors the Tablighi understanding of pious authority as distinct from invocations of Islam in statist and market variants of Islam that permeate Pakistani life (see Anderson 2011). It is by drawing on this logic of sacrifice for God that Tablighis construct and define themselves against what they see as the self-interested exercise of power in the world. As mentioned earlier, the figure of the market (bazaar) emerges routinely as a space of self-interest and ruthless and cutthroat competition against the mosque as a space of sacrifice, moral cultivation, and pious relationality. Importantly, the market is also conceived as a feminized space where men and women must interact in ways that challenge and threaten gendered segregation of pardah as well as a place where the temptations of the tongue run rampant. Crucially, as noted in chapter 1, many Tablighis come from the trader classes, and this construction of the market in Tablighi discourse becomes immediately representative of an experience of moral ambivalence toward the pursuit of money and power, while the mosque becomes a site of purification from this ambivalence and a space of moral certainty. When Tablighis give each other gifts of *ikraam*, they enact an ethics of care that involves voluntary acts of kindness toward fellow Muslims. These acts of care are precisely the inversion of the relations generated in the world overrun by self-interest. The acts of ikraam typify dawat as sacrifice for God and one enacted willfully. The pious authority generated from this willful sacrifice is understood by Tablighis as the basis for transcending the conflict and competition of the world.

For Tablighis in Pakistan, the uptake of Islam in modernist institutions of state and corporations is morally charged because it blurs the distinction between religion and the world. It can thus compromise Islam's standing in the eyes of Muslims and lead them away from Islam. What is central to the world in Tablighi construction is that it centers the individual as a locus of agency and moral value in a way that Tablighis see as anathema to Islam. Two entangled issues arise for Tablighis when religion and the world become entangled. First, the invocation of Islam in institutions of the state and corporations is seen as sites of constant innovation because Islam insofar as it is shaped by material interests comes to be constantly molded to the demands of those interests. Second, the relationships established in modernist institutions like political parties or corporations are not seen as voluntary but instead structured by political and economic necessity. As one Tablighi explained in no uncertain terms, "A person feels compelled to stay in the Tablighi Jamaat because they have faith in Allah and because they can feel a closeness to Allah but in 'worldly institutions' [*dunyavi idare*] people are there because they have to earn a living and have no choice. In dawat, a person is there because he feels closeness to Allah." In Tablighi ritual ideology, then, by contrast, the space of the congregation is simultaneously one of enactment of an original Islam, free from innovation, as well as one in which submission to authority is freely enacted. The Tablighi congregation thus escapes the twin ills of the world: self-interest and domination.

In Pakistan, state-driven Islamization from the late 1970s through the 1980s has given rise to a range of new Islamic actors and institutions, including corporations, banks, new education institutions, televangelists, and NGOs, all of which claim the mantle of Islamic authority. This Islamic revivalist activity has placed Islamic piety at the center of social and political life, but it has also proliferated claims and counterclaims to Islamic authority, leading to an intense fragmentation of Islamic authority in the public sphere (Eickelman and Piscatori

1996). The process of state Islamization and marketization of Islam has produced deep anxieties that Islamic authority is becoming a ruse for the pursuit of self-interest and domination and thus unmoored from ethical life. Stereotypes about "the mullah" with a fat stomach preying on innocent and naive worshippers abound in Pakistani public discourse, and such discourses are not just from those who advocate for a liberal or secular public sphere (see Khan 2012). One of the key failures of the Islamization of political and economic life is that it has engendered deep concerns across many segments of the population that Islamic authority has been emptied of its ethical substance and become a ruse for the pursuit of base desires and interests (Roy 1994).

It is against this political backdrop that dawat's popularity as a pure sacrifice for God and the pious authority generated in dawat comes to be seen as a solution to the crisis of political fragmentation and the basis for the moral regeneration of Islamic life. In his work on Sufi Islam in Turkey, Brian Silverstein (2011) argues that the expansion of mass-mediated forms of Islam has created a "nostalgia for immediation," a desire to return to the original voiced presence of God embodied in the face-to-face interaction (176–78). Indeed, the Tablighi investment in the face-to-face nature of dawat and embodied co-presence in the mosque reflects this nostalgia for immediation against not only mass-mediated forms of Islam but also their entanglement with modernist institutions and profit-driven aims. In a context where state Islamization has generated deep divisions and conflicts, the commitment to the ritual immediacy of dawat is also a "structural nostalgia" for a sacred hierarchy that is separate from the social and political hierarchies of political and economic life (P. Silverstein 2004; see also Hickel 2015). This nostalgia for hierarchy is also what Charles Piot (2010) aptly describes as a "nostalgia for the future" insofar as hierarchy is the means for moral transformation of the self and the creation of an Islamic moral order in the future.

The ethics of hierarchy that I have outlined in this book is a reflexive response to what is understood, broadly, as a corruption of the hierarchies of religious and political authority. The ethics of hierarchy provides a structure for the growth and expansion of pious authority as well as a regulatory framework that aims to keep pious authority anchored in ethical life. It is against the backdrop of political fragmentation that the ritual immediacy of dawat, the constitution of a sacred hierarchy, and the regulatory power of the ethics of hierarchy comes to be seen as an alternative form of sovereignty to that of the Islamic state and a means for transcending the political fragmentation and violence of life in postcolonial Pakistan.

The Tablighi concerns about the corruption of politiks does not mean there are no overlapping goals and concerns with other Islamic movements in Pakistan.

Pakistani liberals and leftists often point out that regardless of how different the means adopted by Islamic movements, they ultimately share the same ends, placing Islam at the center of life and displacing all other forms of being Muslim. The consequence of Islamic movements, many say, is ultimately the "religious violence" that permeates life in Pakistan. In the next and final chapter, we take up the question of religious violence in one of its most glaring forms, the growing moral panic around blasphemy accusations and the violence of blasphemy politics. I show that blasphemy politics occurs at the intersection of state sovereignty and populist Islamic movements, and that the division that Tablighis draw between religion and the world and dawat and politiks structures a reflexive ethical stance on blasphemy politics that, while recognizing blasphemy to be a moral injury, bypasses the moral outrage of blasphemy politics and provides an alternative response to moral injury. This opens the space to think about the sources of religious violence in postcolonial Pakistan.

7

THE ETHICAL AFFORDANCES OF PIETY AND THE SPECTER OF RELIGIOUS VIOLENCE

"We're all gathered here, and we are here to show our love for the Prophet," declared Owais Noorani, vice president of the Jamaat-e-Ulama-e-Pakistan, a political organization of the Barelwi denomination. In the background, one could hear the crowd of nearly fifty thousand men chanting "Allah ho Akbar." Cameras zoomed in on flushed faces. Reporters scribbled furious descriptions of fiery speeches by well-known Islamist leaders. It seemed like a spontaneous gathering of zealous Muslims, a heated, groundswell rejection of the government's timid nods toward amending Pakistan's blasphemy laws, but this was a carefully staged event for mass viewing. The Islamist organization Jamaat-ud-Dawa, well known as a front for the banned militant outfit Lashkar-e-Taiba, sponsored this rally near the Quaid-e-Azam's *mazar* in Karachi to reject any hint of amending the blasphemy laws. The area was cordoned off, traffic was blocked, and the police were deployed in full force for the security of attendees. Journalists were hailed in through the blockade. Islamist leaders from across Sunni denominations were in attendance like Qazi Hussain Ahmed of the Jamaat-e-Islami and Maulana Fazl-ur-Rahman of the Jamiat-e-Ulama-e-Islam, the former a modernist party and the latter attached to the Deobandi tradition. United in their defense of blasphemy laws, they delivered impassioned speeches from atop a footbridge, while the rank and file sat on the street below draped in green and white flags embellished with political slogans and Quranic *ayats*. It was a meticulously planned event that brought together Islamist parties from across Sunni denominational boundaries.

My research on the Tablighi Jamaat overlapped with heightened local and global concerns about the human rights abuses around the blasphemy laws. This interest had been surging because of the well-publicized case of Asia Masih popularly known as Asia Bibi, a Christian mother of five who had been accused of blasphemy in a small Punjabi village. The accusers claimed that she uttered blasphemous words about the Prophet, but reports suggest that the tensions were sparked after she drank water from a public well using the same utensils that were used by Muslims, which outraged the caste sensibilities of the latter. In a case that took on global significance and became evidence of an absence of religious freedom in Pakistan, Asia Bibi was convicted and sentenced to death by hanging in November 2010.[1] On January 4, 2011, less than a year into my research, Salman Taseer, the governor of the Punjab province and a well-known liberal politician, was assassinated by a guard in his own security detail for publicly defending Asia Bibi. The murderer, Mumtaz Qadri, was hailed as a hero by many Pakistanis, and Islamist parties brought out rallies in his defense.[2] Islamist activists at the rally insisted that the laws could not be changed because they are prescribed in the Quran and Prophetic tradition and are thus "sacred." No human being, they insisted, has the power to amend these laws. In such a scenario, to call them a "black law" as Taseer had declared, they insisted, was itself an act of blasphemy.

One of the most significant changes brought about under Zia's Islamization was the expansion of Pakistan's blasphemy laws. The Indian Penal Code of 1860 introduced laws protecting places of worship and sacred objects from damage and defilement (Section 295), religious assemblies from disturbance (Section 296), funeral remains and burial sites from malicious trespass (Section 297), and religious feelings of any person from deliberate insult (Section 298). Zia sought to bolster his Islamic credentials by expanding the laws to explicitly protect Islamic symbols and sentiments, including Section 295-B against defiling of the Quran and Section 295-C, which prescribes death for defilement of the sacred personage of the Prophet. The passing of these laws has undeniably created a surge of blasphemy cases, many of which have led to mob violence, and while Sunni Muslims make up the majority of the accused, religious and sectarian minorities are disproportionately affected by these laws (International Commission of Jurists 2015). According to a recent report by the Jinnah Institute, nearly a thousand cases of blasphemy have been registered since 1986. Of these cases, 476 have been registered against Muslims (various denominations), 479 against Ahmadis (who by law are classified as non-Muslim), and 180 against Christians. The report notes that in 2010 alone, sixty-four people were charged under the so-called "blasphemy law," and thirty-two people were killed extrajudicially either by mobs or individuals (Jinnah Institute 2015). In August 2009, a mob of at least 150 attacked a Christian community in Gojra, setting forty houses and a church on fire, burning eight people alive including four women and a child, and injuring at least eighteen others. Earlier the same year, trained militants opened fire on Ahmadis as they prayed, massacring ninety-three people. These are only some of the most dramatic incidents of violence and persecution in recent years, but everyday discrimination against religious minorities in schools, universities, and the workplace is ubiquitous.

Human rights activists have long argued that the blasphemy laws are readily weaponized against minorities, but many recognize that abolition may not be a politically feasible possibility in the current political climate. With fears of reprisals against those who call for reform of the laws, there is good reason for caution.[3] Such cases show that the law itself has become an object of intense affective force. Many human rights activists and workers, therefore, accept that what is needed is to reform the laws to eliminate those aspects of the law that lend them most readily to abuse. Significant in this is the fact that the blasphemy laws, unlike many other criminal laws, have no place for recognizing or probing the "intention" of the accused. Because of this feature, the blasphemous act can never be repeated in a court of law, and this makes it impossible to determine what specifically was said and the context of its utterance. This necessarily means that people's guilt is determined more by their identity as it is perceived by others than by evidence, which allows them to be wielded readily against religious minorities, both Muslim and non-Muslim. This coupled with the extreme punishments ranging from imprisonment for a minimum of two years to a life sentence and in the case of 295-C, the law against defiling the sacred personage of the Prophet, the death penalty has made these laws into a great source of fear and insecurity for religious minorities.

The blasphemy laws and the moral outrage and violence created around them have generated a sizeable body of academic literature. Talal Asad (2009) argues that the response to blasphemy among Muslims in events like the Danish cartoon controversy has become a source of civilizational identity through which the West defines itself as a space of freedom against an intolerant Islam. From this perspective, the response among Muslims and around the Muslim world demonstrates to liberal secularists the incompleteness of the secularization of Muslims. Muslim societies from this perspective need to reform Islam and encourage critical reasoning and tolerance for free speech. Asad argues that the moral injury experienced in cases of blasphemy is inscrutable from the vantage point of this liberal-secular framework because it presupposes a self-owning individual who is entitled to the expression of his or her own beliefs. Liberal secularism places ultimate value on "authentic belief" and sees the right to expression as inalienable and the quintessence of freedom, which makes commitments to religious normativity a forfeiture of the self. For Muslims, by contrast, Asad (2009) argues, "blasphemy is neither 'freedom of speech' nor the challenge of a new truth but something that seeks to disrupt a living relationship," and this makes it "impossible to remain silent in the face of blasphemy" (46).

In the same volume, Saba Mahmood expands on this line of reasoning. Drawing on Keane's (2007) notion of a semiotic ideology, or cultural understanding of what signs are and how they work, Saba Mahmood argues that liberal secularism draws a sharp distinction between signified and signifier and one in which the relationship between the former and the latter is a relationship of arbitrariness. Such a semiotic ideology, as Keane argues, creates a "representational" understanding of language in that signs stand for already given material realities. The Islamic tradition, by contrast, Mahmood argues, is built on the structuring and constitutive power of sacred signs. It is through the sacred personage of the Prophet that one establishes a relationship to God, and blasphemy disrupts this living relationship and thus represents for Muslims a form of moral injury (Mahmood 2009).

These arguments, however, come perilously close to suggesting that blasphemy politics and violence are direct consequences of the Islamic tradition and run the risk of suggesting that the moral outrage and panic around blasphemy that we see at an escalating scale in countries like Pakistan is an inevitable product of a provocation rather than a moral panic. This can easily end up reproducing the notion that there is an unbridgeable chasm between the West and Islam when it comes to speech acts and sacred objects. Asad Ali Ahmed, by contrast, shifts the focus away from such categorical differences between the Islamic tradition and Western thought and focuses instead on the mediating role of the colonial state in creating the conditions for the rise of new affective publics centered on the defense of the Prophet. Ahmed shows that the blasphemy laws were originally conceived under British colonialism as a means for regulating what were presumed to be uncontrollable religious passions that led to communal conflicts between religious communities, and thus as sites of creating public order, but ultimately ended up escalating communal conflict.

In Pakistan, as Islam and state sovereignty become entangled, the laws shift from generally defending religious symbols of different religious communities to the specific and focused protection of Islamic symbols. Ahmed argues that while the framers of the laws argued that they preserved intercommunal harmony, the laws themselves engender the very passions that they are meant to regulate. The blasphemy laws, he argues, depend on evidence that "religious sentiments" have been hurt, and thus the degree of moral outrage generated by the affront itself becomes the basis for restitution and punishment. In this sense, the laws constitute a "structure of incitement and regulation" generating the very passions that they are meant to regulate (Ahmed 2009). This argument takes us into the law as a technique of governance that has a constitutive role in generating "religious violence" away from the reductive and commonly held notion that blasphemy politics is simply an extension of the Islamic tradition. The law as an embodiment of state sovereignty becomes a basis for the escalation of intercommunal rivalries, and legal punishment is itself invoked as a duty of sovereign authority. Vigilantism follows when the state, or the actors within the state, are seen as failing to act in accordance with the law and with their role as an Islamic sovereign. Indeed, this is precisely how Salman Taseer's murderer, Mumtaz Qadri, was transformed into a heroic martyr (*shaheed*) for Islam whose love for the Prophet compelled him to act when the state failed to fulfill its duties.

In a detailed study, Farhat Haq (2019) argues that blasphemy politics entails simultaneously the sacralization of the state and the secularization of the shariah. She argues that the blasphemy laws have come to be construed by proponents of blasphemy politics as having a status of being divine and therefore not changeable, when in fact they reflect the modern transformation of the shariah from a broad and flexible moral framework in the precolonial period to a law in the modern sense backed by state power (Haq 2019; see Hallaq 2013).[4] The constitutive role of the laws in the violence of blasphemy and the need to dismantle them is also recognized as a necessity among human rights activists and legal scholars in Pakistan (Siddique and Hayat 2008). It, then, is not surprising that blasphemy accusations have surged in Pakistan since the codification of these laws. The sacralization of the law and, by extension, state sovereignty is presupposed in blasphemy politics and in the acts of vigilante violence against those accused of blasphemy.

Indeed, blasphemy politics has become a key performative arena in which claims to Islamic authority are played out as various groups jostle to demonstrate that they are the true "lover of the Prophet" (*ashiq-e-Rasool*). As I noted earlier, blasphemy politics draws Islamist groups from across Sunni denominations and thus is not reducible to doctrinal differences and commitments. Instead, blasphemy politics has become a means for claiming sovereign authority in popular politics and is thoroughly entangled with the defense of the Islamic nation from both internal and external threats. Not surprisingly many of the same Islamic parties and groups that take up blasphemy politics formed the Defence of Pakistan Council (*Difa-e-Pakistan* Council) in response to the US-led NATO attack in Pakistan that left dead twenty-four Pakistani soldiers in 2011. Many of the blasphemy controversies that took on national significance have been framed around the idea of foreign conspiracies against Islam and Pakistan, including the Danish Cartoon Controversy mentioned earlier, the publications of Charlie Hebdo, and the anti-France protests around the alleged presentation of blasphemous caricatures by a French teacher who was subsequently murdered. Blasphemy politics in Pakistan represents what Richard Handler (1988) calls the "negative vision" of nationalism, the fear that the nation will be dismembered by internal and external threats through attacks on the cultural or religious basis of unity. Blasphemy politics is, therefore, comparable to the moral panics in defense of the sacred symbols of nationhood that we see throughout the world, including the racialized violence of Christian nationalism in the United States, Hindutva moral panic and vigilante violence around cow slaughter, fears of Rohingya invasion among Buddhist nationalists in Myanmar, and fears of Islam and particularly women's veiling practices as a threat to the French Republic.

The question, however, that arose for me in my fieldwork is: if Tablighis understand the model of the Prophet to be the constitutive basis for the creation of the sacred ties that bind the Islamic community, why do they not seem to take up blasphemy politics with the same alacrity that other Islamic movements do? In the previous chapter, I outlined the Tablighi critique of politiks as a fount for moral chaos because it violated the terms of pious relationality and thus was a source of political fragmentation. In this chapter, I take up the question of how Tablighis draw on this perspective to respond to the surge of blasphemy politics. While Tablighis were deeply troubled by what they believed was a proliferation of blasphemous materials in the world, they recognized the moral outrage and violence around blasphemy to be a troubling sign that Muslims had lost control of their passions and affirmed the importance of dawat as a means for creating moral order. While blasphemy politics depends on treating state law as a sacred object and thus collapsing the difference between religion and the world, Tablighis draw on this distinction to insist that what is paramount is reproducing the conditions for the flourishing of dawat. Dawat redirects the passions for enacting transcendent principles in blasphemy politics and thus mitigates the violence of blasphemy politics. The ethical stance that Tablighis take on blasphemy highlights the limits of liberal and secular framings of religious violence which are predicated on a division between private and public that collapses the diverse constructions of religion into a single monolith, eliding the ethical affordances of religion in public life. This not only obscures the roots of religious violence in Pakistan but also makes it impossible to understand how Islamic piety comes to be seen by so many Muslims as a basis for addressing the crisis of religious violence in postcolonial Pakistan.

Blasphemy Politics and the Ethical Affordances of Islamic Piety

The Tablighi Jamaat is explicit that the focus of dawat should be on Muslims. In Pakistan, where sectarian tensions run high, Tablighi Elders explicitly instruct practitioners not to pursue dawat directly with non-Sunnis. If a non-Sunni finds their way into a congregation, they should be encouraged to pursue dawat and not turned away, but the Elders caution Tablighis that preaching to anyone other than Sunni Muslims can escalate conflicts. Instead, they are encouraged to draw non-Muslims and non-Sunnis to dawat primarily by modeling exemplary behavior. Where sectarian divisions are woven into geography, as they often are in major urban centers in Pakistan, Tablighis avoid pursuing dawat in those areas so as not to exacerbate sectarian tensions. Itinerant Tablighis rely on a designated Tablighi from the local neighborhood who serves as a guide (*rahbar*). One of the central duties of the guide is to direct Tablighis to avoid houses of Shia and non-Muslim residents. As with trying to draw kinship authorities like parents to the movement, modeling the behavior of the Prophet becomes an indirect means to spread the movement without placing too much strain on delicate relationships. The major conflicts that arise for Tablighis in Pakistan are with fellow Sunnis, like the Islamists from the previous chapter, but also with Sunnis from different denominations (maslak) as they compete for control of mosques and neighborhoods.

These tensions do, in fact, escalate into open conflicts that turn into blasphemy accusations. On the outskirts of Multan, a region known as a hotbed for sectarian tensions and violence in Pakistan, we encountered a young man of about twenty years of age from the local jamaat named Ahmed who was acting as our guide (rahbar). The area was mostly poor and dilapidated, and most residents were working class or at the lower end of middle-class status who worked in outlying farms, traveled to the city to work as laborers, or were small traders. If educated, they had low-level clerical jobs. As we walked through the neighborhood, Ahmed recounted a recent incident about a conflict in a local mosque between Tablighis and the Barelwi imam of a mosque. He explained that the imam was trying to stop Tablighis from holding their daily reading sessions (taaleem) at the mosque. The Tablighis were trying to reason with him, but in a fit of rage, the imam had grabbed the Fazail-e-Amal, a book of accounts (*qissa*) of the Prophet and the Companions that Tablighis read as part of their core religious instruction, and flung it across the room. A few of the Tablighis had become enraged and had manhandled the imam for what they regarded as an act of grave disrespect and potential blasphemy given that the Fazail-e-Amal carries the name of the Prophet. Fellow Tablighis, however, subdued the outraged ones, and the imam was not seriously injured. According to Ahmed, there had been tensions brewing in the community for weeks before this. The Tablighi congregation decided this matter should be taken up in their own consultation (*mashwara*). In the consultation, he told us, it was agreed that the matter should be resolved without escalation because divisiveness in the community would undermine the prospects of dawat in the area. The decision was taken to acquire alternative accommodations for the daily readings, appeasing the imam and giving the mosque over to the Barelwi segment of the community.⁵

It was clear that Ahmed recounted this story to seek our advice on how to proceed because he understood us to be a congregation from a higher plane of pious authority with closer proximity to the Elders. The issue was brought up again later in the evening during the formal consultation with both the itinerant and local congregation. The Tablighis in the itinerant congregation affirmed that the decision was correct as nothing is worse for dawat than such communal tensions since they "make the heart hard" and therefore make it difficult for people to be affected by dawat. In such conversations, the solidifying of communal boundaries was discussed through the metaphor of the hardening of hearts. The hardening of the heart becomes in this discourse a blockage in the path of the sacred word, which leads Muslims away from realizing the virtues of Islamic piety. The Tablighi goal of creating a transcendental Islamic community requires that hearts be opened and softened through dawat, but a hardened heart would be unmoved by God's word.

Sectarian and ethnic conflicts, like other modes of fragmentation of the Islamic community, are understood through this idiom of closed and hard hearts and thus as obstacles in the path of the sacred words of dawat. These conflicts, then, must be de-escalated, hearts opened and softened, and the path of the sacred word cleared for circulation. Tablighis often noted that what is paramount in circumstances of conflict among Muslims is de-escalation, and, in cases like the one above where the affront is to one's religious sensibilities and passions, then it becomes imperative to emphasize the shared relationship to the Prophet and the importance of belonging to the Islamic community.

The conflict within the mosque was an intra-Sunni conflict and because Sunnis are the primary target of dawat, one might say that there was motivation to de-escalate. But, what about cases in which the accused is not seen as being within the boundaries of the larger moral community of Sunni Islam? Since they are not the target of dawat, does this mean that non-Sunni lives are disposable? Let me turn briefly to a conversation I had about the case of Asia Bibi and the subsequent assassination of Salman Taseer with Samad, a committed Tablighi in his early thirties who had been involved in the movement for many years. Samad did not know many details about the case against Asia Bibi. "Why did he [Taseer] not try to go through the proper Islamic channels?" Samad asked me when I raised the brutal murder of the governor. "He should have consulted the ulama on this, right? Instead, he made public statements that the law is a black law. This created outrage." I explained to Samad that Asia Bibi was convicted through a law that had some deep flaws. Specifically, I explained that because the law does not account for the intentionality of the speaker, one cannot even repeat the words that are being deemed blasphemous, so nobody even knows what precisely she is accused of saying. Such a law is rife for abuse, I explained, because there is no way to disprove the accusation. Samad conceded the point. "Arsalan, taking law into your own hands is absolutely not acceptable in any case but here you are right that such laws should be changed if they are being abused. They must be brought into line with shariat and the ulama should play a part in making sure that they are not abused."

While the Multan congregation concluded that the conditions for dawat would be undermined through the hardening of sectarian boundaries, for Samad, on the other hand, it was the gap between the current instantiation of the Islamic state and specifically Islamic law and the future ideal that came to be the focus of ethical reflection. The idealized state of Islam depends on the formation of a moral community, and, since that had not come to pass, there is considerable space for reformulating the law of the state, which is not divine and fixed but a project that can be changed in keeping with the needs of the time and according to the wisdom of Islamic authorities. The state law is not isomorphic with divine law here. Crucially, this position retains the notion that blasphemy is a moral injury and a threat to the Islamic community, but blasphemy is recognized as an effect of the hardening of hearts and the growing sectarianism of public life. Tablighis stress how the goal is not to punish in the here and now but to work for a future in which no acts of blasphemy occur, which depends on growing the Tablighi congregation through dawat.

Samad's position was significantly different from the Islamists parties and groups that have organized their politics around the creation of Islamic law and state. The rallying cry in blasphemy politics is that "there can be no revision in the law for the protection of the respect of the Prophet" (*namoos-e-risalat ke qanoon mein koi tarmeem nahin ho sakti*). The politics of moral outrage for Islamic political parties depends on collapsing the gap between divine and state law and insisting that the sacred then-and-there exists in the Islamic state as it exists in the here-and-now. It is this temporal collapse that undergirds the Islamist insistence that Taseer's critical statement about the laws is itself a blasphemous act. But, for many Tablighis, such a temporal collapse between the immanent and transcendent, human and divine, state law and sacred law is tantamount to usurping divine power, hence Samad's claim that one cannot take violence into one's own hands. For Samad, the temporal gap between the sacred then-and-there and the here-and-now created the potential for a different ethical stance on the problem of moral injury, one that emphasized the conceptualization of the Islamic state as an aspirational form and a process of becoming, a state to be realized in the future through dawat (cf. Khan 2012).

Tablighis' recognition of blasphemy as a moral injury that not only hurts the individual Muslim but destroys the potential for creating an Islamic community does not inevitably lead to the violence of blasphemy politics. Instead, Tablighis focus on an Islamic future made possible by dawat, and this focus on the future keeps at abeyance the escalation of conflict that ensues from blasphemy accusations. The escalation of conflict depends on creating an identity between the law of the Pakistani state in the here-and-now and the sacred law of the shariat as it existed at the time of the Prophet. Ensuring the creation of an Islamic future depends on reproducing the conditions for dawat, and this requires managing sectarian and religious conflict. The ethical stance on sectarian and religious boundary making and the desire to open the path of the sacred word reorients and channels religious passions toward dawat and away from sectarian violence and attacks that target sectarian and religious minorities.

Pakistan's blasphemy laws are a structuring condition for blasphemy politics, and the law can be seen as constituting violence, but this is not an inevitable product of the Islamic tradition. Rather, it depends on how the blasphemy laws are understood and how the injuries of blasphemy are thought to be best addressed. We can think of blasphemy laws as creating an ethical affordance. As Webb Keane (2016) notes, an affordance is a material property of an object that serves as a guide for how an object can or should be used. A chair, for instance, invites one to sit, but of course one need not take up this affordance. Similarly, legal structures like the blasphemy laws can be thought of as carrying ethical affordances, and the question to be asked is under what circumstances are such affordances taken up by different actors? When Islamic parties and movements take to the streets, as they did in defense of Mumtaz Qadri, they are claiming to be the embodiments of transcendental principles of Islam and defenders of the honor of the Prophet (*namoos-e-risalat*). They are claiming that the Islamic state has failed to uphold the transcendental principles of Islam and thus has relinquished its position as a mediator between the people of Pakistan and God. The moral outrage is inevitable, they claim, in that any "lover of the Prophet" would be moved to act in his defense, but it is also necessary because it compels the state to uphold the transcendental principles as enshrined in the constitution and the blasphemy laws. In other words, the moral outrage presupposes the sovereign power of the state as a mediating power between people and God and a keeper and enforcer of public morality and demands that it fulfill its divine mandate. Indeed, such logic can reasonably be called "populist" in that it construes the crowds that gather to defend the honor of the Prophet as the true subjects of the Islamic nation, the lovers of the Prophet, and the bearers of the transcendental principles of Islam, and thus the keepers of sovereign authority (see Laclau 2005).

It is beyond the scope of this book to provide a comprehensive explanation of the moral panic around blasphemy gripping Pakistan. Only a comprehensive study of the Islamist political parties and Islamic movements mobilizing in blasphemy politics can provide this understanding, but a few words are in order. Islamist mobilizations in blasphemy politics, as I noted earlier, index a pervasive fear of the dismemberment of the nation through an attack on the sacred symbols of Islam. Like populist forces around the world, Islamist movements perceive these threats from both religious "Others," as represented by Asia Bibi, and cosmopolitan elites, whom they see as disdainful toward Islam, represented by figures like the late Governor Salman Taseer, who was widely perceived to be living a Westernized and un-Islamic life. Islamic movements are mixed in terms of caste and class makeup; they draw from lower-middle to middle classes, from classes of traders who have historically been religious and conservative, and from the rural and urban poor. New middle classes are deeply invested in forms of Islamic piety and pious consumerism that provide a means for creating an alternative form of Islamic cosmopolitanism to that of the upper classes (Maqsood 2017). For the trader classes, Islamic piety has historically served as a basis to offset the stigmas associated with the management of money and the perceived lack of purity of the high caste (ashraf) and educated classes in Pakistan (Pernau 2013). For the rural and urban working classes, education in Islamic madrassas has been one of the few if not only bases for economic and social mobility. Islam is, therefore, entangled with all manner of class and caste mobility and aspiration in Pakistan. Blasphemy politics indexes anxieties about these class and caste aspirations in the face of various economic and political pressures. In the violence of blasphemy politics, we see the reassertion of the sovereign authority of Islam in public life against perceived and fabricated threats, internal and external, to Islam and Pakistan.

Tablighis come from the same middle classes, traders, and rural and urban working classes that are drawn to blasphemy politics, and yet, as I have suggested, Tablighis did not take to the streets to assert the sovereign authority of Islam. It behooves us to ask why this assertion of sovereign authority in blasphemy politics did not appeal to Tablighis. As I have argued, the ritualized construction of "directness" to God in dawat furnishes a different template for how to respond to the moral injury of blasphemy. We have seen how dawat finds in pious relationality and the ethics of hierarchy the presence of transcendence and thus the sacred means for mediating a relationship to God. This construction of transcendence does not sacralize the mediating power of the law and the state since, as I noted in the previous chapter, the state is also the biggest idol and thus incapable of creating a relationship to God. Instead, the Tablighi focuses on dawat as a sacred, transcendental means for the moral reproduction of the Islamic community.

The affordances of the Islamic law and the pious affordances of dawat despite being in tension are of course not mutually exclusive. Even in Samad's response, we can see these affordances jockeying for position. Samad notes that if there is a problem with Islamic law in Pakistan then it should be reformed and made to conform with the interpretation of the ulama. Tablighis remain committed to the authority of the Deobandi ulama, but the Deobandi ulama have also become actively involved with the project of creating an Islamic state. This makes it difficult for any Tablighi in Pakistan to unequivocally express a rejection of the Islamic state. Nevertheless, one can detect the ambivalence that afflicts many Tablighis over the very notion of the Islamic state. Like many Tablighis, Samad remained committed to the role of the state as a keeper and enforcer of public morality even if he recognized that the laws are subject to reform and that they are not fixed for all times and places. Yet, the ambivalence was enough to keep him and other Tablighis away from the pursuit of blasphemy politics. Instead, Tablighis worried like the rest of us about the destructive force of blasphemy politics and focused instead on reproducing the conditions for the moral reproduction and growth of the Islamic community.[6]

Islamic Piety and the Specter of Religious Violence

Nowhere is thinking about religious violence more important than in Pakistan. This requires thinking beyond some common framings of the problem of religious violence. In chapter 1, I argued that the formulation and codification of Islamic law was integrally bound up with colonial secularism and that this was a key element in creating the separation between religion and custom, and thus spurring the drive for purification of religion. The law 295-A inherited by the Pakistani Penal Code was formulated under British colonialism to manage "communal" tensions between religious communities, Hindu and Muslim, that were by virtue of religious differences seen as intrinsically prone to violence and conflict (Ahmed 2009). The law itself, however, is entangled in intercommunal rivalries as appeals come to be made to the sovereign state to adjudicate issues of religious affront.[7] As Islam becomes central to the definition of the nation in Pakistan and is progressively linked to state sovereignty through Islamization, the laws around the protection of religion come to be oriented primarily toward protecting Islamic symbols. One important line of continuity links the present Pakistani context to its colonial past. As with colonial secular governance, the Pakistani state and its representatives continue to claim that it is the presence of the law that maintains intercommunal harmony and that without the laws regulating religious affront, the religious passions of rival communities would be unleashed, and one would see a breakdown of public order. Whenever an incidence of mob lynching occurs over blasphemy, state representatives insist that the laws are being "misused" and claim that only the courts can adjudicate incidents of blasphemy. Ironically, the very mob made possible by the blasphemy laws comes to be used as unassailable evidence of the need for blasphemy laws and the reassertion of the sovereign authority of the state over the regulation of religious disputes, eliding the mediating role of law and state sovereignty in the creation of blasphemy politics.

The logic of state actors is not unlike dominant liberal and secular framings of religious violence in which it reflects a surfeit of religious zeal or passion that is born of properties intrinsic to religion. The liberal solution is making religion a private rather than public matter. Liberalism is far from hegemonic in Pakistan, but one certainly finds the same understanding of religious violence that one hears throughout the world. For instance, the columnist Khaled Ahmed (2012a) writes, "religion is based on certainty. It is certainty that breeds extremism and consequent violence." A respondent to the op-ed objects to the association between certainty and violence arguing that religious certainty is not the source of violence but its opposite: "Religion demands certainty when it comes to the tenets of imaan. It is absolute certainty about Allah Almighty and the Last Day that becomes the basis of guidance. Guidance cannot lead to extreme behaviour. It leads to patience, tolerance, compassion, kindness, wisdom, knowledge, etc. All these are essential for the development of a civilised society" (Ahmed 2012a). This response is quite similar to Tablighi conceptions that certainty (yaqeen) of faith (iman) must be cultivated as a condition for ethical action in the world. Certainty and faith here refer to a relationship to God that gives one the guidance to act in accordance with God's will and to act with balance and justice. To this, Khaled Ahmed (2012b) responds: "I am asked why I said that 'uncertainty' about one's held belief leads to tolerance of others' points of view. I was, in fact, referring to the rise of European relativism based on empirical evidence. In other words, starting with Enlightenment, nothing was certain unless proved by science." Ahmed's suggestion here is that Western science creates a culture of rationality and self-criticism that in turn becomes the basis for tolerance and mutual respect. By contrast, religion forecloses the possibility for self-reflection and, therefore, leads to intolerance and violence.

The movement from religiosity to violence in the previous statement construes religion as mindless, uncritical, and characterized by passional excess. Charles Hirschkind (2006) argues that liberal secularism, with its commitment to a privatized conception of religion, sees the presence of bodily signs of religiosity as affective excess that signals a lack of reason and rationality and is thus a threat to public order. By these standards, Tablighis, with their focus on bodily markers like beards and on highly conventionalized speech genres and gestures, have given themselves over to some external authority, a forfeiture of the self. Such religiosity implies excess commitment to and certainty about oneself and thus appears to harbor the threat of "communalist" identities deemed intrinsically hostile to religious and cultural differences (see Fernando 2014). This liberal framework also carries the secular commitment to limiting such "nonrational" forms of life to the private domain and the belief that such religiosity becomes a threat when it acts as the basis for public reason. It is the desire of the Islamic pietist to make Islam the basis of public life that, to borrow a phrase from Susan Harding (1991), makes him "the repugnant cultural other" of the liberal subject.

As William Cavanaugh (2009) has argued, commentators often treat "religious violence" as a unique form of violence based on a quest for transcendental truth, a feature commonly found in the writing on terrorism (see Juergensmeyer 2000). Cavanaugh notes that the very notion of religious violence presupposes a transhistoric object called "religion" that can be separated from "the secular," and thus erases the distinct processes through which religion is constituted in different contexts. The fears and anxieties around religious violence, however, are not provoked by all instances of the religious. It is nonliberal forms of religiosity like those of Tablighis that create liberal–secular moral panic about domination and violence. When nonliberal religiosity like that of the Islamic pietist adopts a stance of universal significance, it threatens the liberal–secular division of private and public, passion and reason, and religious and secular domains. In doing so, nonliberal religiosity comes to be seen as antirational and antimodern, and therefore a harbinger of intolerance, violence, and death.

This framework underpins approaches to "radicalization" and Islamic jihad in Western policy and intelligence discourses that have viewed Islamic piety movements like the Tablighi Jamaat as a steppingstone to Islamic militancy. If violence is a product of excess religious zeal, then it makes sense that Islamic movements that promote passions for religion are seen as creating the conditions for religious violence. This is why one analyst has described the Tablighi Jamaat as "jihad's stealthy legion" (Alexiev 2005), while another has described dawat as a "planned conquest of the world" (Gaborieau 1999, 21). Even if such perspectives do not exhaust liberal and secular understandings in Pakistan, they are common enough. I was told routinely that the "blind" devotion to Islamic authorities in the Tablighi Jamaat and the "brainwashing" of Tablighis primed them for Islamic militancy. In other words, the very ethics of hierarchy that I have described as anchoring an alternative to blasphemy politics was seen by many as the basis for the creation of blind and mindless crowds demanding the death of blasphemers. Acquaintances often described the signs of Islamic iconicity like beards as signs of dangerous and surplus religious passions. On one occasion, an elderly activist who is well known in liberal and progressive circles in Karachi, upon seeing my beard growing longer, said to me, "please shave, you are beginning to scare me."

I have shown in this chapter how the ethical affordances of Islamic piety defy these framings of religious violence as simply products of surplus religious passions, but of course it is not that there is no basis for the concerns expressed about Islamic movements in Pakistan. Feminist critiques that the Tablighi Jamaat promotes a patriarchal worldview are undeniable. As I have argued, Islamic piety in the Tablighi Jamaat is premised on distinct and hierarchical gender roles for men and women. Dawat, as we have seen, naturalizes these gender roles, reproduces gender hierarchy, and limits the place of women to the domestic sphere. If the terms of gender hierarchy are violated, this can undermine the conditions for moral order, and thus disruptions to gendered hierarchy must be averted. Thus, women's bodies must be regulated for moral order to be created. This certainly can produce patriarchal violence as it creates the impression, widespread already in Pakistan, that women's presence in public life, particularly without the requisite covering, represents a threat to family honor and public order. While acknowledging this potential for violence, it nevertheless behooves us to recognize the forms of care and mutuality within the domestic sphere that inspire the commitment of both men and women to Islamic piety movements like the Tablighi Jamaat. Tablighis claim that Islamic piety is a model for care that tames the animalistic impulses of men and thus creates men who can fulfill their responsibilities as pious sons, husbands, and fathers. While such claims should not be taken at face value, it is undeniable that many women embrace Islamic piety movements and adamantly defend its attendant patriarchal values and gender hierarchy for precisely this reason. Several pietist women explained to me that Islam alleviates many of the bad habits of men and that learning about Islam affords women greater—rather than less—leverage in their relationships with their fathers, brothers, and husbands. For these women, the absence of Islam in the lives of families means that men adopt much more aggressive forms of patriarchal domination and that Islam grants them a place from which to claim gendered rights (*haqooq*). This conception of hierarchical care and responsibility in the domestic sphere is why Islamic piety carries such moral force in social life (Khan 2018; see also Malara and Boylston 2016).

The moral intervention of Islamic piety also aims to manage and reformulate political hierarchies, but this too has important limitations. The notion that politiks is separate from religion and should not be engaged while posing a challenge to Islamist politics nevertheless leaves the state largely intact and accepts rather than directly confronts state violence. There is no reason to believe that blasphemy politics, let alone other forms of violence in Pakistan, can possibly be resolved without addressing the role of the state and law in social life. Moreover, while Tablighis insist that the spheres of religion and politics are different, political actors covet affiliation with Tablighis to shore up their own Islamic credentials, and this serves to reinforce their political power by converting it into moral righteousness. In the restive and militarized province of Balochistan and in the tribal areas of Khyber Pakhtunkhwa, many people suspect that the activities of the Tablighi Jamaat are facilitated by the military establishment to discourage participation in ethno-nationalist movements demanding ethnic autonomy and political rights. Indeed, the framework of a transcendent Islamic unity that stands above ethnolinguistic identity can articulate with the narrative of the Pakistani state as an enforcer of Islamic unity against ethnic nationalist forces. While Tablighis contend that dawat can transform the powerful, we can also see how the powerful can draw legitimacy from Islamic piety and thus can reaffirm political hierarchies and reinforce the very authoritarian state policies that are the source of many of Pakistan's most pressing problems.

If Tablighis' piety does not directly confront political violence, it is also largely silent on economic inequality and exploitation. Tablighis emphasize charitable giving as an Islamic duty from those above to those below in socioeconomic hierarchies. Moreover, it also encourages acceptance of one's "worldly" status and a belief that such status reflects God's will. The notion of patience (sabr) entails an acceptance of one's place in the world, while stressing the need to focus on fulfilling one's ritual duties. Tablighi piety, therefore, places the onus of moral transformation on the individual rather than targeting the sources of capitalist exploitation. Indeed, it can be understood as a variant of "moral neoliberalism," which emphasizes personal and familial responsibility and interpersonal ethics rather than broad transformations of underlying political and economic structures (Muehlebach 2012; see Iqtidar 2017). The appeal of the Islamic piety framework to many wealthy traders and merchants is evidence enough that it does not challenge the imperatives of capitalist accumulation.

The argument here, then, is not that Islamic piety can address the crisis of moral reproduction in Pakistan. The crisis of political fragmentation and violence that permeates life in Pakistan is entangled with patriarchal authority in domestic life, with state centralization and authoritarianism, particularly by the Pakistani military, and with rampant economic inequality and exploitation by capitalist classes. One cannot genuinely transcend the political fragmentation and violence that permeates everyday life in Pakistan without a radical democratization of power and economic redistribution. What, then, might we say about the moral and political intervention of Islamic piety as a response to the effects of these underlying processes?

The moral intervention of Islamic piety is an effort to manage and reformulate domestic, political, and economic hierarchies to make them more habitable. Dawat aims to produce a form of pious masculinity that encourages men to enact their responsibilities as fathers, sons, and husbands in the domestic domain. This pious masculinity also provides the model of benevolent rule of the state and for charitable giving in economic life. Islamic piety places a model of hierarchical care at the heart of sovereign power. Through the enactment of the Prophetic model and the cultivation and spread of pious virtue, the Tablighi Jamaat aims to domesticate the powers of modern life, political and economic, and make them capable of fulfilling their function of hierarchical care. Rather than aiming to eliminate worldly hierarchies, Islamic piety is an approach that presumes the existence of and naturalizes these hierarchies, but in doing so it invokes a model of pious relationality that can transform self-interest and domination into care and responsibility by anchoring social life in pious authority and through that in the transcendent will of God. By foregrounding hierarchical care and responsibility, Tablighis aim to create a sacred hierarchy that is separate from but also capable of domesticating the powers of the modern world.

It is the regulatory power of the ethics of hierarchy and the everyday affordances of Islamic piety that gives it its moral force in social and political life in Pakistan. The Tablighi Jamaat's promise of transcendence draws millions of Pakistani Muslims from across class, caste, and ethnicity to dawat. The broad respect enjoyed by Tablighis in Pakistan shows why Islamic piety becomes an object of such immense emotional investment for Tablighis in their hopes to become genuine Islamic subjects and agents of Islamic moral order. It is precisely the moral force of hierarchy and its promise to bring about a more harmonious world that is the source of its appeal, and it is precisely this that is erased by liberal-secular constructions of religious violence built as they are on the division between private and public and the suspicion of religiosity in public life. Understanding Islamic piety as a model of hierarchical care and responsibility grants us insight into a broader place of hierarchical imaginaries in modernity. It is the place of hierarchy in modernity to which we turn in the conclusion.

Conclusion

THE POLITICS OF SOVEREIGN TRANSCENDENCE IN MODERNITY

The train came to a stop at the Pattoki station only two stops from the Raiwind station. The conductor informed us that a protest was being staged on the tracks by residents of the surrounding *basti*. They had not had electricity for a week and had blocked the trains in the hope that the political authorities would heed their demands and turn the electricity back on. An hour turned into two and two hours into four. Our train full of Tablighis on their way to the annual congregation in Raiwind waited patiently. After hours of waiting, a small group of Tablighis exited their train cabin and walked toward the protestors. Suddenly a skirmish broke out between the Tablighis and the protestors. A young Tablighi in his mid-twenties, seemingly the leader of the congregation, could be heard screaming and cursing at the protestors. He rushed to a broken gate and proceeded to try to break out an iron bar from the fence to use as a weapon, while other Tablighis held him and pulled him away from it. They managed to subdue him, and the Tablighis retreated to the train. Suddenly the protestors began hurling stones at the train, and we all took cover. A stone flew through an already broken window into our compartment nearly hitting a fellow passenger. After ten minutes, the stones stopped. After about an hour of further waiting, the train began its departure to Raiwind.

Nobody knows why the protestors allowed the train to proceed. A few Tablighi companions speculated that the Elders had sent an emissary from Raiwind to press the importance of the path of God. A few said that God had softened the hearts of the protestors and made them realize the importance of our journey. As the train approached the Raiwind station, the amir of our congregation stood at the front of the cabin to address us. In a manner reminiscent of the sermon (bayan), he explained that what happened back at the previous station should not have happened, that we are on God's path, and that we are heading to the greatest of religious events where we can gain great religious merit (sawab). He said that a few words uttered by the Elders of the congregation can bring a total transformation to our lives, and we must prepare ourselves to receive the words of the Elders. He implored us to forget any ill thoughts that may have accumulated in our hearts from the incident. He said that there are obstacles in the path of God, but it is God who removes obstacles. We must never forget that it is God who has opened this path to us. Our amir was identifying this as an incident of moral failure, a loss of patience, and a lapse of faith in God's power to open the hearts of others. It was a breakdown in the frame of dawat as moral order. After isha prayers, as we sat down at our dastarkhwan to eat dinner, one of our companions, Aftab, turned to me and said:

> Look at all this, Arsalan. There are hundreds of thousands of Muslims here from all over the world. Each has made unknown sacrifices to be here. They have all worked together with members of their mosques to coordinate their travels and to arrive here. They will depart from here to spread Allah's religion all over the country and the world. Did you see how everyone helped each other on the train and in the travels, how we cared for each other and made sure everyone's needs were met? This is what Allah wants of us and this is how our congregation is. Look how organized everything is here. Everyone is even waiting patiently in lines for the bathroom. Have you seen anything like this anywhere else in Pakistan? This is all the power of Allah's dawat.

Aftab was gently reminding me, as many had done before, that lapses in moral judgment are a product of human frailty and that what is important is how one responds to them and moves forward (Kloos and Beekers 2018). Such moral failures, he wanted me to know, do not negate the power of dawat to create moral order against the backdrop of moral chaos.

I began this book with the claim that Islamic piety in the Tablighi Jamaat is an ethical aspiration that fits within the broad architecture of modernity. To say that Tablighi conceptions of Islamic piety are modern leaves us with some important concluding questions: What precisely is modern about Islamic piety in the Tablighi Jamaat, and how does this conception of Islamic modernity relate to the more canonical and hegemonic forms of liberal and secular modernity?

I traced our story of the Tablighi Jamaat back to the context of British colonialism and to the efforts to define the boundaries of religion in colonial secularism. The Tablighi Jamaat emerged in the 1920s, a time of intense competition with Christian missionaries and Hindu revivalists over the bodies of what were seen as religiously ambiguous or nominally Muslim subjects. This was also a period of intense internal debate and contestation over the meaning and form of Islam in a newly emergent Islamic public sphere. The emphasis on embodiment and the face-to-face nature of dawat was also set against the growing possibilities of disembodied and mass-mediated forms of Islam made possible by the objectification of Islamic law by the colonial state and the availability of print technology (Ingram 2018). In postcolonial Pakistan, Islam has become entangled with state sovereignty. State- and corporate-driven Islamization have created new possibilities for the objectification of Islam that have created an even more intense climate of competition over Islamic authority. This has, I argued, engendered a deep and pervasive sense that Islam is being unmoored from ethical life. The immense nostalgia for the immediation of the face-to-face and embodied connection as well as a desire to return to hierarchical form of pious relationality materialized in dawat is one response to this condition. Dawat is a reflexive site for moral reproduction against what Tablighis perceive to be a state of moral chaos reflected in the disembedding of Islam from its ritual context, the intense competition over Islamic authority, and the political fragmentation and violence that characterizes life in postcolonial Pakistan.

Dawat, I argued, is a ritual of transcendence that allows the Tablighi to create a direct relationship to God and thus shares with many other religious and political forces throughout the world an emphasis on creating a direct, immediate relationship to transcendental power (Engelke 2007; Eisenlohr 2018). In creating this direct relationship to God, the Tablighi can radically reimagine his place in the world and become an agent of moral order. Materializing this relationship to transcendence and creating a divine presence requires performative acts of submission in pious companionship and discursive acts of citation in everyday life, or what I have called the ethics of hierarchy, and this in turn allows the Tablighi to stand apart from the the world and faithfully spread Islamic virtue. This is the promise of piety in dawat, realizing a transcendental relationship to God and thus acting on the world to create moral order. This is the promise of piety that inspires men from all walks of life but especially those marginalized by the exclusionary terms of Pakistani nationalism along caste, ethnic and class lines, and by those denied access to political and economic power, to acquire the value of piety, elevating themselves in a hierarchy of religious virtue and transforming themselves into the creators and custodians of a transcendental Islamic moral order. The widespread appeal of the Tablighi Jamaat in Pakistan derives from the fact that it allows all Muslims, primarily male, to reinvent themselves as virtuous subjects of the Islamic community.

Anthropologists working in diverse social and political contexts have returned to the question of the value of hierarchy as a moral framework and ethical resource rather than simply as a form of inequality in modernity (Ansell 2014; Ferguson 2015; Hickel 2015; Haynes and Hickel 2016; Keeler 2017; Khan 2016, 2018; Piliavsky 2020). The argument I have developed here is that the quest for Islamic piety in the Tablighi Jamaat is based on the egalitarian premise of the Tablighi Jamaat, that all Muslims, specifically men, can and should achieve transcendence through the enactment of a Prophetic model, but arriving at a realization of transcendence depends on participation in the sacred hierarchy of the Tablighi congregation. Hierarchy here is not a fixed location but is instead understood as a process of ascent in which the Tablighi connects to the original generative movement of Islam, and this gradually moves him upward in proximity to God. In doing so, the Tablighi abandons his un-Islamic past and moves forward into a pious future. I showed that the sacred hierarchy created in the congregation becomes the basis for reconfiguring the domains of kinship and politics and provides the means for ethical engagement in these spheres. Tablighis understand Islamic piety to be a solution to what they regard as the breakdown of moral relationships between kin, ethnic communities, nations, and within the Islamic community. Dawat constitutes religion (din) on the basis of hierarchical form of pious relationality and establishes the ascendancy of religion (din) over the world (dunya). The reform of the world from the vantage point of religion is, for Tablighis, the basis for the regeneration of moral relationships and the creation of an Islamic moral order, one that Tablighis believe can transcend the political fragmentation and violence of life in postcolonial Pakistan.

I noted in the introduction that my field site was characterized by cultural intimacy, the potentiality of interchangeability between perspectives between me and my interlocutors based on shared cultural sensibilities and a broad sense of belonging to a common religious tradition. Tablighis in Pakistan and beyond operate in a dense and diverse web of relationality. Tablighis draw Muslims from all manner of backgrounds, thus making it a space of immense diversity in terms of caste, class, and ethnicity. Moreover, Tablighis have relationships of kinship and friendship with all manner of people. I met Tablighis whose families were Islamists, liberals who were former Tablighis, and socialists who had Tablighi siblings. Relationships across these differences are a source of great tension in people's lives, but they are also characterized by mutual understanding and even affection. I argued that a Tablighi's recognition of the limits of pious agency and the valorization of individual striving allows the Tablighi to live with religious and cultural differences in domestic and political life and regulates the response to provocations and affronts like those of blasphemy. Hence, the ethics of hierarchy provides the ethical means for managing religious and cultural differences without foregoing the project of transforming those relationships in the direction of pious ideals. It is precisely this, I argue, that allows the Tablighi Jamaat to grow and spread in diverse social and political contexts and is therefore a key aspect of the globalization of the movement. It is the capacity for the reproduction and growth of the movement that Tablighis see as threatened by state- and corporate-driven Islamization with its tendencies to essentialize and reify ethnic and religious differences and thus engender political fragmentation and conflict.

This book has focused on Tablighi efforts to reformulate Islamic practices associated with saint worship and Prophetic intercession, while also focusing on the boundary that Tablighis draw around religion to challenge the uptake of Islam by the state and corporations and a range of other Islamic actors in Pakistan. The key question, then, is how does this Tablighi effort to divide religion and the world and dawat and politiks relate to liberal and secular conceptions of modernity? The anthropological work on Islamic piety movements has focused primarily on the tensions between the Islamic tradition and liberal secularism rather than on the tensions over the meaning and form of Islam. A touchstone for this work has been Talal Asad's (2003) seminal argument that secularism, far from simply limiting religion to the private sphere, in fact reformulates religion as a matter of private belief, a conception drawn from the model of Protestantism, that creates a disembodied religiosity that runs against the embodied practices of Islam. Far from being neutral toward religion, secularism regulates religious practices that do not abide by the terms of a privatized conception of religiosity. Drawing on this framework, Hussein Ali Agrama (2012) argues that secular law is a "questioning power" in that it must determine where the line between religion and politics is located and thus define the legitimate parameters of religion. Agrama argues that this process of delineating the line is never complete because the exigencies of secular governance, the intervention into the sphere of religion, disrupts the line between religion and politics, and thus religion becomes an object of constant intervention by the secular state. Agrama (2012) calls this power to determine the boundaries of religion the "active principle" of secularism (30). The regulatory power of secularism explains why the work on Islamic piety like that of Saba Mahmood (2005) and Charles Hirschkind (2006) have framed Islamic piety as a "counterpublic" to that of the liberal-secular public sphere and its enforcement by the secular state in Egypt.

These arguments are correct in identifying the role of the secular state in regulating religious life, but as Katherine Lemons (2019) argues in her study of Islamic legal adjudication in India, groups outside of the state and especially religious minorities are in fact deeply invested in the preservation of the divide between religion and politics. Lemons shows that Islamic legal adjudication in

India depends on such a division and that "secularity" or the commitment to preserve the divide between religion and politics precedes and generates secularism in India. In Pakistan, we have seen how Tablighi Jamaat's division between religion and the world and dawat and politiks aims to anchor pious authority in moral and ethical life against state- and corporate-driven Islamization. This does not lead Tablighis to a commitment to secularism as such, but it does produce a certain acceptance or accommodation of secular governance. The divide between religion and the world creates the possibility, necessary for a transnational Islamic movement, to allow the Tablighi to live in and operate across very different political systems and forms of government, including ones defined by secularism. Tablighis do not see their main task as being one of dismantling political secularism. Moreover, while secularism does intrude into the domains of religion, the Pakistani context reveals how state- and corporate-driven Islamization is centrally concerned with a redefinition of religion and reformulation of its sites of production. Humeira Iqtidar (2011) argues that Islamists are themselves "secularizing" insofar as they transform religion in ways that are in conformity to modernist conceptions. Indeed, the entanglement of Islam with modern institutions does transform religion. We have seen how this can produce individuated forms of agency that Tablighis regard as unruly and dangerous. This means that while Tablighis foresee and aim to create a world beyond secularism, a pious future in which all Muslims and ultimately all people live a life based on the Prophetic model, one of their primary concerns is the drive to reformulate Islam in terms of modernist conceptions, whether that is pursued by liberals or Islamists.

The Tablighi response to state and corporate Islamization tells us that political secularism is not the only or even the primary threat to traditionalist and orthodox visions of moral order. It is, therefore, important not to overdetermine the regulatory power of secularism, but instead to focus on how various social and political actors pick up secular principles in various contexts in order to posit specific conceptions of religion (see Bangstad 2009). This focus on the politics of religion gives us a better sense of when and how the regulatory power of secularism becomes an intrusive force in the religious lives of nonliberal and nonsecular people and how, alternatively, people can draw on the affordances of secularism to secure religious rights and authority and lay claim to alternative forms of life and visions of moral order. This, again, allows us to retain the insight that secularism is not neutral and aims to define and redefine religion while also recognizing that the state does not possess a totalizing power. As Ashley Lebner (2015) notes, the critique of secularism also tends to treat it as a transcendental object, which can make us lose sight of the diverse ways that people engage with secularism. We need to recognize that the indeterminacy of secularism makes it not just a regulatory project but also a site of hegemonic struggle by competing social forces, including traditionalist and orthodox Muslims. To define the boundaries of religion is to articulate a claim to sovereign authority and it is critical that we focus on how such claims are emergent in social life (see McAllister and Napolitano 2021)

This is important to recognize because secularism can manifest in significantly different ways with serious implications for religious and cultural minorities. In India, for instance, recent decades have witnessed a significant shift from Nehruvian secularism, in which the state recognized the autonomy of religious communities, to majoritarian Hindu nationalism that views the purification of India of Muslims and others to be the basis of recuperating India's lost glory and its political and economic ascent. The former emphasized the autonomy of religious communities, while the latter has mobilized the regulatory power of secular governance toward the creation of a public sphere free of Muslims and Islam.[1] Both of these stances contain the powers to regulate religious differences, but they do not have the same implications for Muslims and other religious minorities in India (Chatterjee 2006; see Bangstad 2009; cf. Mahmood 2016). This means that while the scholarship is correct to point to the regulatory powers of secularism (Asad 2003; Agrama 2012), the contradictions of secularism (Fernando 2014), and the capacity of secularism to reify religious communities and thus become one of the "enabling conditions of religious conflict today" (Mahmood 2016, 22), it is critical in this current political conjuncture of resurgent right wing forces to recognize secularism as a capacious formation in which many different political and ethical stances can arise and a contested political terrain on which all manner of social and political actors, including traditionalist Muslims, lay claim.

The context of postcolonial Pakistan shows how the features noted about secularism, whether regulation, contradiction, or reification, are all also all features of Islamization in Pakistan. State-driven Islamization in Pakistan has failed to create a unity based on Islam against ethnic fragmentation, has created laws designed to subordinate sectarian minorities and non-Muslims, has thoroughly exacerbated the sectarianization of life, and has had deleterious effects on the rights of women. Islamic pietists like Tablighis, although not formally committed to secularism, are also capable of seeing the laws of the state as humanly authored and thus subject to change and recognize the mediation of the Islamic state as an obstacle to the realization of a pious Islamic community. It would be a stretch to say that this commits them to a secular vision of modernity, but it certainly allows them to accommodate one. We must, therefore, avoid totalizing claims about secularism and violence, just as we should avoid totalizing claims about Islam and violence, and instead interrogate the specific political implications of drawing the boundary between religion and nonreligious spheres whether done by liberals, socialists, Islamists, or Tablighis.

The anthropological scholarship on Islamic piety movements has taken shape in a post-9/11 world and in the shadow of the Global War on Terror. In this highly charged political context, liberal principles of individual liberty and freedom were invoked by the United States and its allies to justify military interventions in Iraq and Afghanistan in the name of spreading freedom and democracy and protecting Muslim women from Islam (Abu Lughod 2013). Government officials, pundits, and analysts drew on these ideas to reinforce anti-Muslim racial animus and Islamophobia across the Western world. It is not surprising, then, that the anthropological literature on Islamic movements to emerge in this period was centrally concerned with the sharp differences between Islam and liberalism in their conception of selves, agency, and ethics (Asad 2003; Mahmood 2005; Hirschkind 2006). This scholarship aimed at creating a deeper understanding and respect for the ontological plurality of modernity and offered a trenchant critique of orientalist and Eurocentric conceptions that structure Western imperialism. Unfortunately, while drawing attention to the particularities of Islam and liberalism, this literature also left the impression that Islam and liberalism are incommensurable and thus fundamentally at odds with one another. This perspective can even reinforce the pernicious logic of an inevitable "clash of civilizations" between the West and Islam that is pushed by various shades of white supremacists, right-wing nationalists, and Islamophobes in the West as well as by Islamists in Muslim societies (cf. Huntington 1996). To move beyond this problem, we must consider both the differences and underlying commonalities of liberalism and Islamic piety movements as frameworks for moral order in modernity.

In liberalism, it is the absence of individual freedom and equality that is the central problem with Islam and particularly with traditionalist forms of Islam. Secularism is understood as the means for securing both freedom and equality as it ensures individual freedom and protects the equality of all people before the law. Ernst Kantorowicz (1997) famously argued that medieval sovereignty was organized around the "king's two bodies," the mortal body that exists in this world and the transcendent body that stood apart from and above society. The sovereign power of the modern state requires that it be an actor in the world but also that it transcend an association with any group or interest and thus maintain an impartiality and universality embodied in the notion of the rule of law. In liberalism, it is the sphere of civil society and the figure of a sovereign individual who, bearing rational-critical faculties, enacts a "reason on and to power rather than by power" (Taylor 2004, 90). In other words, the sovereign individual of liberalism, as David Gilmartin (2012) notes, must stand apart and above society to reform and regulate it.

If liberalism construes the sovereign subject as an autonomous individual who acts on the world through the exercise of reason and rationality, Tablighis and other Islamic pietists understand the sovereign subject as one who can materialize a relationship to God through the enactment of Quranic norms and the Prophetic model. In liberalism, the gravest threat to moral order is the erosion of individual liberties and freedoms and the loss of selfhood to the collective, which means that the bodily conformity and hierarchy of Islamic piety augurs the dangers of moral decay and death. For the Islamic pietist, the gravest threat, by contrast, is posed by liberalism's valorization of the self-authorizing individual. The sovereign individual of liberalism challenges the hierarchies and particularly gender hierarchy that is seen as the condition for piety as well as unleashing the inventive possibilities that vitiate the connection to the sacred past and through that the relationship to God. Liberalism and Islamic piety thus harbor specific threats to each other's conception of sovereign subjects and visions of moral order.

These different conceptions of sovereign subjects and visions of moral order shape a range of political issues from the rights of women and minorities to debates about war and empire, but they also share in some key aspects of modernity that draw them into competition. I have argued in this book that central to modernity is the possibility of creating a "direct" relationship to transcendental power, and this potential to materialize transcendence is what makes modernity a contested field of aspiration. Islamic piety and liberalism are different means of mediating a relationship to transcendence and thus distinct aspirational forms, but both posit a sovereign and transcendent subject that stands apart from and above ordinary life to reform and regulate it. The sovereign subject, in both cases, is a disciplined, self-regulating subject who is therefore capable of moral action in and on the world and is therefore the fount for moral order. Both Islamic piety and liberalism presume formal equality, but in their constitution of sovereign subjects they generate their own forms of authority and hierarchy, which in turn shape how they imagine moral order (Piliavsky 2020). The pious subject acquires pious agency through the relationships of the congregation and by committing to the spiritual hierarchies of congregational life. The sovereign self of liberalism, while presumed to exist prior to and independently of social relationships, nevertheless must acquire authenticity and agency through all manner of bodily, psychological, and spiritual disciplines, creating its own hierarchies of transcendence (see also Hoesterey 2015). Crucially, both Islamic piety and liberalism aim to secure the ascendence of their form of sovereign subject by transforming and subordinating all other forms of relationality. Liberalism and Islamic piety are therefore both hegemonic and universalistic projects aimed at creating moral order (see also Li 2020). These two universal and hegemonic projects build on competing conceptions of sovereign subjects, relationality, and moral order and thus produce deep anxieties in one another not because they are fundamentally different but because they both lay claim to what we can call the sovereign transcendence of modernity.

Pakistan is an important site to understand competing forms of sovereign transcendence in modernity. Created in the name of protecting the Muslims of South Asia, Pakistani nationalism was explicitly set up against parochial loyalties of kinship, caste, clan, and ethnicity, with the state explicitly claiming to embody a transcendent unity organized around Islam. Authoritarian modernization in the first decades of Pakistan created the ground for robust ethnic nationalist and secessionist opposition that led to the violent civil war of 1971 and the dismembering of the nation. Islamization of the state in the late 1970s and 1980s arose to recuperate this transcendental unity but unleashed fierce contestation over the mantle of Islamic authority in a bourgeoning Islamic public sphere.

Islamic movements in Pakistan materialize the directness of modernity in a variety of ways. Islamists in Pakistan see the Islamic state and especially Islamic law as the medium through which to create a relationship to God and thus to materialize an Islamic nation and community. We saw how blasphemy politics and becoming a "Lover of the Prophet" (ashiq-e-Rasool) was another mode of making transcendence manifest in the people. Many militant Islamic groups see "jihad" as a primary individual duty and as a form of transcendence above and beyond any worldly duties, a logic that is mobilized against both traditional Islamic authorities and the Islamic state (Devji 2005; Khoja Moolji 2021). One of the most robust claims to sovereign transcendence is the popular political party the Pakistan Tehreek-e-Insaf (Movement for Justice in Pakistan) organized around the cricketer turned politician Imran Khan who claims to be establishing a *Naya Pakistan* (new Pakistan) that will be free of corruption and modeled on the "state of Medina" (*riyasat-e-medina*) of the Prophet's time. Finally, claims to Islamic authority are distributed a range of modern institutions like corporations, media houses, banks, new educational institutions, and NGOs.

The competition and fragmentation of the Islamic public sphere have deepened the sense that Islamic authority has become emptied of moral substance and unmoored from ethical life. The growth and popularity of Tablighi Jamaat reflects a widespread desire to create an Islamic community that can transcend the political fragmentation and violence that characterizes life in postcolonial Pakistan. The division Tablighis draw between religion and the world and dawat and politiks is an effort to return to an authentic Islam untainted by the machinations of power and thus capable of regulating and domesticating the powers of modern life. The aspiration to become a pious agent of moral order is what explains the hundreds of thousands if not millions of Muslims who flock through the gates of the Tablighi Jamaat. In a world of deepening political, economic, and ecological crises, the promise of piety in the Tablighi Jamaat in Pakistan points to how religious and hierarchical aspirations for sovereign transcendence shape the politics of moral order in modernity.

Notes

INTRODUCTION

1. There is a large body of work across disciplines on the Tablighi Jamaat (Masud 2000; Metcalf 1993, Reetz 2006; Sikand 2002; Van der Veer 1992), including a number of full-length ethnographies in countries as diverse as Indonesia (Noor 2012), Gambia (Janson 2014), Kyrgyzstan (Pelkmans 2017), and the United Kingdom and Bangladesh (Siddiqi 2018). This body of scholarship provides a rich source of knowledge on the organization of the Tablighi Jamaat and the political significance of the movement in diverse social and political contexts. The theoretical concerns that animate this book are the hierarchical relationality constituted in the ritual practices of the movement and the ways this becomes a basis for ethical engagement with social and political life in Pakistan.

2. The approach to semiotic mediation dovetails with recent works in Pakistan that draw on affect theory to show how affective attachments and connections are forged between soldiers and their families and the Pakistani army (Rashid 2020), between citizens and the Islamic state (Khoja-Moolji 2021), and between religious practitioners and saints (Kasmani 2022). These works, like my own, are concerned with how affective relationships are fashioned.

1. COLONIAL SECULARISM AND THE MAKING OF SCRIPTURAL TRADITIONALISM IN BRITISH INDIA

1. Richard Eaton (2003) argues that the Mongol invasions dispersed a great many Persianized Turks and devastated the central institutions of Islam in West and Central Asia, including the raising of the Abbasid Caliphate in Baghdad, and left a deep sense of loss and rupture among Indo-Persian chroniclers from the thirteenth century onwards. This, he argues, pushed them to associate Muslim rule in India with Islam. However, Sanskrit sources show that this sentiment was not shared even by other Indian elites who mostly thought of the Muslim rulers as Turkic. Eaton argues that the notion of Islam being "foreign" to India and the focus on an "Islamic conquest" and "Muslim era" that became important under colonialism were largely a product of Orientalist scholars who privileged the work of Indo-Persian chroniclers over other kinds of data. It can be argued that the sense of diasporic yearnings among Muslim elites in the nineteenth century are refracted Orientalist conceptions about the essential foreignness of Islam to India.

2. The point here is not that genealogy is the only principle that defined political power in the precolonial period, or that textual authority had no role, as both sources of authority have surely existed throughout Islamic history, but that colonialism reconfigured their relationship in South Asia such that the latter could be imagined as autonomous and supreme. The conditions for imagining a sharp contrast between religious and customary and textual and genealogical authority inaugurated a reform of the latter by the former based on an idea of pure religion, as we will see later in this chapter. It is important to recognize that some of the most prominent Sufi silsilas like the Chistiyya silsila are not committed to a vision of bio-spiritual descent but instead knowledge and ritual mastery (Ernst and Lawrence 2002).

2. DAWAT AS A RITUAL OF TRANSCENDENCE IN AN ISLAMIC NATION

1. Pathan is a term used interchangeably with Pashtun throughout Pakistan and many Pashtuns also use it for themselves. However, the term is also regarded as derogatory by some segments of the Pashtun community.

2. The annual congregations are attended by Tablighis from around the world, but the swelling of the ranks has necessitated that the Raiwind ijtima be split into two distinct events, one international and one national, each happening every alternate year rather than every year.

3. ISLAMIC ICONICITY, MORAL RESPONSIBILITY, AND THE CREATION OF A SACRED HIERARCHY

1. In a programmatic theorization of ethics in anthropology, James Laidlaw (2014) argues that critics of Foucault's notions of the care of the self often wrongly attribute to him a failure to attend to the "social." Laidlaw argues that while Foucault places primacy on the relationship with the self, he does not ignore the relational dimension of ethics. Rather, the focus on the relationship to the self introduces Foucault's understanding of ethical deliberation as a product of freedom in that ethical decision-making requires some degree of choice between alternative possibilities. Laidlaw goes on to argue that Mahmood and Hirschkind fail to attend to the freedom and reflexivity involved in ethical life. My argument here is that the backgrounding of the relational and intersubjective aspects of ethical subject formation in this work creates the impression of an individual acting on themselves in Islamic practice, which erases the ethical deliberation and reflexivity involved in ethical self-formation. As we will see, the limits of pious agency itself becomes the object of ethical reflection.

4. THE ETHICS OF HIERARCHY AND THE MORAL REPRODUCTION OF CONGREGATIONAL LIFE

1. Drawing on Bakhtin (1981), Matt Tomlinson (2017) argues that while all discourses are dialogically constituted in the sense that they carry multiple voices that "interanimate" each other, a feature Bakhtin called heteroglossia, many authoritative discourses adopt a monological framework in which the dialogical aspects are displaced. One key feature of monologism is that it aims to limit the change that happens in the uptake of a discourse across contexts. We saw in the previous chapter how Tablighis erase the intersubjective aspects of speech in dawat by emphasizing the ritual process through the sacralization of words. Moreover, the effort in dawat is to contain the changes that occur in the discourse as it moves across distinct contexts, hence the central importance of repetition (takrar) in the creation and circulation of piety. In this sense, dawat shares features with other forms of monologism (see Tomlinson and Millie 2017).

2. What I am describing here is not unique to Tablighis or even to Islam and can be found anywhere where tradition must be faithfully replicated. In her work among the Mopan Maya of Belize, Eve Danziger (2013) notes that the Mopan Maya place tremendous emphasis on establishing a relationship of faithful obedience toward traditional authority. Danziger draws on Goffman's (1981) categorization of three types of stances in a speech event: the animator or person voicing the speech, the principle or person responsible for the speech, and the author or the person seen as creating the speech. Danziger adds to this the idea of being an "acceptor," which involves recognizing the speaker as an animator and principal but not the author or source of the speech. This requires both downplaying one's own inner mental state as well as not questioning the inner states of the authority in question. When the most valued forms of speech are seen to origi-

nate from outside the speaker, the emphasis is placed on becoming a trusting and obedient "acceptor." Pious listening is an effort to enact such obedience to pious authority in order to faithfully replicate tradition.

5. CERTAIN FAITH, THE PIOUS HOME, AND THE PATH TO AN ISLAMIC FUTURE

1. Partha Chatterjee (1993) argues that the struggle against colonialism produced a division between the inner, spiritual sphere in which Indians were morally superior against the outer material world in which the British had gained ascendancy. It was the task of anticolonial nationalism, Chatterjee argues, to gain mastery over the material world while retaining one's spiritual essence. Chatterjee shows that it is indeed the realm of kinship, and particularly the place of women, that came to define this spiritual essence. This theme, much like the themes of Hindu reform on which Chatterjee elaborates, also runs through narratives of Islamic reform where the material aspects must be the cultivation of spiritual potency. This theme also ran through the Tablighi Jamaat though the emphasis was on reconfiguring the domain of kinship to create spiritual potency (*roohani quwwat*) that would bring about moral and economic well-being.

6. PIOUS SOVEREIGNTY IN TIMES OF MORAL CHAOS

1. I mark the term *politiks* here to highlight for the reader the specific meanings that Tablighis assign to the category. Tablighis use the term politiks interchangeably with the Urdu term for "politics" (siyasat).

7. THE ETHICAL AFFORDANCES OF PIETY AND THE SPECTER OF RELIGIOUS VIOLENCE

1. Asia Bibi was acquitted in 2018 on the grounds of insufficient evidence and surreptitiously evacuated to Canada where she now lives in exile.

2. Mumtaz Qadri was convicted and subsequently executed in 2016. He is widely heralded as a martyr by right-wing Islamic groups, particularly in the Barelwi denomination to which he belonged. The case of Asia Bibi spawned the emergence of the Tehreek-e-Labbaik (TLP) party, which has placed zeal around blasphemy at the center of its political project. In the 2018 general elections, the TLP won 2.2 million votes and emerged as the fifth-largest political party in the country, evidencing growing Barelwi militancy and the new centrality of blasphemy politics in the democratic arena.

3. The risks to those who challenge the blasphemy laws were made evident by the murder of both governor of Punjab Salman Taseer and the subsequent murder of the Minister of Minority Affairs, Shahbaz Bhatti, a Christian politician, in 2011. In 2014, Rashid Rahman, a prominent progressive lawyer who took up the case of Junaid Hafeez, a university lecturer and former Fulbright student who had been accused of blasphemy, was murdered in the very courtroom where he came to represent his client.

4. A thorough report by the organization Engage directed by Arafat Mazhar on the history and politics of Pakistan's blasphemy laws shows that the 1986 parliamentary proceedings that led to the passing of 295-C and the prescription of the death penalty cite a range of sources from Hanafi jurisprudence. The report shows through a careful examination of the sources that the parliamentary proceedings wrongly claimed that the sources prescribe death for non-Muslims (*dhimmi*) for defiling the sacred personage of the Prophet when in fact non-Muslims are consistently excluded from the death penalty by these sources on account that being non-Muslim (*kufr*) represents a greater sin than blasphemy. Such nuances of the history of Islamic jurisprudence and debates around blasphemy are suppressed by Islamic groups pursuing blasphemy politics in Pakistan and claiming the sacred nature of the law.

5. Barelwi-Deobandi tensions, as we've noted earlier, center on the model of Prophethood. Barelwis consider the Prophet to be "present and observant" (*hazir-o-nazir*) and thus capable of intervening in the world. Deobandis claim this elevates the Prophet to the status of God and thus constitutes a form of idolatry (shirk) (see Tareen 2020).

6. In response to the Asia Bibi case and the Tehreek-e-Labbaik party's mobilization in defense of Governor Salman Taseer's assassin, Mumtaz Qadri, the popular Islamic preacher Maulana Tariq Jameel, who is strongly affiliated with the Tablighi Jamaat, spoke out against the disorder being created by describing it as a greater disrespect to the honor of the Prophet than any act of blasphemy.

7. Among the most famous episodes is the publication of pamphlet entitled *Rangila Rasul*, a biography of the Prophet Muhammad published in Lahore in 1924 that contained lurid accounts of the Prophet's marriages. The publication created outrage and led to widespread disturbances and conflicts between Hindus and Muslims. A legal case was lodged against the publisher Rajpal leading to the expansion and amendment of the Indian Penal Code and the addition of 295-A. Farhat Haq (2019, 14–44) argues that the urgency to pass IPC 295-A sprang from the fact that many such publications were circulating and conflicts between Hindus and Muslims were escalating. In other words, the religious tensions forged in the emergent public sphere were being resolved through the law. It is then not the law alone but broader colonial policies that intensified competition and conflict between religious communities. The acquittal of Rajpal by Justice Dalit Singh led to attacks on him and calls for his resignation, which Haq (2019) argues represents an "'insurgent public' interacting with the rational-legal institutions of the British state" (27). In 1929, Rajpal, after surviving two other assassination attempts, was murdered by Illum-ud-Din, a carpenter who was convicted and hanged, and is widely lionized in Pakistan as a heroic martyr (shaheed) for having defended the "honor of the Prophet" (namoos-e-risalat). Mumtaz Qadri who assassinated Governor Salman Taseer is often compared to Illum-ud-Din by proponents of blasphemy politics.

CONCLUSION

1. We see this, for instance, in the 2022 ruling in Karnataka court's ruling upholding the ban on Muslim women wearing the headscarf in schools on the basis that headscarves are not "essential" to Islam, arguments that draw on and mimic ones in France ("India Court Upholds Karnataka State's Ban on Hijab in Class," *Al Jazeera*, March 15, 2022, https://www.aljazeera.com/news/2022/3/15/india-court-upholds-karnataka-states-ban-on-hijab-in-class).

References

Abu Lughod, Lila. 1986. *Veiled Sentiments: Honor and Poetry in a Bedouin Society.* Berkeley: University of California Press.
Abu Lughod, Lila. 2013. *Do Muslim Women Need Saving?* Cambridge, MA: Harvard University Press.
Agha, Asif. 2007. *Language and Social Relations.* Cambridge: Cambridge University Press.
Agrama, Hussein A. 2012. *Questioning Secularism: Islam, Sovereignty, and the Rule of Law in Modern Egypt.* Chicago: University of Chicago Press.
Ahmed, Asad. 2009. "Specters of Macaulay: Blasphemy, the Indian Penal Code and Pakistan's Postcolonial Predicament." In *Censorship in South Asia: Cultural Regulation from Sedition to Seduction*, edited by Raminder Kaur and William Mazzarella, 172–206. Bloomington: University of Indiana Press.
Ahmed, Khaled. 2012a. "Our 'Reactive' Extremism." *Express Tribune*, August 4. https://tribune.com.pk/story/417591/our-reactive-extremism/.
Ahmed, Khaled. 2012b. "Certainty and Intolerance." *Express Tribune*, August 14. https://tribune.com.pk/story/422048/certainty-and-intolerance/.
Alam, Muzaffar. 2004. *The Language of Political Islam in India c. 1200–1800.* New Delhi: Permanent Black.
Alavi, Hamza. 1972. "Kinship in West Punjab Villages." *Contributions to Indian Sociology*, New Series 6, no 1: 1–27.
Alexiev, Alex. 2005. "Tablighi Jamaat: Jihad's Stealthy Legions." *Middle East Quarterly* 12, no. 1: 3–11. https://www.meforum.org/686/tablighi-jamaat-jihads-stealthy-legions.
Anderson, Benedict. 1991. *Imagined Communities.* London: Verso.
Anderson, Michael R. 1993. "Islamic Law and the Colonial Encounter in British India." *Institutions and Ideologies: A SOAS South Asia Reader* 15, no. 10: 165.
Anderson, Paul. 2011. "'The Piety of the Gift': Selfhood and Sociality in the Egyptian Mosque Movement." *Anthropological Theory* 11, no. 1: 3–21.
Ansell, Aaron. 2014. *Zero Hunger: Political Culture and Anti-Poverty Policy in North Eastern Brazil.* Chapel Hill: University of North Carolina Press.
Antoun, Richard T. 1989. *Muslim Preacher in the Modern World: A Jordanian Case Study in Comparative Perspective.* Princeton, NJ: Princeton University Press.
Appadurai, Arjun. 1996. *Modernity at Large: Cultural Dimensions of Globalization.* Minneapolis: University of Minnesota Press.
Asad, Talal. 1993. *Genealogies of Religion: Discipline and Reasons of Power in Christianity and Islam.* Baltimore, MD: Johns Hopkins University Press.
Asad, Talal. 2003. *Formations of the Secular: Christianity, Islam, Modernity.* Stanford, CA: Stanford University Press.
Asad, Talal. 2009. "Free Speech, Blasphemy and Secular Criticism." In *Is Critique Secular?: Blasphemy, Injury, and Free Speech*, edited by Talal Asad, Wendy Brown, Judith Butler, and Saba Mahmood, 20–63. Berkeley: University of California Press.
Asad, Talal, Wendy Brown, Judith Butler, and Saba Mahmood. 2009. *Is Critique Secular?: Blasphemy, Injury, and Free Speech.* Berkeley: University of California Press.
Austin, John L. 1975. *How to Do Things with Words.* Cambridge, MA: Harvard University Press.

REFERENCES

Ayres, Alyssa. 2009. *Speaking like a State: Language and Nationalism in Pakistan.* New York: Cambridge University Press.
Bakhtin, Mikhail. 1981. "Discourse in the Novel." In *The Diaological Imagination: Four Essays*, edited by Michael Holquist, translated by Caryl Emerson and Michael Holquist, 259–422. Austin: University of Texas Press.
Ball, Christopher. 2014. "On Dicentization." *Journal of Linguistic Anthropology* 24, no. 2: 151–173.
Bangstad, Sindre. 2009. "Contesting Secularism/s: Secularism and Islam in the work of Talal Asad." *Anthropological Theory* 9, no. 2: 188–208.
Basu, Helene. 1998. "Hierarchy and Emotion: Love, Joy and Sorrow in a Cult of Black Saints in Gujrat, India." In *Embodying Charisma*, edited by Pnina Werbner and Helene Basu, 117–139. New York: Routledge.
Bauman, Richard, and Charles Briggs. 1990. "Poetics and Performance as Critical Perspectives on Language and Social Life." *Annual Review of Anthropology* 19: 89–88.
Boddy, Janice. 1989. *Wombs and Alien Spirits: Women, Men, and the Zar Cult in Northern Sudan.* Madison: University of Wisconsin Press.
Breckenridge, Carol. A., and Peter Van der Veer, eds. 1993. *Orientalism and the Postcolonial Predicament: Perspectives on South Asia.* Philadelphia: University of Pennsylvania Press.
Briggs, Charles, and Richard Bauman. 1992. "Genre, Intertextuality, and Social Power." *Journal of Linguistic Anthropology* 2, no. 2: 131–72.
Carrier, James. 1995. *Gifts and Commodities: Exchange and Western Capitalism since 1700.* New York: Routledge.
Cavanaugh, William. 2009. *The Myth of Religious Violence: Secular Ideology and Roots of Modern Conflict.* New York: Oxford University Press.
Chatterjee, Partha. 1993. *The Nation and Its Fragments: Colonial and Postcolonial Histories.* Princeton, NJ: Princeton University Press.
Cohn, Bernard S. 1996. *Colonialism and Its Forms of Knowledge: The British in India.* Princeton, NJ: Princeton University Press.
Combs-Schilling, M. E. 1989. *Sacred Performances: Islam, Sexuality, and Sacrifice.* New York: Columbia University Press.
Danziger, Eve. 2013. "Conventional Wisdom: Imagination, Obedience, Intersubjectivity." *Language & Communication* 33: 251–62.
Das, Veena. 1997. *Critical Events: An Anthropological Perspective on Contemporary India.* Delhi: Oxford University Press.
De Castro, Eduardo Viveiros. 2004. "Perspectival Anthropology and the Method of Controlled Equivocation." *Tipiti* 2, no. 1: 3–22.
Deeb, L. 2015. "Thinking Piety and the Everyday Together: A Response to Fadil and Fernando." *HAU: Journal of Ethnographic Theory* 5, no. 3: 93–96.
Delaney, Carol. 1991. *The Seed and the Soil: Gender and Cosmology in Turkish Village Society.* Berkeley: University of California Press.
Devji, Faisal. 2005. *Landscapes of the Jihad: Militancy, Morality, Modernity.* London: Hurst.
Devji, Faisal. 2013. *Muslim Zion: Pakistan as a Political Idea.* Cambridge, MA: Harvard University Press.
Dhulipala, Venkat. 2015. *Creating a New Medina: State Power, Islam and the Quest for Pakistan in Late Colonial India.* Delhi: Cambridge University Press.
Dirks, Nicholas. 2001. *Castes of Mind: Colonialism and the Making of Modern India.* Princeton, NJ: Princeton University Press.
Dumont, Louis. 1980. *Homo Hierarchicus: The Caste System and Its Implications.* Chicago: University of Chicago Press.

Dumont, Louis. 1986. *Essays on Individualism: Modern Ideology in Anthropological Perspective*. Chicago: University of Chicago Press.
Dumont, Louis. 2013. "On Value. The Radcliffe-Brown Lecture in Social Anthropology, 1980." *HAU: Journal of Ethnographic Theory* 3, no. 1: 287–314.
Eaton, Richard. 2002. *Essays on Islam in Indian History*. New Delhi: Oxford University Press.
Eaton, Richard. 2003. *India's Islamic Traditions 711–750*. New Delhi and New York: Oxford University Press.
Eglar, Zekiye Suleyman. 2010 [1960]. *A Punjabi Village in Perspective*. Karachi: Oxford University Press.
Eickelman, Dale F. 1978. *The Art of Memory: Islamic Education and its Social Reproduction*. Cambridge: Cambridge University Press.
Eickelman, Dale F. 1992. "Mass Higher Education and the Religious Imagination in Contemporary Arab Societies." *American Ethnologist* 19, no. 4: 643–55.
Eickelman, Dale F., and James Piscatori. 1996. *Muslim Politics*. Princeton, NJ: Princeton University Press.
Eisenlohr, Patrick. 2006. "As Makkah Is Sweet and Beloved, So Is Madina: Islam, Devotional Genres, and Electronic Mediation in Mauritius." *American Ethnologist* 33, no. 2: 230–45.
Eisenlohr, Patrick. 2010. "Materialities of Entextualization: The Domestication of Sound Reproduction in Mauritian Muslim Devotional Practices." *Journal of Linguistic Anthropology* 20, no. 2: 314–33.
Eisenlohr, Patrick. 2011. "Introduction: What Is a Medium? Theologies, Technologies and Aspirations." *Social Anthropology* 19, no. 1: 1–5.
Eisenlohr, Patrick. 2018. *Sounding Islam*. Berkeley: University of California Press.
Engelke, Matthew. 2007. *A Problem of Presence: Beyond Scripture in an African Church*. University of California Press.
Engelke, Matthew. 2010. "Religion and the Media Turn: A Review Essay." *American Ethnologist* 37, no. 2: 371–79.
Ernst, Carl W., and Bruce B. Lawrence. 2002. *Sufi Martyrs of Love: The Chisti Order in South Asia and Above*. New York: Palgrave MacMillan.
Ewing, Katherine Pratt. 2010 "Anthropology and Pakistani National Imaginary." In *Beyond Crisis: Re-Evaluating Pakistan*, edited by Naveeda Khan, 531–40. London: Routledge.
Fader, Ayala. 2009. *Mitzvah Girls: Bringing up the Next Generation of Hasidic Jews in New York*. Princeton, NJ: Princeton University Press.
Fader, Ayala. 2017. "Ultra-Orthodox Jewish Interiority, the Internet, and the Crisis of Faith." *HAU: The Journal of Ethnographic Theory* 7, no. 1: 185–206.
Fadil, Nadia, and Mayanthi Fernando. 2015. "Rediscovering the "Everyday" Muslim: Notes on an Anthropological Divide." *HAU: Journal of Ethnographic Theory* 5, no. 2: 59–88.
Ferguson, James. 2015. *Give a Man a Fish: Reflections on the New Politics of Distribution*. Durham, NC: Duke University Press.
Fernando, Mayanthi. 2014. *The Republic Unsettled: Muslim French and the Contradictions of Secularism*. Durham, NC: Duke University Press.
Fischer, Michael M. J., and Mehdi Abedi. 1990. *Debating Muslims: Cultural Dialogues in Postmodernity and Tradition*. Madison: University of Wisconsin Press.
Foucault, Michel. 1994. "Technologies of the Self." In *The Essential Works of Michel Foucault 1954–1984 Vol. 1*, edited by Paul Rabinow, translated by Robert Hurley and others, 223–52. The New Press: New York.

Gaborieau, Marc. 1999. "Transnational Islamic Movements: The Tablighi Jama'at in Politics." *ISIM Newsletter*, 21. https://scholarlypublications.universiteitleiden.nl/handle/1887/17321.
Gaonkar, Dilip Parameshwar. 2001. *Alternative Modernities*. Durham, NC: Duke University Press.
Gayer, Laurent. 2014. *Karachi: Ordered Disorder and the Struggle for the City*. New York: Oxford University Press.
Gilmartin, David. 1981. "Kinship. Women, and Politics in Twentieth Century Punjab." In *The Extended Family: Women and Political Participation in India and Pakistan*, edited by Gail Minault, 151–73. Varanasi: Chanakya Publications.
Gilmartin, David. 1988. *Islam and Empire: Punjab and the Making of Pakistan*. Berkeley: University of California Press.
Gilmartin, David. 1998. "A Magnificent Gift: Muslim Nationalism and the Election Process in Colonial Punjab." *Comparative Studies in Society and History* 40, no. 3: 415–436.
Gilmartin, David. 2012. "Towards a Global History of Voting: Sovereignty, The Diffusion of Idea and the Enchanted Individual." *Religions* 3: 407–23.
Gilsenan, Michael. 1982. *Recognizing Islam*. London: Croom Helm.
Goffman, Erving. 1959. *The Presentation of Self in Everyday Life*. New York: Anchor Books.
Goffman, Erving. 1981. *Forms of Talk*. Philadelphia: University of Pennsylvania Press.
Graeber, David. 2001. *Toward an Anthropological Theory of Value: The False Coin of Our Own Dreams*. New York: Palgrave MacMillan.
Graeber, David. 2015. "Radical Alterity Is Just Another Way of Saying "Reality." A Reply to Eduardo Viveiros de Castro." *HAU: Journal of Ethnographic Theory* 5, no. 2: 1–41.
Graham, William. 1993. *Beyond the Written Word: Oral Aspects of Scripture in the History of Religion*. Cambridge: University of Cambridge.
Haeri, Niloofar. 2003. *Sacred Language, Ordinary People: Dilemmas of Culture and Politics in Egypt*. New York: Palgrave MacMillan.
Hallaq, Wael. 2013. *The Impossible State: Islam, Politics and Modernity's Moral Predicament*. New York: Columbia University Press.
Handler, Richard. 1988. *Nationalism and the Politics of Culture in Quebec*. Madison: University of Wisconsin Press.
Hansen, Thomas Blom. 1996. "Recuperating Masculinity: Hindu Nationalism, Violence, and the Exorcism of the Muslim 'Other.'" *Critique of Anthropology* 16, no. 2: 137–72.
Hansen, Thomas Blom. 1999. *The Saffron Wave: Democracy and Hindu Nationalism in Modern India*. Princeton, NJ: Princeton University Press.
Haq, Farhat. 2019. *Sharia and the State in Pakistan: Blasphemy Politics*. New York: Routledge.
Harding, Susan. 1991. "Representing Fundamentalism: The Problem of the Repugnant Cultural Other." *Social Research*: 373–93.
Haynes, Naomi, and Jason Hickel. 2016. "Introduction: Hierarchy, Value and the Value of Hierarchy." *Social Analysis* 60, no. 4: 1–20.
Hickel, Jason. 2015. *Democracy as Death: The Moral Order of Anti-Liberal Politics in South Africa*. Berkeley: University of California Press.
Hirschkind, Charles. 2006. *The Ethical Soundscape: Cassette Sermons and Islamic Counterpublics*. New York: Columbia University Press.
Ho, Engseng. 2006. *The Graves of Tarim: Genealogy and Mobility across the Indian Ocean*. Berkeley: University of California Press.

Hoesterey, James Bourk. 2015. *Rebranding Islam: Piety, Prosperity, and a Self-Help Guru.* Stanford: Stanford University Press.
Holbraad, Martin, and Morten Axel Pedersen. 2017. *The Ontological Turn: An Anthropological Exposition.* Cambridge: Cambridge University Press.
Human Rights Commission Pakistan. 2011. *The State of Human Rights Annual Report.*
Huntington, Samuel. 1996. *The Clash of Civilizations and the Remaking of World Order.* New York: Simon & Shuster.
International Commission of Jurists. 2015. *On Trial: The Implementation of Pakistan's Blasphemy Laws. International Commission of Jurists.* https://www.refworld.org/docid/565da4824.html.
Ingram, Brannon. 2014. "The Portable Madrassa: Print, Publics and the Authority of the Deobandi Ulama." *Modern Asian Studies* 48, no. 4: 845–71.
Ingram, Brannon. 2018. *Revival from Below: The Deoband Movement and Global Islam.* Berkeley: California University Press.
Iqtidar, Humeira. 2011. *Secularizing Islamists? Jama'at-e-Islami and Jama'at-ud-Da'wa in Urban Pakistan.* Chicago: University of Chicago Press.
Iqtidar, Humeira. 2017. "How Long Is Life? Neoliberalism and Islamic Piety." *Critical Inquiry* 43, no. 4: 790–812.
Jakobson, Roman. 1971. *Selective Writings, Vol II (Word and Language).* The Hague: Mouton.
Jaffrelot, Christophe. 2002. *Pakistan: Nationalism without a Nation.* Zed Books.
Jalal, Ayesha. 1985. *The Sole Spokesman: Jinnah. The Muslim League and the Demand for Pakistan.* Cambridge: Cambridge University Press.
Jalal, Ayesha. 1995. "Conjuring Pakistan: History as Official Imagining." *International Journal of Middle East Studies* 27, no. 1: 73–89.
Janson, Marloes. 2014. *Islam, Youth and Modernity in the Gambia: The Tablīghī Jama'at.* New York: Cambridge University Press.
Jinnah, Mohammad Ali. Address to Constituent Assembly, August 11, 1947. https://pakistan.gov.pk/Quaid/messages_page2.html.
Jinnah Institute Research Report. 2015. *A Question of Faith: A Report on the Status of Religious Minorities in Pakistan.* https://jinnah-institute.org/publication/a-question-of-faith-a-report-on-the-status-of-religious-minorities-in-pakistan/.
Juergensmeyer, Mark. 2000. *Terror in the Mind of God: The Global Rise of Religious Violence.* Berkeley: University of California Press.
Kantorowicz, Ernst H. 1997. *The King's Two Bodies: A Study in Medieval Political Theology.* Princeton, NJ: Princeton University Press.
Kasmani, Omar. 2022. *Queer Companions: Religion, Public Intimacy, and Saintly Affects in Pakistan.* Durham, NC: Duke University Press.
Keane, Webb. 2003. "Semiotics and the Social Analysis of Material Things." *Language and Communication* 23: 409–25.
Keane, Webb. 2007. *Christian Moderns: Freedom and Fetish in the Mission Encounter.* Berkeley: University of California Press.
Keane, Webb. 2016. *The Ethical Life: Its Natural and Social Histories.* Princeton, NJ: Princeton University Press.
Keeler, Ward. 2017. *The Traffic in Hierarchy: Masculinity and its Others in Buddhist Burma.* Honolulu: University of Hawaii Press.
Khan, Arsalan. 2016. "Islam and Pious Sociality: The Ethics of Hierarchy in the Tablighi Jamaat in Pakistan." *Social Analysis* 60, no. 4: 96–113.
Khan, Arsalan. 2018. "Pious Masculinity, Ethical Reflexivity and Moral Order in an Islamic Piety Movement in Pakistan. *Anthropological Quarterly* 91, no. 1: 53–78.

Khan, Naveeda. 2010. "Introduction." In *Beyond Crisis: Re-evaluating Pakistan*, edited by Naveeda Khan, 1–30. London: Routledge.
Khan, Naveeda. 2012. *Muslim Becoming: Aspiration and Skepticism in Pakistan*. Durham, NC: Duke University Press.
Khan, Nicola. 2010. *Mohajir Militancy in Pakistan: Violence and Transformation in the Karachi Conflict*. New York: Routledge.
Khan, Taimur. 2013. "Cooking in Karachi." *Foreign Policy*, September 3. https://foreignpolicy.com/2013/09/03/cooking-in-karachi/.
Khoja-Moolji, Shenila. 2021. *Sovereign Attachments: Masculinity, Muslimness, and Affective Politics in Pakistan*. Oakland: University of California Press.
Kirmani, Nida. 2015. "Fear and the City: Negotiating Everyday Life as a Baloch Man in Karachi." *Journal of Economic and Social History of the Orient* 58, no. 5: 732–55.
Kloos, David. 2018. *Becoming Better Muslims: Religious Authority and Ethical Improvement in Aceh Indonesia*. Princeton, NJ: Princeton University Press.
Kloos, David, and Daan Beekers, 2018. "Introduction: The Productive Potential of Moral Failure in Lived Islam and Christianity." In *Straying from the Straight Path: How Senses of Failure Invigorate Lived Religion*, edited by Daan Beekers and David Kloos, 1–20. New York and Oxford: Berghahn.
Knauft, Bruce. 2002. *Critically Modern: Alternatives, Alterities, Anthropologies*. Bloomington: Indiana University Press.
Kurin, Richard. 1980. "*Person, Family and Kin in Two Pakistani Communities*." PhD diss., University of Chicago.
Kurin, Richard. 1986. "Morality, Personhood and the Exemplary Life: Popular Conceptions of Muslims in Paradise." In *Moral Conduct and Authority: The Place of Adab in South Asian Islam*, edited by Barbara Metcalf, 196–220. Berkeley: University of California Press.
Kurin, Richard. 1988. "The Culture of Ethnicity in Pakistan." In *Shariat and Ambiguity in South Asian Islam*, edited by Katherine Ewing, 220–47. Berkeley: University of California Press.
Laclau, Ernesto. 2005. *On Populist Reason*. London and New York: Verso.
Laidlaw, James. 2014. *The Subject of Virtue: An Anthropology of Virtue and Freedom*. Cambridge: Cambridge University Press.
Lambek, Michael. 1993. *Knowledge and Practice in Mayotte: Local Discourses of Islam, Sorcery, and Spirit Possession*. Toronto: University of Toronto Press.
Lambek, Michael. 2010. *Ordinary Ethics: Anthropology, Language, and Action*. New York: Fordham University Press.
Lebner, Ashley. 2015. "The Anthropology of Secularity beyond Secularism." *Religion and Society: Advances in Research* 6: 62–74.
Lefebvre, Alain. 2014. *Kinship, Honour and Money in Rural Pakistan: Subsistence Economy and the Effects of International Migration*. New York: Routledge.
Lelyveld, David. 1978. *Aligarh's First Generation: Muslim Solidarity in British India*. Princeton, NJ: Princeton University Press.
Lelyveld, David. 1993. "The Fate of Hindustani: Colonial Knowledge and the Project of a National Language." In *Orientalism and the Postcolonial Predicament: Perspectives on South Asia*, edited by Carol Breckenridge and Peter van der Veer, 189–214. Philadelphia: University of Pennsylvania Press.
Lemons, Katherine. 2019. *Divorcing Traditions: Islamic Marriage Law and the Making of Indian Secularism*. Ithaca, NY: Cornell University Press.
Li, Darryl, 2020. *The Universal Enemy: Jihad, Empire, and the Challenge of Solidarity*. Stanford: Stanford University Press.

Lindholm, Charles. 1998. "Prophets and Pirs: Charismatic Islam in the Middle East and South Asia." In *Embodying Charisma*, edited by Pnina Werbner and Helene Basu, 209-33. New York: Routledge.
Mahmood, Saba. 2001. "Rehearsed Spontaneity and the Conventionality of Ritual: Disciplines of Salat." *American Ethnologist* 28, no. 4: 827-53.
Mahmood, Saba. 2005. *Politics of Piety: The Islamic Revival and the Feminist Subject*. Princeton, NJ: Princeton University Press.
Mahmood, Saba. 2009. "Religious Reason and Secular Affect: An Incommensurable Divide." In *Is Critique Secular?: Blasphemy, Injury, and Free Speech*, edited by Talal Asad, Wendy Brown, Judith Butler, and Saba Mahmood, 64-100. Berkeley: University of California Press.
Mahmood, Saba. 2016. *Religious Difference in a Secular Age: A Minority Report*. Princeton, NJ: Princeton University Press.
Maine, Henry Sumner. 1861. *Ancient Law*. London: Murray.
Malara, Diego Maria, and Tom Boylston. 2016. "Vertical Love: Forms of Submission and Top-Down Power in Orthodox Ethiopia." *Social Analysis* 60, no. 4: 40-57.
Mani, Lata. 1998. *Contentious Traditions: The Debate on Sati in Colonia India*. Berkeley: University of California Press.
Maqsood, Ammara. 2017. *The New Pakistani Middle Class*. Cambridge, MA: Harvard University Press.
Marsden, Magnus. 2005. *Living Islam: Muslim Religious Experience in Pakistan's North-West Frontier*. New York: Cambridge University Press.
Marsden, Magnus, and Kostas Retsikas. 2012. *Articulating Islam: Anthropological Approaches to Muslim Worlds*. Springer Science & Business Media.
Masud, Muhammad Khalid. 2000. *Travellers in Faith: Studies of the Tablīghī Jamā'at as a Transnational Islamic Movement for Faith Renewal*. Brill.
Mauss, Marcel. 1954. *The Gift: Forms and Functions of Exchange in Archaic Societies*. Translated by W. D. Halls. W.W. Norton.
Mazzarella, William. 2006. "Internet X-Ray: E-Governance, Transparency and the Politics of Immediation in India." *Public Culture* 18, no 3: 473-505.
McAllister, Carlota, and Valentina Napolitano. 2021. *Annual Review of Anthropology* 50: 109-24.
Mernissi, Fatima. 1975. *Beyond the Veil: Male-Female Dynamics in Modern Muslim Society*. New York: John Wiley and Sons.
Mertz, Elizabeth. 1985. "Beyond Symbolic Anthropology: Introducing Semiotic Mediation." In *Semiotic Mediation: Sociocultural and Psychological Perspectives*, edited by Elizabeth Mertz and Richard Parmentier, 1-19. London: Academic Press.
Messick, Brinkley. 1992. *The Calligraphic State: Textual Domination and History in a Muslim Society*. Berkeley: University of California Press.
Metcalf, Barbara. 1978. "The Madrassa at Deoband: A Model for Islamic Education in Modern India." *Modern Asian Studies* 12, no 1: 111-34.
Metcalf, Barbara. 1982. *Islamic Revival in British India: Deoband, 1860-1900*. Princeton, NJ: Princeton University Press.
Metcalf, Barbara. 1993. "Living Hadith in the Tablighi Jama'at." *Journal of Asian Studies* 52, no. 3: 584-608.
Metcalf, Barbara. 1998. "Women and Men in Contemporary Pietist Movements: The Case of the Tablighi Jamaat." In *Appropriating Gender: Women's Activism and Politicized Religion in South Asia*, edited by Amita Basu and Patricia Jeffrey, 107-21. New York: Routledge.
Metcalf, Barbara. 2003. "Travelers' Tales in the Tablighi Jamaat." *The Annals of the American Academy of Political Science* 588, no. 1: 136-48.

Metcalf, Barbara. 2004. *Islamic Contestations: Essays on Muslims in India and Pakistan*. New Delhi: Oxford University Press.
Meyer, Birgit. 2006. "Religious Sensations: Why Aesthetics, Media and Power Matter in the Study of Contemporary Religion." *Inaugural Lecture*. Vrije, Universiteit, Amsterdam (6-10-2006).
Meyer, Birgit, ed. 2009. *Aesthetic Formations: Media, Religion, and the Senses*. New York: Palgrave Macmillan.
Meyer, Birgit. 2011. "Mediation and immediacy: Sensational Forms, Semiotic Ideologies and the Question of the Medium." *Social Anthropology* 19, no. 1: 23–39.
Meyer, Birgit, and Annelies Moors. 2006. *Religion, Media, and the Public Sphere*. Bloomington: Indiana University Press.
Mitchell, Timothy. 2006. "State, Economy, and the State Effect." In *The Anthropology of the State: A Reader*, edited by Ardhana Sharma and Akhil Gupta, 169–89. Blackwell Publishing.
Mittermaier, Amira. 2011. *Dreams That Matter: Egyptian Landscapes of the Imagination*. Berkeley: University of California Press.
Moin, Azfar. 2012. *The Millenial Sovereign: Sacred Kingship & Sainthood in Islam*. New York: Columbia University Press.
Muehlebach, Andrea. 2012. *The Moral Neoliberal: Welfare and Citizenship in Italy*. Chicago: University of Chicago Press.
Munn, Nancy. 1986. *The Fame of Gawa: A Symbolic Study of Value Transformation in Massim (Papua New Guinea) Society*. Cambridge: Cambridge University Press.
Murata, Sachiko. 1992. *The Tao of Islam: A Sourcebook on Gender Relationships in Islamic Thought*. New York: State University of New York Press.
Nakassis, Constantine. 2016. *Doing Style: Youth and Mass Mediation in South India*. Chicago: University of Chicago Press.
Nelson, Matthew J. 2011. *In the Shadow of Shari'ah: Islam, Islamic Law, and Democracy in Pakistan*. New York: Columbia University Press.
Noor, Farish. 2012. *Islam on the Move: The Tablighi Jamaat in Southeast Asia*. Amsterdam: Amsterdam University Press.
Pakistan Census. 2017. Pakistan Bureau of Statistics, Government of Pakistan. https://www.pbs.gov.pk/content/final-results-census-2017-0.
Pandey, Gyan. 1990. *The Construction of Communalism in Colonial North India*. Oxford University Press.
Peirce, Charles Sanders. 2011. *Philosophical Writings of Peirce*, edited by Justus Buchler. New York: Dover Publications.
Pelkmans, Mathijs. 2017. *Fragile Conviction: Changing Ideological Landscapes in Urban Kyrgyzstan*. Ithaca, NY: Cornell University Press.
Pernau, Margrit. 2013. *Ashraf into Middle Classes: Muslims in Nineteenth-Century Delhi*. Oxford University Press.
Piliavsky, Anastasia. 2020. *Nobody's People: Hierarchy as Hope in a Society of Thieves*. Stanford: Stanford University Press.
Piot, Charles. 2010. *Nostalgia for the Future: West Africa after the Cold War*. Chicago: University of Chicago Press.
Qasmi, Ali Usman. 2014. *The Ahmadis and the Politics of Religious Exclusion in Pakistan*. London and New York: Anthem Press, 2014.
Rahman, Fazlur. 1979. *Islam*. Chicago: University of Chicago Press.
Rappaport, Roy. 1999. *Ritual and Religion in the Making of Humanity*. Cambridge: Cambridge University Press.
Rashid, Maria. 2020. *Dying to Serve: Militarism, Affect, and the Politics of Sacrifice in the Pakistan Army*. Stanford, CA: Stanford University Press.

Reetz, Dietrich. 2006. *Islam in the Public Sphere: Religious Groups in India, 1900–1947.* Delhi: Oxford University Press.
Reetz, Dietrich. 2008. "The 'Faith Bureaucracy' of the Tablighi Jama'at: An Insight into Their System of Self-Organization (Intizam)." In *Colonialism, Modernity, and Religious Identities: Religious Reform Movements,* edited by Gwilym Beckerlegge, 98–124. New Delhi: Oxford University Press.
Ring, Laura. 2006. *Zenana: Everyday Peace in a Karachi Apartment Building.* Bloomington: Indiana University Press.
Robbins, Joel. 2001. "God Is Nothing but Talk: Modernity, Language, and Prayer in a Papua New Guinea Society." *American Anthropologist* 103, no. 4: 901–12.
Robbins, Joel. 2001. "Ritual Communication and Linguistic Ideology: A Reading and Partial Reformulation of Rappaport's Theory of Ritual." *Current Anthropology* 42, no. 5: 591–614.
Robbins, Joel. 2004. *Becoming Sinners: Christianity and Moral Torment in a Papua New Guinea Society.* Berkeley: University of California Press.
Robinson, Francis. 1974. *Separatism among Indian Muslims: The Politics of the United Provinces' Muslims, 1860–1923.* London and New York: Cambridge University Press.
Robinson, Francis. 2001. *The 'Ulama of Farangi Mahall and Islamic Culture in South Asia.* Hyderabad: Orient Blackswan.
Rock-Singer, Aaron. 2022. *In the Shade of the Sunna: Salafi Piety in the Twentieth-Century Middle East.* Oakland: University of California Press.
Roy, Olivier. 1994. *The Failure of Political Islam.* Cambridge, MA: Harvard University Press.
Rudnyckyj, Daromir. 2009. "Market Islam in Indonesia." *Journal of the Royal Anthropological Institute* 15: S183–S201.
Sanyal, Usha. 1996. *Devotional Islam and Politics in British India. Ahmad Riza Khan: Barelwi and his Movement, 1870–1920.* Delhi: Oxford University Press.
Schimmel, Annemarie. 1992. *Islam: An Introduction.* Albany: State University of New York Press.
Shaikh, Farzana. 2009. *Making Sense of Pakistan.* New York: Columbia University Press.
Schielke, Samuli. 2009. "Being Good in Ramadan: Ambivalence, Fragmentation and the Moral Self in the Lives of Young Egyptians." *Journal of Royal Anthropological Institute,* 24–40.
Schielke, Samuli. 2015. *Egypt in the Future Tense: Hope, Frustration and Ambivalence before and after 2011.* Bloomington: Indiana University Press.
Shryock, Andrew. 1997. *Nationalism and the Genealogical Imagination: Oral History and Textual Authority in Tribal Jordan.* Berkeley: University of California Press.
Siddiqi, Bulbul. 2018. *Becoming "Good Muslim": The Tablighi Jamaat in the UK and Bangladesh.* Singapore: Springer.
Siddique, Osama, and Zahra Hayat. 2008. "Unholy Speech and Holy Laws: Blasphemy Laws in Pakistan: Controversial Origins, Design Defects and Free Speech Implications." *Minnesota Journal of International Law* 17, no. 2: 305–85.
Sikand, Yoginder. 2002. *Origins and Development of the Tablighi Jamaat (1920–2000): A Cross Country Comparative Study.* London: Sangam Books.
Silverstein, Brian. 2003. "Islam and Modernity in Turkey: Power, Tradition and Historicity in the European Provinces of the Muslim World." *Anthropological Quarterly* 76, no. 3: 497–517.
Silverstein, Brian. 2008. "Disciplines of Presence in Modern Turkey: Discourse, Companionship and the Mass Mediation of Islamic Practice." *Cultural Anthropology* 23, no. 1: 118–53.

Silverstein, Brian. 2011. *Islam and Modernity in Turkey*. New York: Palgrave Macmillan.
Silverstein, Michael. 1976. "Shifters, Linguistic Categories, and Cultural Description." In *Meaning in Anthropology*, edited by Keith H. Basso and Henry A. Selby, 11–55. Albuquerque: University of New Mexico Press.
Silverstein, Paul. 2004. "Of Rooting and Uprooting: Kabyle Habitus, Uprooting and Structural Nostalgia." *Ethnography* 5, no. 4: 553–78.
Simon, Gregory M. 2014. *Caged In on the Outside: Moral Subjectivity, Selfhood, and Islam in Minangkabau, Indonesia*. Honolulu: University of Hawaii Press.
Sinha, Mrinalini. 1995. *Colonial Masculinity: The "Manly Englishmen" and the "Effeminate Bengali" in the Late Nineteenth Century*. Manchester: Manchester University Press.
Stasch, Rupert. 2011. "Ritual and Oratory Revisited: The Semiotics of Effective Action." *Annual Review of Anthropology* 40: 159–74.
Stephens, Julia. 2018. *Governing Islam: Law, Empire, and Secularism in Modern South Asia*. Cambridge: Cambridge University Press.
Strathern, Marilyn. 1988. *The Gender of the Gift: Problems with Women and Problems with Society in Melanesia*. Berkeley and Los Angeles: University of California Press.
Streets, Heather. 2004. *Martial Races: The Military, Race, and Masculinity in British Imperial Culture, 1857–1914*. Manchester: Manchester University Press.
Tapper, Nancy. 1991. *Bartered Brides: Gender and Marriage in an Afghan Tribal Society*. Cambridge: Cambridge University Press.
Tareen, Sher Ali. 2020. *Defending Muhammad in Modernity*, Notre Dame, IN: University of Notre Dame Press.
Taylor, Charles. 2004. *Modern Social Imaginaries*. Durham, NC: Duke University Press.
The Quran. 2004. Translated by Saheeh International. Jeddah: Al-Muntada Al-Islami. https://asimiqbal2nd.files.wordpress.com/2009/06/quran-sahih-international.pdf.
Thomas, Todne, Asiya Malik, and Rose Wellman, eds. 2017. *New Directions in Spiritual Kinship: Sacred Ties across the Abrahamic Religions*. New York: Palgrave MacMillan.
Tomlinson, Matt. 2017. "Introduction: Imagining the Monologic." In *The Monological Imagination*, edited by Matt Tomlinson and Julian Millie, 1–18. Oxford: Oxford University Press.
Tomlinson, Matt, and Julian Millie. 2017. *The Monological Imagination*. Oxford: Oxford University Press.
Toor, Saadia. 2011. *The State of Islam: Culture and Cold War Politics in Pakistan*. Pluto Press.
Torab, Azam. 2007. *Performing Islam: Gender and Ritual in Iran*. Leiden: Brill.
Turner, Victor. 1977. *The Ritual Process: Structure and Anti-Structure*. Ithaca, NY: Cornell University Press.
Van der Veer, Peter. 1992. "Playing or Praying; A Sufi Saint's Day in Surat." *Journal of Asian Studies* 51, no. 3: 545–64.
Van der Veer, Peter. 1993. "The Foreign Hand: Orientalist Discourse in Sociology and Communalism." In *Orientalism and the Postcolonial Predicament*, edited by Carol Breckenridge and Peter Van der Veer, 23–45. Philadelphia: University of Pennsylvania Press.
Van der Veer, Peter. 1994. *Religious Nationalism: Hindus and Muslims in India*. Delhi: Oxford University Press.
Verkaaik, Oscar. 2004. *Migrants and Militants: Fun and Urban Violence in Pakistan*. Princeton, NJ: Princeton University Press.

Verkaaik, Oscar. 2016. "Violence and Ethnic Identity Politics in Karachi and Hyderabad." *South Asia: Journal of South Asian Studies* 39, no. 4: 841–54.
Warner, Michael. 2002 "Publics and Counterpublics." *Public Culture* 14, no. 1: 49–90.
Washbrook, David A. 1981 "Law, State and Agrarian Society in Colonial India." *Modern Asian Studies* 15, no. 3: 649–721.
Watt, Montgomery. 1998 [1973]. *The Formative Period of Islamic Thought*. London: Oneworld Publications.
Werbner, Pnina. 2005. *Pilgrims of Love: The Anthropology of a Global Sufi Cult*. Bloomington: Indiana University Press.
Werbner, Pnina, and Helene Basu, eds. 1998. *Embodying Charisma: Modernity, Locality, and the Performance of Emotion in Sufi Cults*. New York: Routledge.
Werbner, Pnina, and Helene Basu. 1998. "Introduction: The Embodiment of Charisma." In *Embodying Charisma: Modernity, Locality and the Performance of Emotion in Sufi Cults*, edited by Pnina Werbner and Helene Basu, 3–30. New York: Routledge.
Wittrock, Björn. 2000. "Modernity: One, None, or Many? European Origins and Modernity as a Global Condition." *Daedalus* 129, no. 1: 31–60.
Woodward, Mark R. 1989. *Islam in Java: Normative Piety and Mysticism in the Sultanate of Yogyakarta*. Tucson: University of Arizona Press.
Wright, Theodore P. 1991. "Center-Periphery Relations and Ethnic Conflict in Pakistan: Sindhis, Muhajirs, and Punjabis." *Comparative Politics* 23, no. 3: 299–312.
Zaman, Muhammad Qasim. 1998. "Sectarianism in Pakistan: The Radicalization of Shi'i and Sunni Identities." *Modern Asian Studies* 32, no. 3: 689–716.
Zaman, Muhammad Qasim. 2002. *The Ulama in Contemporary Islam: Custodians of Change*. Princeton, NJ: Princeton University Press.
Zaman, Muhammad Qasim. 2018. *Islam in Pakistan: A History*. Princeton, NJ: Princeton University Press.

Index

Page numbers in italic indicate figures.

Abbas, Sadia, 16
Abdullah (Tablighi), 83–84, 136–37, 144
Abid (Tablighi), 65–67, 70–71, 109–10, 164–65, 168
Abraham. *See* Ibrahim
affordances, 22, 178–83, 186, 188, 194
Aftab (Tablighi), 109, 190
agency, 6, 12, 13, 15, 65, 68–69, 103, 123, 149–52, 194; divine, 20, 96–97; surplus, 136, 156–59. *See also* pious agency
agnatic theory, 36, 39–40, 83
Agrama, Hussein Ali, 193
Ahl-e-Hadith, 46, 109
Ahmadiyya community, 31, 46, 160, 173–74
Ahmad Khan, Sir Syed, 46, 51–52
Ahmed (Tablighi), 178–79
Ahmed, Asad Ali, 175–76
Ahmed, Khaled, 184
Ahmed, Qazi Hussain, 172
ajlaf, 19, 28, 31, 35, 49, 159
Akbar (Mughal emperor), 35
Alam, Muzaffar, 37
Al-Aqsa Mosque (Karachi), 9, 61, 115, 117–19, 121, 125, 139, 146, 153
Aligarh Muslim University, 52, 55
All-India Muslim League, 50, 52–54
alterity, 11–13
amal, 29, 32, 43, 47, 64, 75, 78–79, 81, 92–94, 101–2; *afzal,* 133; *dini,* 4; *ijitmai,* 88; *infiradi,* 88
ambiguity, 16, 30, 76, 87, 95
ambivalence, 16, 30, 76, 87, 95, 144, 150, 155, 169, 183
amir, 88, 139, 145, 146, 165, 189, 190
Anderson, Benedict, 48–49
Anderson, Michael R., 40
Anglo Muhammadan Law, 40
anxiety, 41, 51, 131, 144
aql. See reason
Arabic language, 17, 51, 104
Arya Samaj, 30–31
Asad, Talal, 14, 63, 174–75, 193
Asghar (Tablighi), 165–66

ashraf, 19, 28, 31, 35, 49, 54–55, 57, 159, 160, 182
authenticity, 30, 44, 197, 199
authority, 120; fragmentation of, 162–63; genealogical, 29, 34, 41, 46; Islamic, 108, 162–63, 165; patriarchal, 187; pious, 22, 132, 167–71; sovereign, 35, 176, 182; textual, 37, 201n2 (chap. 1); traditional, 106–7. *See also* pious authority
Awami National Party, 59
azaan, 90, 133

Ball, Christopher, 94–95
Bangla, 56
Bangladesh, 160. *See also* East Pakistan
baniya, 62
Barelwis, 18, 31, 59–60, 66, 141, 143, 144, 157, 178, 204n5
Basharat bhai (Tablighi), 146
bayan, 1, 84, 88, 90, 104, 111
beard, 10, 61, 93, 153, 185, 186
Bengalis, 55–56
Bhutto, Zulfiqar Ali, 56, 160
Bibi, Asia, 173, 179–80, 203nn1–2, 204n6. *See also* Qadri, Mumtaz; Taseer, Salman
biddat, 20, 278, 102, 104–7, 110, 143, 154, 169
blasphemy, 22; politics of, 176–83, 187, 204n7
blasphemy laws, 172–76, 184, 203nn3–4
boundaries, 5, 14, 16, 22, 29–30, 46, 47, 141, 154, 172, 179–80, 190–91, 193, 195
British administrators, 37–39
British rule, 27, 30
buzurg. See Elders

care, 6, 133–38, 186–88; ethics of, 167–69. *See also* hierarchy; moral responsibility; responsibility
Carrier, James, 168
caste, 6, 28, 31, 47, 52–54, 69–72, 151–52, 159, 182, 192, 198. See also *ajlaf; ashraf*
Cavannaugh, William, 185
certain faith, 21, 129–52
Chatterjee, Partha, 49, 203n1 (chap. 5)

217

chilla, 61, 85, 88, 97–98, 117, 120, 136. See also *dawat*: tours
Chisti order, 9, 108, 201n2 (Introduction)
Christians, 31, 77, 173
civilization, 30, 50, 196
class, 12–13, 19, 29, 47–48, 49, 52, 55, 57, 151–52, 182, 192; agricultural, 39; capitalist, 187; merchant, 70–71
closeness, 3, 32, 48, 79, 136, 169
collectiveness, 105, 122
colonialism, 19, 28, 34, 37, 40, 45, 49, 55–57, 175, 183, 190–91, 201nn1–2 (chap. 1)
common law, 42
community, 15, 151, 166; Islamic, 4, 15, 21, 33, 46–49, 60, 63–65, 69, 134–36, 148, 150, 151, 155, 164–66, 179–83, 195, 198
companion, 85, 88, 99, 124, 131
companionship, 17, 105, 108, 111, 119; ethic of, 110. See also *sohbat*
Companions of the Prophet, 4, 106, 122, 125, 129, 166
conflict, 164–66, 178–79
congregation, 47, 61; dinner, 113–14, 190; life of, 124–26. See also Tablighi Jamaat: annual congregations
consultation, 96, 178–79
control, 82, 121–22, 161
coolness, 135
cosmology, 35, 76, 82
cosmopolitanism, 160, 182
courts, 40, 164, 184
creed paradigm, 20, 76, 92
cricket, 129–30, 142–43
cultural intimacy, 7–13, 192
custom, 40, 50, 55–57, 63–69, 71, 143, 165
customary law, 19, 34, 38–40

Danish Cartoon Controversy, 176–77
Danziger, Eve, 202n2 (chap. 4)
darja, 76, 96, 98
Dar-ul-Uloom madrassa, 41–42. See also Deobandi ulama
dawat, 2, 136; act, 76; as bodily discipline, 87; as duty, 32, 89; disciplinary power of, 135; face-to-face nature of, 170; and gender, 81–85; and Islamic authority, 166; as Islamic practice, 7–8, 131; as mandatory practice, 153–54; as performative, 94–95; act, 76; *politiks* and, 155, 193–94; Tablighi conception of, 3, 13–14, 87, 153; tension within, 104; tours, 83, 85, 97, 132; and transcendence, 48–72, 65–72, 191; transformative power of, 80

decline, 30
Defence of Pakistan Council, 176
Delaney, Carol, 82
denominations, 153–54, 178. See also *maslak*
Deobandi ulama, 5, 19, 27–29, 64–65, 141, 143, 183, 204n5; Department of Preaching, 31; tradition of, 82, 110, 155. See also Zaman, Muhammad Qasim
descendants of the Prophet, 35–36
desire, 79, 82, 90–91, 102, 104, 121–22, 125, 137, 170, 181; sexual, 83
Devji, Faisal, 54
din. See religion
directness, 18, 19, 68–70, 75–76, 99, 109, 182, 198; regulation of, 125
direct relationship, 13, 17–18, 48, 65–68, 87, 108, 109, 111, 143, 191, 197
direct rule, 30
disjuncture, 91–92, 138–45
divine light, 36
doubt, 21, 87, 95, 131–33, 138–45, 150–52
dried out. See *khushka*
Dumont, Louis, 6, 13
dunya. See world

East Pakistan, 55, 160. See also Bangladesh
Eaton, Richard, 201n1 (chap. 1)
education, 41, 50, 52, 54–55
egalitarianism, 96, 192
Egerton, Sir Robert, 38
Eickelman, Dale, 42, 163
Eid-e-Milad-un-Nabi, 144
Eisenlohr, Patrick, 18
Elders, 2, 9, 99, 109, 112, 118–19, 125, 132, 139, 154, 166, 178, 189–90; authority of, 150
embodied practices, 15, 33, 45
embodied process, 117
embodiment, 32, 43, 45, 54, 78, 118, 176, 181, 191
Engelke, Matthew, 17–18
English language, 51, 117, 130, 131
equality, 84, 196, 197
ethical reflexivity, 6–7, 16
ethical voices, 151
ethics, 15; of listening, 106–7. See also care: ethics of; hierarchy: ethics of
ethnicity, 62, 192; worship, 62–63
ethnic joking, 62. See also humor
ethnographic approach, 8
ethnolinguistic identity, 160
everyday: acts, 5; affordances, 188; citationality, 17, 20, 100, 124–25; concerns, 16; discourse, 90, 123, 134; life, 14, 16, 44, 95,

123, 124, 131–32, 150–51, 187, 191; discrimination, 174; miracles, 8; practice, 108, 125
Ewing, Katherine, 60

faith, 14–15, 33, 62–63, 118, 120, 129, 157; cultivation of, 118; materiality of, 81. See also certain faith
faith bureaucracy, 96
family, 132, 133, 135–36, 140, 144–46, 150
Fazail-e-Amal, 90, 122, 178
Fazl-ur-Rahman, Maulana, 172
fitna, 2, 21, 53, 60, 69, 83, 153–71
Foucault, Michel, 15, 75–76, 92, 202n1 (chap. 3)
free speech, 174. See also Danish Cartoon Controversy
friendship, 8, 62, 117, 118, 145, 166, 192

gangster, 161–62
gasht, 88, 98, 156
Geertz, Clifford, 14
gender, 76, 82–86, 148, 186; labor and, 148–49. See also *pardah*
genealogy, 35, 49, 55, 201n2 (chap. 1); and Islamic Habitus, 61–65. See also authority: genealogical
gestation, 85, 98
ghaflat, 86
ghaib, 143
ghunda. See gangster
gift economies, 168
gifts, 167–68
Gilmartin, David, 5, 39, 53–54, 197
Global War on Terror, 8, 196
Goffman, Erving, 18, 202n2 (chap. 2)

hadith, 44–45, 62, 77, 122
Haeri, Niloofar, 17, 103–4
hafiz-e-Quran, 146. See also recitation of the Quran
Hagar. See Hajra
Hajra, 133–34, 148
Handler, Richard, 176–77
Hansen, Thomas Blom, 161
Haq, Farhat, 176
Harding, Susan, 185
hardness, 135, 158, 161, 179
hardship, 88, 96, 106, 133
Hastings Plan (1772), 40
Hazrat, 9–10, 108, 115–17, 119, 121, 123–25, 129, 131, 134–35, 139, 146, 164
headscarf, 204n1
heart, 15, 36, 67, 69, 79, 81–82, 85, 87–90, 93, 97, 109, 116, 118, 135, 137, 161–62, 179

hierarchy, 15, 192; ethics of, 5–7, 101–26, 135, 170, 185, 188; gender, 186; religious, 162; sacred, 95–100, 119, 124, 188, 192; socioeconomic, 187
Hindi, 51
Hinduism, 28, 30–31, 32, 35, 37, 40, 46, 57, 64, 143
Hindu nationalism, 195
Hindu reform, 30, 203n1 (chap. 5)
Hindus, 29–31, 35, 36, 37, 40, 50–51, 62, 64, 204n7
Hirschkind, Charles, 14–15, 75, 86, 106, 184–85, 193
Ho, Engseng, 36
home, Islamic, 21, 133–52
hubris, 89, 103–5, 111, 120–22, 157
Hudood Ordinances, 160
humility, 15, 20, 75, 81, 84, 86, 105, 122–23, 158
humor, 130, 131, 141, 161
hypocrite, 107–8

Ibrahim, 133–34, 148
iconicity, 20, 76, 86–95, 108. See also indexicality: iconic
ideology: ritual, 8, 16, 33, 87; semiotic, 12, 17, 93, 175
idol, 69, 159, 182
idolatry, 143, 204n5
ijtima. See Tablighi Jamaat: annual congregations
ikraam, 97, 169
Illum-ud-Din, 204n7
Ilyas, Muhammad, 3, 27–28, 31–33, 91
Imaad bhai (Tablighi), 139–40, 151
Iman. See faith
immediacy, 18, 65–72, 87, 108–9, 170. See also directness; direct relationship
impious people, 11, 132
indeterminacy, 15, 18, 76, 95, 99, 108, 194–95
indexicality, 20, 76, 94–95, 97, 107; iconic, 95, 123, 125. See also Peirce, Charles; semiotics
Indian Penal Code (1860), 173, 204n7
individual, the, 151–52, 162, 169, 174, 187, 196–97, 202n1 (chap. 3)
Ingram, Brannon, 33, 42, 44–45, 57, 110, 155
innovation. See *biddat*
intention, 88, 92, 157, 174; purity of, 87–88, 90
intercession, 35, 109, 157. See also saints: intercession by
interchangeability, 10, 12, 192
interpretation, 104
intimacy, 7–13, 192

INDEX

Iqbal, Muhammad, 52
Iqtidar, Humeira, 194
Irfan (Tablighi), 93–94, 145–49, 150
islah, 9, 27, 33, 57, 79, 84, 151. *See also* Islamic reform
Islam, 52–57, 60, 62–64, 65, 67, 69–75, 77–79, 82, 91–92, 101, 104–5, 116–17, 120, 140–42, 157–59, 162–63, 169–71, 174–77, 181–83, 191–96
Islamic future, 129–52, 181
Islamic governmentality, 159–64
Islamic habitus, 15, 47, 61–65, 69, 94, 133, 145–49
Islamic law, 4, 5, 19, 29, 160, 180, 183, 191, 198; codification of, 33–34, 37
Islamic public sphere, 45–57, 191
Islamic reform, 5, 19, 27, 28, 49, 57, 64, 192, 203n1 (chap. 5)
Islamic revival, 4–5, 14–15, 57, 160
Islamic state, 4, 6, 22, 46, 154, 159–60, 170, 180–83, 195, 198, 201n2 (intro)
Islamic statehood, 50–58
Islamism, 46, 57, 156, 158, 159
Islamists, 4, 154, 156–59, 194
Islamization, 57, 163, 167–71, 173, 191, 194–95
Islamophobia, 196
Ismail, 134
isnad, 44, 77, 122

Jalal, Ayesha, 50
Jamaat-e-Islami, 4, 46, 56, 58, 154, 156–57, 160, 166, 172
Jamaat-e-Ulama-e-Islam, 155, 172
Jamaat-e-ulama-e-Pakistan, 172
Jamaat-ud-Dawa, 156, 172
Jameel, Maulana Tariq, 204n6
jihad, 58, 185, 198
Jinnah, Mohammad Ali, 50, 52
Jinnah Institute, 173
jor, 1, 8, 15, 118, 130, 148

kalima, 89–90
Kantorowicz, Ernst, 196
Karachi, 1–2, 58–60, 120, 161
Keane, Webb, 68, 92–93, 151, 175, 181
Khan, General Ayub, 55–56
Khan, Imran, 198
Khan, Naveeda, 60, 70
Khandalwi, Maulana Muhammad Zakariyya, 90–91
khanqa. *See* spiritual house
khidmat, 76, 84, 105, 121, 129, 145
Khilafat Movement, 155

Khoja-Moolji, Shenila, 161
khushka, 131, 144
khutba, 90
kinship, 34–35, 39, 62–63, 141, 149, 162, 166. *See also* relationships: kin
Kloos, David, 16, 151
knowledge, 77–80, 103; religious, 44–45; textual, 34
Kurin, Richard, 56
Kyrgyzstan, 132, 148, 201n1 (intro)

labor, 147–48
Laidlaw, James, 202n1 (chap. 3)
Lambek, Michael, 77
land, 39–40
language, 50–61, 63, 89–90, 104, 142; suspicion of, 107
Lashkar-e-Taiba, 172
Lebner, Ashley, 194
Lelyveld, David, 50, 54
Lemons, Katherine, 193–94
liberalism, 22, 184, 196–98
liberals, 14–15, 22
listening, 20. *See also* pious listening
literacy, 42
loss, 140–41
love, 105–6, 107, 137
lower self, 33, 48, 49, 56, 81–82, 85, 86, 91, 104, 135, 148, 158–59, 164

Madni Masjid, 8, 111–12, *114*, *115*, 118
Mahmood (Tablighi), 61–62
Mahmood, Saba, 6, 14–15, 75, 86, 163, 175, 193
Maine, Henry, 38, 39
Makki Masjid, 7–8
Maqsood (Tablighi), 67–68, 70–71, 157–58
markaz, 1–3, 71, *112*, 125, 167
market, 91–92, 168–69
masculinity, 161. *See also* pious masculinity
Masih, Asia. *See* Bibi, Asia
maslak, 46, 109, 178
Masowe Apostolics, 17
Maududi, Abu Ala, 46
maulvi, 7
Mauss, Marcel, 63, 168
media, 4, 51, 60, 99, 163; compact disc, 99, 118; print, 33, 37, 42, 46; radio, 4, 163; television, 4, 79; internet, 4, 79, 99
mediation, 17–18; of Islam, 162–63; of conflicts, 164; pious, 21–22, 122, 164–67; semiotic, 201n2 (intro)
Memons, 62–63, 71, 145

Meos, 31–32
Messick, Brinkley, 17, 43–44, 87, 104
Metcalf, Barbara, 5, 84, 122, 154–55
Meyer, Birgit, 5, 17, 68
middle talk, 88, 97–98
modernism, 49, 169, 194; Muslim, 46, 47, 54, 57
modernist, 21, 29, 43, 46, 48, 51, 57, 65, 109, 154, 155, 157, 160, 169, 170, 194. *See also* Muslim modernism
modernity, 11, 13, 17, 19, 22–23, 189–99; colonial, 45, 47
modernization, 160
Mohsin (Tablighi), 2
Moin, Azfar, 35
monologism, 202n1 (chap. 4)
moral chaos. *See fitna*
moral disjuncture, 91–92
morality, 16, 34; public, 42
moral order, Islamic, 13–14, 19, 72, 191
moral outrage, 180, 181
moral panic, 175, 182
moral reproduction, 159–64
moral responsibility, 20, 76, 86–95. *See also* responsibility
Morgan, Lewis Henry, 38
mosque, 91, 138, 158, 165, 168
motorcycles, 1, 111, *113*
Mughal empire, 30, 34–37, 62
Muhajir Quami Movement (MQM), 58–59
Muhajirs, 58–59, 161
Multan, 120, 180
music, 144
Muslim modernism, 46, 47, 54, 57
Muslim rule, 30, 201n1 (chap. 1)
Muslims, 42, 46–47, 62–63, 69, 77, 79, 86, 120, 157, 169, 174, 192; abroad, 146–47; division among, 60; as foreigners, 30–31; of India, 45, 50; of Pakistan, 72, 89, 188; political life of, 52. *See also ajlaf*; *ashraf*; Shia Muslims; Sunni Muslims

naat, 18, 144, 146
nafs. *See* lower self
Nakassis, Constantine, 123
namaz, 32, 44, 67, 90
nation, the, 4, 47, 54, 161; Islamic, 19, 54, 57, 176, 181–83, 198
nationalism, 48–49; Bengali, 160; ethnic, 56; Muslim, 50–58; Pakistani, 33, 47–48, 58, 68–69, 151, 159, 191, 198; religious, 49; Sindhi, 56
native law, 40
Nazimabad (neighborhood of Karachi), 10

neighborhood, 8, 71, 88, 97–98, 112, 119, 139, 162, 178
neoliberalism, 187
new Muslims. *See ajlaf*
Noorani, Owais, 172
norms, 10, 15–16, 38, 92, 197
nostalgia, 170, 191
nur. *See* divine light

objectification, 41–47, 191
old Muslims. *See ashraf*
ontology, 11–13
openness, 72, 76, 135
orality, 33, 43, 104. *See also* recitational logocentrism
Order of the Prophet, 56–57, 160
Ordinance XX, 160
orientalism, 196, 201n1 (chap. 1)
orthodoxy, 77
orthopraxy, 43, 45, 75, 77–86, 87, 117, 119, 124
Other, the, 11–12

Pakistan, 4, 12; 1956 constitution of, 160
Pakistan Civil War, 56
Pakistani Penal Code, 183
Pakistani Taliban, 161
Pakistan National Alliance, 57, 160
Pakistan People's Party, 59
Pakistan Tehreek-e-Insaf, 198
pardah, 82–84, 136, 142, 148, 168–69
Pashtuns, 58–59. *See also* Pathans
passion, 79, 81, 156, 184, 185–86
Pathans, 59, 61–63, 201n1 (chap. 2). *See also* Pashtuns
patience, 187
patriarchy, 21, 39, 82–86, 186–87
Pattoki, 189
Peirce, Charles, 94
Pelkmans, Mathijs, 15, 132, 148, 150
performance, 20, 76, 87, 92–95
performative act, 94, 102, 124, 191
Pernau, Margrit, 55
Persian language, 51, 129
personhood, 49, 81–82, 85; moral, 34, 43–44, 82
pietists, 6, 12, 15, 86, 95, 185–86, 195–97
piety, 5–6, 10, 58–61; citationality of, 120–24; Islamic, 177–88, 190, 197; performance of, 94; semiotics of, 13–18, 20; signs of, 93
Piot, Charles, 170
pious agency, 21, 76, 85–86, 132, 149–52, 192, 197, 202n1 (chap. 3)
pious becoming, 147, 149

INDEX

pious companionship, 132, 164, 191. *See also* companionship; *sohbat*
pious listening, 102–8, 121–22, 202n1 (chap. 4)
pious masculinity, 85, 133–38, 167, 188
pious relationality, 5, 18, 20, 154
pir-muridi, 66, 68, 109
pirs, 34, 37–38, 66–68, 162
Piscatori, James, 163
Plato, 102–3
political fragmentation, 163–64, 170
political rally, 158
politics, 4, 7, 48, 187, 193–94, 203n1 (chap. 6). See also *politiks*
politiks, 21, 155, 156–59, 162, 170–71, 177, 186, 203n1 (chap. 6). *See also* politics
population growth, 58
populism, 182–83
procreation, 35, 85
Prophet, the, 3, 32, 104–6
proselytizing, 29, 92
protest, 176, 189
Protestants, 14, 92–93, 193
Punjab, 37–39, 53, 55, 58
Punjab Alienation of Land Act (1901), 39
purity, 6, 29, 57; hierarchy of, 64, 65; of intentions, 87–88

qabza, 65–66
Qadri, Mumtaz, 173, 176, 181, 203n2, 204nn6–7
Quran, 43–44, 77, 97, 104, 109, 116, 133–34, 143. *See also* recitation of the Quran
qurbani. *See* sacrifice

radicalization, 185
Raheem (Tablighi), 61–63, 69
Rahman, Fazlur, 44
Raiwind, 71, 115, 129, 138–45, 189, 202
Rajpal, 204n7
Rangila Rasul, 204n7
rank, 54, 76, 98, 99, 108
Rappaport, Roy, 94
reading sessions. *See taleem*
reason, 67, 81–82, 103, 154
Rebellion of 1857, 27, 30
recitational logocentrism, 87. *See also* orality
recitation of the Quran, 42–44, 130
Reetz, Dietrich, 96
relationality, 125, 132; hierarchical, 6–7, 201n1 (intro). *See also* pious relationality
relationships, 117–18; kin, 134
relativism, 184

religion, 2, 4–5, 14, 37–42, 192; materiality of, 81; of practice, 116; privatized conception of, 184–85
religious law, 34
renewal, 27
replication, 44, 47, 106–7
research, 11, 75, 101
respectability, 54–55
responsibility, 19, 97, 133, 186–87. *See also* care; hierarchy; moral responsibility
ritual, 12, 88, 94–95; of transcendence, 48–72
ritual practices, 67, 82, 86–87, 92, 118
robbers, 1
Robbins, Joel, 13
Robinson, Francis, 50
rope of God, 89
ruh, 33, 56, 81
rural, 37–38, 143

saati, 124. *See also* companion
sacrifice, 96–97, 140, 142, 147, 168
saints, 36, 193; intercession by, 56–57, 65–66, 143
Samad (Tablighi), 179–80, 183
sawab, 112
Schielke, Samuli, 16, 150
Schimmel, Annemarie, 78
scripture, 29
secularism, 7, 14, 174–75, 184, 193–95; colonial, 27–47, 183
sehroza, 97–98. *See also dawat*: tours
self, 81, 143, 202n1 (chap. 3); forfeiture of, 185; worship of the, 157–58, 162. *See also* lower self
self-control, 82–83
self-cultivation, 15–20, 76, 87, 92, 99, 124
semiotics, 7, 12, 17–18, 20, 68, 92–99, 111, 149, 175, 201n2 (Introduction). *See also* iconicity; indexicality; Peirce, Charles; piety: semiotics of
sensational form, 19, 31, 20, 68, 70, 75, 109
sermon. *See bayan*
shab-e-jumma, 1, 111–16, 121, 147–48
Shah Waliullah, 37
Shahzaib (Tablighi), 117–24, 120–26, 131, 140, 145
Shakil (Tablighi), 61
shalwar kameez, 80
sharafat, 54
shariat, 4, 5, 22, 28, 52, 66, 67, 77, 160, 180–81
Shia Muslims, 46, 59
Silverstein, Brian, 110, 170
Singh, Justice Dalit, 204n7

INDEX

six points, 90, 167
siyasat. See politics
softness, 76, 121, 135, 158, 162
sohbat, 17, 20, 102, 105, 108–19, 141, 155.
   See also companionship
solicitation. See *tashkeel*
sovereignty, 189–99; Islamic, 41; medieval, 196; muslim, 27; pious, 153–71; state, 4, 22, 57, 183, 191
spirit. See *ruh*
spiritual house, 9, 131
spiritual potency, 96
Srinivas, M. N., 30
state law, 180
Stephens, Julia, 34, 37
stereotypes, 55
subjectivity, 15, 155
Sufis, Naqshbandi, 110. See also Chisti order
Sufism, 19, 29, 34–36, 40, 55–57, 108–9, 160; cosmology of, 82. See also *pirs*
Sultan (Tablighi), 61
sunnat, 3, 7, 44, 61, 78
Sunni Muslims, 46, 109, 173, 178
syeds. See descendants of the Prophet

Tablighi Jamaat: annual congregations, 71, 138–41, 202n2 (chap. 2); and Barelwis, 178; history of, 3; Islamist critiques of, 156; moral authority of, 167; as "walking madrassa," 78
tahqiqat. See research
tajdid. See renewal
takabbur. See hubris
taleem, 83, 91, 98, 149
Talha (Tablighi), 1, 7–9, 64, 121, 132, 139, 141–45
talk, 81, 101–8, 120, 124–25, 158
taqlid, 40–41, 52
tariqa, 2, 32, 78, 118
Taseer, Salman, 173, 176, 179, 203n3, 204nn6–7
tashkeel, 92
technologies of the self, 15, 75, 95. See also Foucault, Michel
Tehreek-e-Labbaik Party, 60, 203n2
Temporality, 20, 48, 64, 79, 86, 102, 120–24, 180–81
terrorism, 59, 185
Thanwi, Ashraf Ali, 31, 155

thingification, 18
Tomlinson, Matt, 202n1 (chap. 4)
tongue, 103–7, 118, 119, 121, 122, 169
traditionalism, scriptural, 34–45
train, 189–90
transcendence, 13, 18, 83, 187, 192; and *dawat*, 48–72; ritual of, 19, 68; sovereign, 189–99
transience, 83
Tupper, C. L., 38–39
two-nation theory, 50

ulama, 37, 162. See also Deobandi ulama
Umer (Tablighi), 129–32, 139–40, 143–45, 147, 150–51
Unionist Party, 53
urban, 37–38, 160
Urdu, 50–51, 59, 160, 161, 165–66
Usman (Tablighi), 114–15

van der Veer, Peter, 30, 49
Verkaaik, Oskar, 56, 160, 161
violence, 22, 58–60, 161, 170–71; political, 187; religious, 172–88
virtue, 8, 47, 61, 78–80, 81, 98, 99, 107, 117, 119, 121, 136, 137, 149, 188; Islamic, 3–4, 15, 21, 27, 67, 75, 83–86, 95, 102, 105, 110–11, 123, 148, 154–55, 159, 191

Waliullah, Shah, 32, 37, 41
Warner, Michael, 46–47
Watt, Montgomery, 77
wealth, 162
West Pakistan, 55–56
Wittrock, Björn, 13
women, 15, 82–86, 135–36, 148
work, 137
world, 2, 10, 14, 82–83, 91, 98, 130, 169, 191, 192
worldview, Brahmanical, 6

Yasin, Surah, 97
Yusaf bhai (Tablighi), 115–17, 120–24

Zaidi, Bushra, 59
Zaman, Muhammad Qasim, 40, 42, 45. See also Deobandi ulama
Zamzam, 134
Zia-ul-Haq, Muhammad, 56–57, 160, 163. See also Islamization